Accounting and Reporting Practices of Private Foundations

Jack Traub

The Praeger Special Studies program—utilizing the most modern and efficient book production techniques and a selective worldwide distribution network—makes available to the academic, government, and business communities significant, timely research in U.S. and international economic, social, and political development.

Accounting and Reporting Practices of Private Foundations

A Critical Evaluation

PRAEGER SPECIAL STUDIES IN U.S. ECONOMIC, SOCIAL, AND POLITICAL ISSUES

Praeger Publishers   New York   London

Library of Congress Cataloging in Publication Data

Traub, Jack, 1936-
   Accounting and reporting practices of private
foundations.

   (Praeger special studies in U.S. economic, social,
and political issues)
   Bibliography: p. 208
   1. Endowments—Accounting.   I. Title.
HF5686.C3T7 1977   657'.98   77-5344
ISBN 0-275-24530-6

PRAEGER PUBLISHERS
200 Park Avenue, New York, N.Y. 10017, U.S.A.

Published in the United States of America in 1977
by Praeger Publishers, Inc.

789   038   987654321

Printed in the United States of America

To Esther

The bible teaches us that a man without a
woman is incomplete. So I thank my wife for her
role in my life.

ACKNOWLEDGMENTS

I wish to express my gratitude to several individuals whose aid was vital to me in the long and difficult task of writing this book. I thank Dr. Leo Rattner for giving me the ego strength to begin the journey. I also thank Dr. Stephen Feldman for consoling me in my many hours of need.

I would also like to express my appreciation to those who helped my complete this project. I am very indebted to Professor Reed Storey, chairman of my dissertation committee, for all his many helpful criticisms and suggestions, and whose standards of academic excellence were matched by his sincerity, patience, and understanding.

Thanks to all the certified public accountants and foundation officials who took the time to allow me to interview them. The library staff of the AICPA under Ms. Katherine Michaelsen, head librarian, provided me with invaluable services in locating the many materials needed in my research project.

This book is based principally on research undertaken for my doctoral dissertation accepted by the faculty of the City University of New York Graduate School of Business in the fall of 1976.

CONTENTS

LIST OF TABLES AND ILLUSTRATIONS

xiii

Accounting and Reporting Practices of Private Foundations

1

INTRODUCTION

PURPOSE OF THIS STUDY

Because this nation regards private philanthropy as important, the federal government generally has provided for the exemption of charitable organizations from federal income taxation. In addition, tax deductions are allowed for the contributions made to such organizations.

Private foundations have been tax-exempt under our federal taxing statutes as far back as the Revenue Act of 1894, which provided tax exemption for corporations, companies, or associations organized and conducted solely for charitable, religious, or educational purposes.[1] The first income tax law in 1913, following the passing of the Sixteenth Amendment, provided for exemption of certain organizations organized and operated exclusively for religious, charitable, scientific, or educational purposes.[2]

Recently, however, private foundations have become controversial social institutions. Although foundations have been credited with doing vital work in many areas, such as medicine, science, and the humanities, they have also been criticized as being havens for "tax dodgers."

A Treasury Department report on private foundations described the role of private philanthropy in our society as follows:

Private philanthropy plays a special and vital role in our society. Beyond providing for areas into which government cannot or should not advance (such as religion), private philanthropic organizations can be uniquely qualified to initiate thought and action, experiment with new and untried ventures, dissent from prevailing attitudes and act quickly and flexibly.

Private foundations have an important part in this
work. . . . Equally important, because their funds
are frequently free of commitment to specific operating
programs, they can shift the focus of their interest
and their financial support from one charitable area
to another. They can, hence, constitute a powerful
instrument for evaluation, growth, and improvement
in the shape and direction of charity.[3]

Not everyone, however, expressed admiration toward foundations. Congressman Wright Patman, chairman of the Subcommittee
on Foundations, Select Committee on Small Business, testified as
follows at hearings on tax reform in 1969:

Put most bluntly, philanthropy . . . one of mankind's
most noble instruments . . . has been perverted into a
vehicle for institutionalized, deliberate evasion of fiscal
and moral responsibility to the nation. . . . The use of
the tax-free status . . . reveals the continuing devotion
of some of our millionaires to greed, rather than conversion to graciousness. . . . And the onerous burden on
65 million taxpayers demand that Congress curb the
tax-exempt foundations which, in unwitting good faith,
it helped to create.[4]

Congressman Patman asked the following question in his report
on foundations:

Are foundations being used as a cloak and a vehicle for
crippling competition and accelerating concentration
of economic power? Are foundations being used to
facilitate the use of economic power disguised as charity,
to obtain ends never intended by the people or the
Congress . . . ends such as taking control of commercial enterprise?[5]

In a later installment of his report on foundations, Congressman
Patman concluded:

The trend to shift the wealth of America's richest
families into tax-exempt foundations and trusts represents a gigantic loophole in our tax laws.[6]

Congressman Patman expressed the fear felt by many others
that "more and more the 'cream' is slipping out of our tax system
as the great fortunes go into tax-exempt foundations."[7]

The public has a legitimate and vital interest in the activities of private foundations. The American people, in granting tax exemption to the foundations, are saying that the benefits to be derived therefrom are significant enough that they are willing to bear the additional burden. They expect, and rightfully, that those granted exemption carry out the objectives for which they are exempted from taxation.

There is no requirement that foundations publish annual reports, although some foundations can compare in size with large, publicly held corporations. Thirteen foundations presently each have assets in excess of 200 million dollars. Moreover, the Revenue Act of 1969 merely requires that a foundation have a copy of its annual tax Form 990 available in its office for public inspection. That secretive approach pervades the whole area of nonprofit organizations. McGeorge Bundy, president of the Ford Foundation, suggested that one reason higher education has not made its case for financial support persuasively enough to the public was "calculated reticence in reporting of financial affairs." He further stated:

> How many colleges or universities . . . public or private, large or small . . . have ever told the whole story of their resources and their obligations, their income and their expenses, their assets and their debts in a way that the public can fully and fairly judge their economic position?[8]

Richard Magat of the Ford Foundation stated: "The proper goal of foundation reporting should be informed public opinion. Opinion should rest on a base of knowledge."[9] He concluded that "for foundations, the principal vehicle and irreducible minimum is the annual report."[10]

Most of the efforts of the accounting profession in the past have concentrated on improving reporting practices of profit-oriented enterprises. The Accounting Research Bulletins and the Opinions of the Accounting Principles Board of the American Institute of Certified Public Accountants dealt primarily with profit-oriented business. The Committee on Accounting Procedure specifically pointed out that it had not directed its attention to accounting problems or procedures of religious, charitable, scientific, educational, and similar nonprofit organizations.[11]

The Accounting Principles Board issued 31 opinions, all of which dealt with profit-oriented enterprise. Opinion Number 22 recognized the existence of nonprofit organizations when the board concluded that accounting policies adopted by nonprofit organizations should be described in their financial statements.[12]

Malvern Gross, a partner in Price Waterhouse & Co. and an authority on nonprofit accounting, criticized the accounting profession for failing to clearly define generally accepted accounting and reporting practices for nonprofit organizations with the result that "complicated statement presentation and fuzzy reporting are frequently encountered."[13]

The body of knowledge in accounting for nonprofit organizations at the present time is deficient in comparison with profit-oriented enterprises. However, the area of nonprofit accounting is starting to receive some attention.

Nonprofit organizations are in the nature of public trusts, since they operate under a tax exemption that the American taxpayer grants to them through the government. The American Council on Education recognized this responsibility on the part of colleges, which are nonprofit, when it recommended the following:

> Thus, the inherent obligations for stewardship and
> accountability necessitate a system of accounts and
> reports that will insure full disclosure of the results
> of their operations and of their financial position.[14]

The report of the Committee on Accounting for Not-for-Profit Organizations of the American Accounting Association stated that profit and nonprofit organizations are important complementary parts of the same economic system and compete for many of the scarce resources to convert into services and goods. The committee recognized the deficiency in reporting for nonprofit organizations and went a step further to recommend that in addition to dollar accountability, the nonprofit organizations should provide operational accountability. The committee suggested the following:

> They [nonprofit organizations] should utilize all avail-
> able analytical techniques to ensure appropriate and
> efficient use of resources in the best interest of society
> as a whole, and require information systems, of which
> accounting is an integral part, to provide all interested
> parties with data bearing upon "operational accountability"
> as well as "dollar accountability" in order that such
> parties at interest may properly plan, direct, control,
> and evaluate the way its scarce resources are utilized.[15]

The committee pointed out that nonprofit organizations, even to a greater degree than profit-oriented enterprises, should be required to justify their existence and activities on the basis of the efficiency and effectiveness of their operations as well as on their fulfillment of the purpose for which they were granted exemption as a nonprofit organization.[1] Furthermore, the rather remote and indirect relation between the contributors of resources and the consumers of these resources can result in the existence of nonprofit entities that operate inefficiently.[17] A profit-oriented business is measured on how it utilizes the assets under its control, and thus the business, acting in its own self-interest, tries to be as efficient as possible. That principle does not hold true for a nonprofit organization. Since the objective of a foundation is to carry out charitable activities, the profit incentive to ensure that the entity will attempt to be as efficient as possible is missing.

The obligation to measure how efficiently the nonprofit organization utilizes the assets under its control is termed "operational accountability" by the Committee on Not-for-Profit Organizations. Since an accountant is in the service of providing information systems and attesting to financial data, society logically expects him to expand his horizons and become involved in the area of "operational accountability," or as it is more popularly called today, "social accountability."

Lee Seidler, in an article in the Journal of Accountancy stated that, "The United States is in the midst of a new revolution . . . a revolution of rising demands for social accountability."[18] Part of the criticism being directed toward the accounting profession, as well as other institutions, is a manifestation of society's desire for a broad-based increase in social accountability. Seidler concurred with the Committee on Not-for-Profit Organizations in concluding that the general welfare actually demands a greater need for accounting measurements in the nonprofit sector than in the private sector.

OBJECTIVES OF STUDY

The purposes of this study are twofold. First, it will involve an attempt to ascertain or formulate objectives of foundation reporting and to describe standards that help meet those objectives. The basic questions are: Who are the users of the information? What information should be communicated by the private foundations to them?

Second, it will investigate the present reporting practices of private foundations to see what kind of information is presently being transmitted from the foundation to the users of the information.

METHODOLOGY AND RESEARCH DESIGN

The objectives of the study will be researched both analytically and empirically. The first objective will be researched analytically, utilizing the following procedures:

1. Review of current accounting, economic, and selected relevant sociological literature.

2. Selected interviews with foundation officials and certified public accountants. The selection process will not be random. Those selected for interview, especially the certified public accountants, will be individuals who have demonstrated an interest in nonprofit accounting. Approximately 15 interviews will be conducted, one-half for each group. No statistical inferences will be or should be drawn from these interviews.
3. Critical analysis of the above.

The second objective will be researched empirically. Approximately 250 private foundations file annual reports and these reports will be studied to determine present reporting practices.

I am concerned with all the relevant variables such as:

I. Accounting standards
   A. Cash basis versus accrual basis.
   B. Valuing assets at cost versus market price or value.
   C. Capitalizing fixed assets versus expense of period of acquisition.
   D. Including depreciation expense versus not depreciating.
   E. Deducting grants made from net income versus deducting them from principal.
   F. Including contributions received as income versus including them in principal.
   G. The extent of fund accounting.
II. Reporting standards
   A. Certified reports versus noncertified reports.
   B. Financial statements commonly included in reports.
   C. Terminology used in financial statements.
   D. Disclosure of investments.
   E. Disclosure of grants made.
   F. Disclosure of investment policies.
   G. Disclosure of the criteria used to determine which projects to finance.
   H. Disclosure of the criteria for applying for grants and the method of selection.
   I. Disclosure of the success or failure of the foundation in performing its function.

LIMITATIONS OF STUDY

First, the study is limited to private foundations and does not attempt to deal with many other types of organizations that are also tax-exempt, such as churches, schools, labor unions, and social clubs.

Second, the emphasis is descriptive rather than judgmental. The approach will be similar to that of an accountant who supplies information on a profit-oriented enterprise for the user to evaluate performance; the study will attempt to provide standards for measurement of foundations, but leave the evaluation of their performance to other interested parties.

Consideration must be given to the performance or output of a nonprofit organization. The problem was stated clearly in an editorial in the Journal of Accountancy: "The overall problem concerns the development of reliable methods of measuring the effectiveness of social programs."[19]

There is presently little research and knowledge concerning this area to draw upon. This study will attempt to deal with developing methods of measuring the performance of the private foundations, some of which may turn out to be nonquantitative. It will inquire into the area of social accountability, but that will not be its primary emphasis; rather, it will be one of the factors that must be considered in evaluating the reporting practices of private foundations.

DEFINITIONS

Private Foundation

There is no singularly accepted definition as to what actually constitutes a private foundation. Thus, when Congressman Patman quoted statistics on private foundations and the U.S. Treasury quoted its own statistics, the reason for the large variance was due to the fact that they were not referring to the same organizations. To add further confusion, certain organizations that call themselves foundations are not what is generally considered to be such. For example, the National Foundation (formerly March of Dimes) does not meet the definition that will be used in this study.

The U.S. Treasury, in its report on private foundations, gave the following definition:

1. Organizations of the type granted tax exemption by Section 501 (C) (3) (that is, generally, corporations or trusts formed and operated for religious, charitable, scientific, literary, or educational purposes, or for the testing for public safety or the prevention of cruelty to children or animals), with the exception of—
   a. Organizations which normally receive a substantial part of their support from the general public or governmental bodies;
   b. Churches or conventions or associations of churches;

      c. Educational organizations with regular facilities, curriculums, and student bodies; and

      d. Organizations whose purpose is testing for public safety; and

2. Nonexempt trusts empowered by their governing instruments to pay or permanently set aside amounts for certain charitable purposes.[20]

    The Tax Reform Act of 1969 for the first time introduces the term "private foundation." The act defines private foundations as follows:

a. General Rule—For purposes of this title, the term "private foundation" means a domestic or foreign organization described in section 501 (C) (3) other than—

    1. an organization described in section 170 (b) (1) (A) . . .;

    2. an organization which—

      A. normally receives more than one-third of its support in each taxable year from any combination of—

        i. gifts, grants, contributions, or membership fees, and

        ii. gross receipts from admissions, sales of merchandise, performance of services . . . ,

      B. normally receives not more than one-third of its support in each taxable year from gross investment income . . . ,

    3. an organization which—

      A. is organized, and at all times thereafter is operated, exclusively for the benefit of, to perform the functions of one or more specified organizations described in paragraph 1 or 2,

      B. is operated, supervised, or controlled by or in connection with one or more organizations described in paragraph 1 or 2, and

      C. is not controlled directly or indirectly by one or more disqualified persons (as defined in section 4946) other than one or more organizations described in paragraph (1) or (2); and

    4. an organization which is organized and operated exclusively for testing for public safety.[21]

    The Foundation Center, which has the most complete collection of information and statistics pertaining to foundations in the United States, provides the following definition of a private foundation:

    The Center defines a foundation as a nongovernmental, nonprofit organization with funds and program managed by its own trustees or directors, and established to

maintain or aid social, educational, charitable, religious,
or other activities serving the common welfare, primarily
through the making of grants. Both charitable trusts and
corporations are included. Excluded are organizations
which bear the name "foundation" but whose primary purposes are other than the awarding of grants, for example
making general appeals to the public for funds; acting as
trade associations for industrial or other special groups;
or which are restricted by charter solely to aiding one
or several named institutions; or which function as endowments set up for special purposes within colleges, churches,
or other organizations and are governed by the trustees
of the parent institution.[22]

The Commission on Foundations and Private Philanthropy's
definition of a private foundation was very similar to the Foundation
Center's definition. The Commission said that in order to be classified as a private foundation, the organization should possess the
following characteristics:

A foundation is primarily a grant-making organization
supported by contributions from an individual, a company,
or a small group of persons. We distinguish foundations
from organizations which are broadly supported by the
general public. Our definition excludes so-called
"feeder" organizations which support only a single
charity, as well as "operating" foundations which devote
most of their funds to the direct conduct of charitable
activities. A foundation, within our use of the term,
may be organized in the form of either a trust or a
nonprofit corporation; it may have an endowment or
distribute contributions for charitable purposes as they
are received.[23]

The Commission specifically noted that their definition differed
from that in the Tax Reform Act of 1969, which includes operating
foundations within the purview of private foundation status. The
comission excluded operating foundations from private foundation
status.[24]

In my opinion, the definition provided by the Foundation Center
and the Commission on Foundations and Private Philanthropy is
more useful because it defines a foundation in a positive sense by
saying what it is, rather than in a negative way as in the case of the
Treasury Department or Congress in the Tax Reform Act of 1969,
both of whom define foundations by saying what they are not. The

definition used in this study is the one provided by the Foundation
Center and the Commission on Foundations and Private Philanthropy.

Community Foundation

The programs of community foundations, in aim and method,
are similar to those of private foundations. The main difference is
that community foundations receive their funding from multiple
sources rather than an endowment from a single source. Under the
tax law, they are classified as "public charities." They do not pay
the 4 percent excise tax, do not have fixed payout requirements,
and are not subject to the same limitations on gifts of new funds.
Their assets are comprised of gifts and bequests from many donors.
Usually their expenditures benefit a limited geographical area and
the governing board represents broad community interests. The
community foundation is of growing importance because it provides
a community with a flexible means for administering many different
kinds of charitable funds for the community's benefit.[25]

Company-Sponsored Foundation

This type of foundation is closely tied to the parent company
that created it. Usually, company officers serve on the foundation's
board of directors. In some company-sponsored foundations, their
annual grants are equal to or exceed assets. Some corporations,
rather than making grants directly, prefer to fund annually a foundation to carry out the corporation's charitable activities. Other
company-sponsored foundations have substantial endowments.[26]
Foundations in this category are classified as private foundations
under the tax law.

Operating Foundation

Operating foundations are foundations that have funds that are
primarily committed to their own ongoing activities rather than for
grant making. Thus, the operating foundation is actively engaged in
carrying out its own programs, the purpose for which the organization was created. The private, nonoperating foundation acts as an
intermediary entity—a conduit for philanthropic giving with no or
insubstantial programs or similar activities of its own. For example,
a private foundation created to operate a museum would be considered
an operating foundation.

The Tax Reform Act of 1969 makes a distinction between "private operating foundations" and "private nonoperating foundations." The distinction is based on mechanical qualifying tests and operating foundations failing to meet the act's tests would not be classified as a "private operating foundation" for tax purposes.

Under the Tax Reform Act of 1969, a private foundation is considered a private operating foundation if it uses substantially all of its adjusted net income (at least 85 percent) directly for the active conduct of activities constituting its charitable, educational, or other similar tax-exempt purposes.[27] In addition, the foundation must meet one of the following qualifications: substantially more than half (at least 65 percent) of the foundation's assets must be devoted directly to the active conduit of activities constituting the foundation's charitable, educational, or other similar exempt purposes, either directly or indirectly; the foundation must make qualifying distributions directly for the active conduit of its activities in an amount not less than two-thirds of its minimum investment return; or substantially all of its support (at least 85 percent) must be normally derived from the general public and from five or more unrelated exempt organizations. Not more than 25 percent of its support can be normally received from any one such exempt organization. In addition, not more than half of its support can be derived from investment income.[28]

Operating foundations, under the Tax Reform Act of 1969, are subject to the excise tax on net investment income but are not subject to the minimum distribution rules.[29] In addition, contributions made to an operating foundation qualify for the 50 percent limit on charitable deductions rather than the more stringent rules applicable to contributions to private foundations.[30]

NOTES

1. J. S. Seidman, Seidman's Legislative History of Federal Income Tax Laws 1938-1861 (New York: Prentice-Hall, 1938), p. 1016.

2. Ibid., p. 1001.

3. U.S. Congress, House, Committee on Ways and Means, Treasury Department Report on Private Foundations, 89th Cong., 1st Sess., 1965, p. 5.

4. U.S. Congress, House, Committee on Ways and Means, Written Statements Submitted by Witnesses on the Subject of Tax Reform (Feb. 18, 1969), p. 1.

5. U.S. Congress, House, Select Committee on Small Business, Tax-Exempt Foundations and Charitable Trusts: Their Impact on Our

Economy, 87th Cong., 2nd Sess., 1962 Chairman's Report to the
Select Committee on Small Business, 1st installment, p. 1.

6. U.S. Congress, House, Select Committee on Small Business,
Tax-Exempt Foundations and Charitable Trusts: Their Impact on Our
Economy, 88th Cong., 1st Sess., 1964 Chairman's Report to the
Select Committee on Small Business, 3rd installment, p. 4.

7. Ibid., p. 1.

8. McGeorge Bundy, "In Praise of Candor," address to the
American Council on Education, Oct. 13, 1967, quoted in Richard
Magat, "Foundation Reporting," New York University Conference
on Charitable Foundations (New York: Matthew Bender, 1969), p. 68.

9. Ibid., p. 65.

10. Ibid., p. 81.

11. American Institute of Certified Public Accountants, Committee
on Accounting Procedure, "Restatement and Revision of Accounting
Research Bulletins," Accounting Research Bulletin No. 43 (New York,
1953), p. 8.

12. American Institute of Certified Public Accountants, Accounting Principles Board, "Disclosure of Accounting Policies," Opinion
No. 22 (New York, 1972), p. 435.

13. Malvern Gross, Jr., Financial and Accounting Guide for
Non-Profit Organizations (New York: Ronald Press, 1972), p. 2.

14. American Council on Education, College and University
Business Administration (Washington, D.C.: ACE, 1968), p. 141.

15. American Accounting Association, Report of the Committee
on Accounting for Not-for-Profit Organizations, Supplement to
vol. 46 of the Accounting Review (1971), p. 86.

16. Ibid., p. 93.

17. Ibid., p. 102.

18. Lee J. Seidler, "Accountant: Account for Thyself," The
Journal of Accountancy, June 1973, p. 38.

19. "Editor's Notebook," The Journal of Accountancy, November
1972, p. 39.

20. Treasury Department Report on Private Foundations, op. cit.,
p. 1.

21. Section 509, Tax Reform Act of 1969.

22. The Foundation Directory, 5th ed. (New York: Foundation
Center, 1975), p. xi.

23. Commission on Foundations and Private Philanthropy,
Foundations, Private Giving, and Public Policy (Chicago, Ill.:
University of Chicago Press, 1970), p. 39.

24. Ibid., p. 40.

25. Foundation Center, op. cit., pp. xviii-xix.

26. Ibid., p. xx.

27. Treas. Reg. 53.4942(b)-1.

28. Treas. Reg. 53.4942(b)-2.
29. Sec. 4942, Tax Reform Act of 1969.
30. Sec. 170(b) (1) (A) (vii), Tax Reform Act of 1969.

2

A HISTORY OF
TAX ABUSE BY
PRIVATE FOUNDATIONS

INTRODUCTION

In studying the private foundation phenomenon, whether it be social output, accounting practices, or its wealth and influence on the economy, an inquiry into its history is essential. This will reveal the forces and events that gave this institution its present structure.

Federal taxation has and does play a major role in the creation, organization, and functioning of private foundations. It has provided the incentive for their creation and for the types of activities engaged in, and in addition presently acts as the major agency for the regulation of these activities.

Much of the publicity received by private foundations has been the result of congressional investigations—investigations initiated by abuses of their tax exemption. The result has been a much greater awareness by the foundations that they are quasi-public organizations with a responsibility to report fully to the general public on their activities. The foundation officials interviewed for this study indicated that foundations will have to operate in a different environment than was the case in the past. The present environment, as they see it, requires foundations to make much more of a disclosure of their economic and social activities. They also indicated that many of their problems have been caused by poor communication between them and the public.

The purpose of this chapter is to outline the history of private foundations under federal income taxation, since this factor more than any other has resulted in the present environment in which foundations operate today. Federal income taxation should be broken down into three eras: prior to 1950; 1950 to 1969; and 1969 to the

present. Each era is one in which foundations have been operating
under different federal tax laws, and this chapter is organized on
the basis of this chronology. A history of foundations under tax law
is really a study of tax abuses by private foundations because most
of the law concerned itself with curbing the abuses. (I want to say
at the outset that this chapter is not intended to imply that tax abuses
are widespread since no one knows the number of foundations that
have engaged in tax abuse. Unfortunately for foundations, a study
of federal income taxation as it pertains to them is mostly a catalogue
of abuses.)

FOUNDATIONS AND TAX LAW PRIOR TO 1950

The Revenue Act of 1913, which followed the adoption of the
sixteenth amendment, provided exemption for

> any corporation or association organized and operated
> exclusively for religious, charitable, scientific, or
> educational purposes, no part of the net income of
> which inures to the benefit of any private stockholder
> or individual . . . .[1]

The applicable law was vague and uncertain. It did not answer the
question as to whether profit-making activities were consistent with
tax exemption. The government immediately made the interpreta-
tion that profit-making activities were not permissible under the
law, and courts had to decide what activities were permissible for
exempt organizations to engage in. The government's position was
tested in the Supreme Court with disastrous results to the government.

The "landmark" Trinidad v. Sagrada case[2] established that the
ultimate test of exemption was the destination of income rather than
its source. The foundation had large properties in the Philippines,
consisting of real estate, stocks in private corporations, money
loaned at interest, and sales of wines, chocolates, and other articles.
The government contended that the foundation was being operated
not exclusively for religious purposes but also for business and
commercial purposes in that it used its property to produce income
and traded in wine, chocolates, and other articles.

Justice Van Devanter, delivering the decision of the Supreme
Court, stated:

> Whether the contention is well taken turns primarily
> on the meaning of the excepting clause, before quoted

from the taxing act. Two matters apparent on the face
of the clause go far towards settling its meaning. First,
it recognizes that a corporation may be organized and
operated exclusively for religious, charitable, scientific
or educational purposes, and yet have a net income.
Next it says nothing about the source of the income,
but makes the destination the ultimate test of exemption.

The Supreme Court in this early case established a doctrine that
became known as the "ultimate destination of income test." This
doctrine, as it developed in later cases, meant that it did not matter
how the tax-exempt organization derived its funds, even if it was
engaged in profit-making activities, as long as the funds were ultimately used exclusively for charitable, religious, scientific, or
educational purposes.

A later case involved a foundation that ran a home and school
for the benefit of poor children and poor, old, and infirm persons.
To produce income with which to carry on its charitable activities,
the foundation operated oil and gas leases, sold oil refineries and
gas to distributing companies, generated and sold electricity for
light and power, maintained a reservoir from which water was sold to
the general public at commercial rates, operated a greenhouse, and
owned and operated a cotton gin and an amusement park. In its
business activities, the foundation traded with the general public
and competed with other corporations. The court held the foundation
(Sands Spring Home) to be operated exclusively for charitable purposes and cited Trinidad v. Sagrada, giving as its reason for the
decision the following:

A corporation otherwise exempt from tax is not deprived
of exemption because it carries on profitable or competitive activities in furtherance of its predominant religious,
charitable, scientific or educational purpose.[3]

While the Supreme Court in Trinidad v. Sagrada stated that the
commercial activities engaged in were of a negligible nature and
not a factor in its decision and it was the destination of income that
was the ultimate test, in the subsequent cases where commercial
activity was not a negligible factor, the courts continued to rely on
and expand the doctrine of the "ultimate destination of income test,"
so that the extent of the business activities did not become a factor
in the court's decisions.

In the cases previously discussed, the foundation owned and
operated the business directly. From an economic viewpoint, it
makes little difference whether the foundation owns the business

directly or alternatively owns a corporation that owns the business.
However, from a legal viewpoint, there is quite a difference between
the two forms. What about a situation in which the foundation owned
all the stock in a corporation that owned and operated the business,
paying its net profits over to the foundation? The government,
realizing that there was a difference in the two situations, took into
court Roche's Beach Inc.,[4] which was owned by a tax-exempt foundation. This corporation ran a bathing-beach business and collected
rents from the houses and garages, turning over any excess of
income over expenses to the foundation for charitable purposes.
The court stated that:

> It seems clear that the Corporation was organized and
> operated exclusively for charitable purposes . . . no
> reason is apparent to us why Congress should wish
> to deny tax exemption to a corporation organized and
> operated exclusively to feed a charitable purpose . . . .

Thus, this type of corporation became known as a "feeder" corporation. The court had extended the rationale of Trinidad v. Sagrada,
in which the foundation owned the business directly, to Roche's Beach,
in which the foundation owned the stock of a corporation involved in
business. The court said in this case that under the doctrine of
"ultimate destination of income test," there was little difference
between the two situations since both ultimately fed some charitable
purpose.

The most celebrated case in the area of "feeder" corporations
was when New York University acquired Mueller Macaroni Co.,
and became involved in the spaghetti business, or as one writer
described it, the macaroni monopoly.[5] New York University
organized a charitable corporation to purchase the business of an
established corporation engaged in the manufacture and sale of
macaroni and similar products for profit in competition with taxable
corporations engaged in the same business. The corporation turned
over its net profits to New York University, an exempt educational
institution. The government lost the case in the Court of Appeals,
which applied the "ultimate destination of income test" and held
that the corporation was exempt from taxes as a corporation organized
and operated exclusively for charitable purposes.[6]

Another practice related to the acquiring of business by foundations was what became known as the "sale and leaseback." As
implied by its name, a "sale and leaseback" involved the purchase
of property by the foundation and then leasing of the property,
usually to the same business from which the property was purchased.
In many cases, the exempt organization, in buying the property, did

not use its own funds to make the payment, but borrowed the purchase price and paid off the loan by applying part or all of the rental
income received for a period of years to this purpose. Thus, the
exempt organization was able to obtain, after a period of time, an
unencumbered title to the property, without having invested any of
its own funds.[7]

The government attempted to revoke a foundation's exempt
status for engaging in this type of transaction and lost. The Shattuck-
Ohio Foundation purchased the stock of the Ohio Furnace Co., for
which it gave the sellers a series of notes. The entire net earnings
of the Furnace Co. were under its charter to inure to the foundation,
and during the years in question, 1948, 1949, and 1950, constituted
the foundation's only income. The foundation was required by the
purchase agreement with the sellers to use substantially all of its
earnings to pay off the notes. The purpose for which the foundation
was established was to give financial assistance to a school. The
court held that the foundation was organized and operated exclusively
for educational purposes and was entitled to its tax exemption.[8]

The "sale and leaseback" constituted a serious tax abuse if
borrowed funds were used for three reasons.[9] First, the foundation
was not merely looking for someplace to invest its funds, since it
was borrowing the funds. Its contribution to the whole transaction
was its tax exemption, since it contributed nothing else. "Therefore, it appears reasonable to believe that the only reason why it
receives the property at no expense to itself is the fact that it pays
no income tax on the rentals received."[10] A second objection to
the "sale and leaseback" was "that it is altogether conceivable that
if its use is not checked, exempt organizations in the not-too-
distant future might own the great bulk of the commercial and
industrial real estate in the country."[11] Third, there was always
the possibility that the exempt organization had paid a higher purchase price for the property or charged lower rents than a taxable
business would in the circumstances. In effect, the tax-exempt
organization had sold part of its tax exemption.

Another abuse was disclosed in a subsequent congressional
investigation into foundations—the use of a private foundation to
preserve control of a business in connection with estate planning.
In a very large estate comprised mainly of the stock of a family-owned
business, the death of the founder of the business may cause severe
problems to family retention of the business. The need for cash to
pay estate taxes may require the sale of the stock of the family
business to pay the estate taxes. An ingenious device was devised
using a private foundation, which resulted in the payment of very
little estate taxes and the retention of the business in family hands.

Ninety percent of the ownership of the Ford Motor Co. was transferred to the Ford Foundation, which was created for this purpose. The family would have almost certainly lost control of the business, since high taxes payable by the Ford estate could not have been paid without liquidating a considerable part of the family business.[12] The above results were achieved by the following steps taken prior to Ford's death:

1. A recapitalization under which the stock was converted into common voting and common nonvoting stock.
2. The establishment of a private foundation. Henry Ford and his family transferred their nonvoting stock to the Ford Foundation, and retained only the relatively small proportion of voting shares. In this manner, Henry Ford's estate, which was estimated as high as $500 million, was reduced by a possible 90 percent, and the family was able to retain control of the Ford Motor Company since they still held the voting stock and were in control of the foundation. Furthermore, the resulting reduction in the taxable estate made it unnecessary to dispose of the stock publicly to meet huge estate taxes.[13]

The use of a foundation to retain control of a business upon the founder's death was quite commonly recognized; however, there was also evidence that private foundations were also being used during the owner's lifetime to salvage control in a critical situation. In one case, a foundation's funds were used to guarantee an investment that enabled the owners to win a proxy fight. In another case, a foundation purchased mortgage notes of enterprises where such financing made possible control of these businesses by the foundation's creators.[14]

Certain foundations made loans that were motivated by the desire to create unwarranted private advantage, and the benefits accruing to the foundation's donors, creators, or managers were sufficiently removed from the loan transactions to be difficult to discover, identify, and prove.[15]

Some donors or creators of private foundations engaged in other transactions with the foundation. Property was rented to or from it; assets were sold to it or purchased from it; money was borrowed from it or loaned to it. These transactions were rarely necessary to the carrying out of the foundation's charitable purposes; they gave rise to the misuse of the foundation's assets for private advantage. The question was whether the economic resources of the foundation were being used in the best interests of charity or to further the private purposes of the donor.

Another problem area was the unreasonable accumulation of income by private foundations. Contributions to the foundation were treated as principal or corpus, and the foundation was expected to maintain its principal. However, foundations also retained the income earned on the principal instead of disbursing it for any charitable purpose. The law permitted the foundation to earn its income tax-free and it also permitted a donor to deduct from his taxable income the amount of his contribution, yet, charity was not being benefited whatsoever until it received funds, and there was nothing in the law requiring foundations to pay out their income.

REVENUE ACT OF 1950

Capsule Summary

It was obvious that new legislation was needed to cope with the tax abuses, and Congress, responding as it had done in other areas of abuse, passed new legislation—the Revenue Act of 1950. New sections were added to the Internal Revenue Code designed to curb foundation activities that were most objectionable or, as the House Committee stated it, "Your committee's bill includes a series of amendments designed to correct certain problems which have arisen in connection with tax-exempt organizations."[16]

To give the reader a capsule view of the corrective legislation enacted, it is presented here in summary form to provide an overall picture of the corrective legislation enacted. The statutory provisions[17] dealing with tax-exempt organizations were Sections 502, 503 and 504, and Sections 511 through 514. Section 502 dealt with feeder organizations. Section 503 dealt with prohibited transactions, and Section 504 dealt with the unreasonable accumulation of income. Sections 511 through 514 imposed a tax on the unrelated business income of tax-exempt organizations. Thus, the provisions dealt with basically four abuse areas—feeder organizations, foundations used for tax avoidance purposes, accumulations of income, and "lease-back" income.

Feeder Organizations

Section 502 provided that an organization operated for the primary purpose of carrying on a trade or business for profit would not be exempt on grounds that all of its profits were payable to one or more organizations exempt from taxation.

The House Committee Report stated:

> The effect of this amendment is to prevent the exemption
> of a trade or business organization under sec. 101 on
> the grounds that an organization actually described in
> sec. 101 receives the earnings from the operations of
> the trade or business organization. In any case, it
> appears clear to your committee that such an organization
> is not itself carrying out an exempt purpose. Moreover,
> it obviously is in direct competition with other taxable
> businesses.[18]

Thus, the ultimate destination of income theory made famous
in the Trinidad v. Sagrada case was discarded. A new concept was
being applied to the tax-exempt area; the exempt organization itself
must be engaged in exempt purposes, and merely receiving money
from a business activity and paying it to charity would not suffice
any longer. Hence, in a situation similar to the relationship of
New York University and Mueller Macaroni Co., the business organization was subject to income tax like any other business.

Prohibited Transactions

The House Committee, recognizing the abuses that may exist
if a donor is to enter into financial transactions with his private
foundations, wanted to take away exemption if there were any financial dealings between a creator or substantial contributor and the
foundation.[19] The Senate version, which was enacted into law,
provided that an organization would lose its tax exemption only if
the dealings between the foundation and the creator or substantial
contributor were not at arm's length. The committee defined prohibited transaction as those transactions in which a donor or a
member of his family was likely to gain some special benefit from
the transaction.[20] The Senate version was enacted into law and it
provided that an exempt organization would not be tax exempt if it
has engaged in a prohibited transaction after July 1, 1950.

Unreasonable Accumulations

The House Committee's studies revealed that in a number of
cases, charitable organizations have obtained the concessions granted
under existing law without distributing a substantial portion of their

current income for exempt purposes. In some cases, the time when charity could expect to benefit appeared extremely remote. The committee said that the tax-exemption privileges with respect to investment income should be restricted to that portion of the income which the organization demonstrated it was using to fulfill its charitable purposes by actual distributions to charity as the income is earned. To eliminate this delay, the House version would have generally taxed the portion of an exempt organization's investment income that the organization did not currently distribute for the charitable purpose for which the exemption was granted.[21] The Senate rejected the House version and in conference, Section 504 was enacted, which provided denial of exemption if the foundation unreasonably accumulated its income.[22] It is interesting to note that the House version was ultimately adopted in the Tax Reform Act of 1969.

Unrelated Business Income

Foundation involvement in business took one of two forms, either owning the business directly or in the alternative, owning the stock in a corporation which owned the business. Congress enacted a tax on unrelated business income to prevent the foundation from dissolving the business corporation and owning the assets directly, since under Section 502, "feeder" corporations were now taxable. Congress recognized the problem of foundations' acquiring commercial ventures which often put competitive business at a serious competitive disadvantage. The House Committee stated:

> The tax-free status of these section 101 organizations enables them to use their profits tax-free to expand operations while their competitors can expand only with the profits remaining after taxes. Also a number of examples have arisen where the organizations have, in effect, used their tax exemption to buy an ordinary business. That is, they have acquired the business with no investment on their own part and paid for it in installments out of subsequent earnings—a practice which usually could not be followed if the business were taxable.[23]

The statute[24] imposed a tax on income derived from a trade or business regularly carried on by a tax-exempt organization if the business was not substantially related to the performance of the function upon which the organization's exemption is based.

Related to the unrelated business taxable income was the "lease-back" problem, in which the tax-exempt organization purchased property and then leased it back to the same business from which it was purchased, without using any foundation funds to make the payments, but borrowing the purchase price and paying off the loan from the rentals received. Congress recognized that under existing law an exempt organization did not need to use any of its own funds in acquiring property through "sales and leasebacks" and that borrowed funds might represent 100 percent of the purchase price, with the result that there was no limit to the property an exempt organization might acquire in this manner.[25] This aspect of the "leaseback" problem was resolved by taxing as unrelated business income certain income received from the lease of real property and personal property. The tax applied only if the property owned was leased for a period of five years or more and the property was acquired or improved by incurring an indebtedness.[26]

The main objective of Congress in passing the Revenue Act of 1950 was basically to prevent unfair competition to business from tax-exempt organizations and the law attempted to deal with the advantages that a tax-exempt organization had over a taxable competitor.

THE EFFECTS OF THE REVENUE ACT
OF 1950

Feeder Organizations

The Revenue Act of 1950 dealt a death blow to "feeder" organizations by taxing them as any ordinary business.[27] In Sico Foundation,[28] the tax-exempt organization sold petroleum products, averaging approximately $5.5 million in sales per year. The foundation distributed funds for educational purposes through the establishment of a scholarship program in several state teachers colleges. The court ruled it to be a "feeder" organization. It is interesting to note that a foundation itself could be considered a "feeder" organization if its primary source of income was from business activities, and even though its funds were used for charitable purposes, it was held to be not exempt from taxation.

In Scripture Press Foundation,[29] the tax-exempt organization was not connected with any particular religious denomination or church. Its main activity was the sale of religious literature. The foundation argued that its purpose was the betterment of the Protestant Sunday schools of America and that it was operated exclusively

for religious purposes under Sec. 501(c)(3). It was a difficult decision
for the court to make. The court ruled that the test should be whether
the sale of religious literature by the organization was incidental to
its religious purposes or the religious purposes were incidental to
the sale of literature. The court concluded that the sale of religious
articles was the primary objective of the organization's activities
and thus the organization was involved in the conduct of a trade or
business; the sale of religious articles was not an exempt purpose.
Since its primary activity was the sale of religious articles, the tax
on unrelated business income did not come into play, and the organization lost its tax exemption. However, if the organization had other
exempt activities, it probably would have merely had to pay a tax on
the sales of religious articles while maintaining its tax exemption.

Involvement in Business

Foundation involvement in business, far from being curbed by
the Revenue Act of 1950, actually grew more extensive. Organizations that paid careful heed to the exceptions prescribed by the 1950
Act were able to shield their commercial ventures from tax. The
law excepted dividends, interest, rents from real property, and
royalties from unrelated business income.[30] The theory was that
these sources were passive and had always been regarded as a
proper type of income for charitable organizations. The difficulty
lies in drawing the line between passive investment and engaging in
an active trade or business.

The seriousness of the problem was reported in a New York
Times article in 1969,[31] which revealed that dozens of foundations
were being used as middlemen by banks and oil companies in deals
in which the Treasury Department calculated that it lost $100 million
annually in tax revenues in each of the previous two years. By
selling oil-production payments, a company could increase depletion-
allowance benefits and inflate its income in one year, and then take
a self-induced loss the next year and avoid payment of any taxes.
The Treasury officials revealed that sales of production payments
had a part in the fact that Atlantic Richfield Company, while earning
$500 million net income for the period 1962-67, owed no federal
income taxes for the same period. An Associated Press check of
foundations in two states[32]—Louisiana and Texas—revealed that more
than 30 foundations had production payments as their sole assets.
Most had directors or officers linked to banks or oil company law
firms. The foundations handled $118.5 million in production pay-
ments in one year, and in the same year contributed $145,635 to
charity, or one-tenth of one percent of the production payments.

The foundations were set up by the interested parties to buy the production payments with the banks lending them the money with the production payments serving as collateral.

Because the unrelated business income tax did not apply to rents derived from property with respect to which the lessor had no outstanding indebtedness, foundations were able to lease business assets owned free of debt to operating subsidiaries, siphon off most or all of the business profits by means of rent, which was deductible by the subsidiary but not taxable to the parent foundation, and thereby accumulate large reservoirs of untaxed capital that could be used to support the future operations of the business. Another exception to the unrelated business income tax immunized rents stemming from a lease whose term was not longer than five years, even if the lessor had an outstanding indebtedness, with respect to the leased assets.[33]

Related to the "sale and leaseback" was the "bootstrap sale" in which the foundation was able to acquire the business, using no assets of its own, and then lease the property back to the same interests from which it had originally purchased the property. Had the foundation chosen to operate the acquired business directly, the profits would clearly have been subject to the unrelated business income tax.[34] Had the foundation, on the other hand, transferred the assets to its controlled corporation in the form of capital, the controlled corporation would be a "feeder"[35] and fully taxable, and the only way the controlled corporation could return the profits to the foundation would be as a dividend, not taxable to the foundation, but not deductible by the controlled corporation. By setting up the transaction in the form of rent, the foundation arranged to receive tax-free rental income and its controlled corporation had a rental deduction.

In Anderson Dairy, Inc.,[36] a dairy was owned by a partnership. The partners were interested in selling the dairy and after negotiating with a few prospective buyers, such as Arden Farms Dairy and Beatrice Foods, they entered into negotiations to sell the dairy to University Hill Foundation. The agreement provided for the sale of the Anderson Dairy for a total purchase price of $1,250,000, with a down payment of $15,000. The foundation agreed to lease the assets to a new corporation (Anderson Dairy, Inc.) of which the original partners were to own 48 percent and the foundation 52 percent. The lease agreement required the corporation to pay 80 percent of the net income from the operation of the business before taxes to the foundation. The foundation agreed to pay 90 percent of all its rentals received to the sellers until they were paid in full. The unpaid balance was to bear no interest, and the lease was for five years. The court ruled that the rentals paid were in fact rentals and were deductible by the corporation and that the trans-

action between the sellers and the foundation constituted a bona fide
sale and not a sham and were thus taxable as capital gains.

Not only were small or medium-sized businesses involved in
these "sale and leasebacks." In St. Paul, Minnesota, three foundations were purchasing gasoline service stations and commercial
buildings and leasing them back to the sellers such as Pure Oil Co.,
Cities Service Oil Co., General Electric, and F. W. Woolworth.
One foundation (Hill Foundation) had acquired, as of February 29,
1960, 15 service stations and 5 commercial buildings in this
manner.[37] Such "sales and leasebacks" were providing these companies with instant capital without these big companies having to go
to the "market" to borrow funds. The foundations were competing
with real estate investors in the commercial investment business.

A variation of the "sale and leaseback" was a sale in which the
business purchased was used to pay for itself, and the seller looked
only to future earnings of the business he had sold. This variation
became known as "bootstrap sales" to charities. In Clay Brown,[38]
the taxpayers sold their stock in a corporate enterprise to a tax-
exempt foundation in consideration for a small amount of cash and
a noninterest bearing note for $1.3 million. Under a prearranged
scheme, the foundation liquidated the corporation, leased its fixed
assets for a period of five years, and paid the taxpayers 90 percent
of the income it received from the lease in payment of the note. The
new corporation was obligated to pay 80 percent of its net profits
before taxes and depreciation to the tax-exempt foundation as rent
for the fixed assets. At the termination of the five-year lease, the
corporate assets were returned to the foundation, which entered
into an agreement with the taxpayers permitting them to negotiate a
sale thereof, even though the promissory note had not been paid in
full.

The main thrust of the commissioner's argument before the
Supreme Court in Clay Brown was that the tax-exempt foundation
invested nothing, assumed no independent liability for the purchase
price, and promised to pay over to the sellers a percentage of the
earnings of the newly formed corporation. The entire risk of the
transaction remained on the sellers; therefore, the transaction
should not be treated as a sale but should be treated as a gratuitous
transfer of the stock to the foundation subject to the retention by the
seller of the right to receive $1.3 million of dividends out of future
earnings of the business. The Supreme Court held that the word
"sale" should be construed in its ordinary significance; that the
instant transaction was clearly a sale under generally accepted legal
principles; that affording capital-gain treatment to the instant transaction would comport with, rather than in any way contradict, the
underlying policy of the capital-gains provisions to guard against

the consequences of taxing in a single year the realization of appreciation in value accrued over a substantial period of time. Thus, the Supreme Court dealt with the tax consequences to the sellers.

The government then tried to revoke a foundation's exempt status for participating in these "bootstrap sales." The government selected University Hill Foundation,[39] a tax-exempt organization that engaged in numerous "bootstrap sales" during the period 1945-54. The Treasury Department tried to take away the foundation's exemption as a "feeder." The Tax Court held that the foundation was not a feeder organization, since the rental by an organization of its real property does not constitute a trade or business. The court also held that the rental income was not subject to the tax on unrelated business income because income from the leasing of real property (including personal property leased with real property) was excluded from the tax on unrelated business income.

On appeal, the Court of Appeals reversed the lower court and concluded that:

> the foundation was engaged in commercial business for profit. That was what it was operated for. Even though the profits were ultimately distributable to an exempt institution, the Foundation was not "operated exclusively for exempt purposes."

The Treasury Department concluded in its report on private foundations that:

> by this expansion of its exemption privilege to borrowed assets and this divorce from dependence upon contributors, the foundation begins a multiplication of its holdings which bears no relation to the Community's evaluation of its charitable works; it embarks upon an extension of its economic empire which is limited only by the financial acumen and commercial skills of its managers.[40]

Prohibited Transactions

The Revenue Act of 1950 prohibited donor-foundation dealings that violated an "arm's length" standard. Sec. 503[41] specifically prohibited the following transactions between the foundation and its creator or substantial contributor:

1. Loans without adequate security or a reasonable rate of interest
2. Payment of excessive compensation

3. Preferential services
4. Purchases by foundation in excess of fair market value
5. Sales by foundation below fair market value

The consequences of having engaged in a prohibited transaction was the loss of exemption for one year following the year in which the prohibited transaction occurred.

Even though the law prohibited loans without adequate security or a reasonable rate of interest,[42] the definition of those terms presented the government with a difficult problem in law enforcement. For example, on May 12, 1954, the Sears, Roebuck Foundation, which was supported by the tax-deductible contributions given to it by the corporation, made a short-term loan of $1,200,000 at 3 percent to Sears, Roebuck & Company. At that time, the foundation could have received 6 percent or more had it made the funds available to other borrowers. As Congressman Patman pointed out with respect to this particular transaction, "it is quite an advantage to have a ready source of cash without having to assume a responsibility to banks or stockholders."[43] The Duke Power Company of Charlotte, North Carolina, was charged only 2.65 percent interest on a $3 million, 20-year loan, while other borrowers paid 6.50 percent; the loan was made by the Duke Endowment Fund, a tax-exempt foundation that owned 57 percent of the Duke Power Company.[44] The Fred L. Emerson Foundation made a loan of $175,000 to the Enna Jettick Corporation in 1951. Only three payments had been made on the demand note by 1960 in what appeared to be a virtually perpetual loan.[45] Another donor and his corporation borrowed $197,300 from his foundation on an unsecured loan. The Internal Revenue Service contended that the foundation should lose its tax exemption because the loans without "adequate" security and "reasonable" rate of interest were prohibited transactions. The court held that even though the foundation's loans to its substantial donors constituted prohibited transactions, they were nevertheless not entered into for the purposes of diverting the foundation's corpus or income from its exempt purpose.[46]

Loans were not the only form of self-dealing that was being engaged in between foundations and their creators and/or donors. Property was sold to and purchased from the foundation, and it was difficult, if not impossible, to ascertain the motivation in these transactions. Was the purpose of the transaction some private gain? In 1952, L. E. Phillips Charities, Inc. sold stock worth $33,600 in Vick Chemical Co. to L. E. Phillips. The same year, it purchased for $1,082,250 stock in Ed. Phillips & Sons Co., another contributor to the foundation. In 1953, the foundation bought and sold several thousand shares of National Pressure in transactions with L. E.

Phillips. In 1954, the foundation sold shares in National Presto Industries Inc. to the creator's relatives and bought National Presto shares from them. In 1955, the foundation sold shares of Reynolds Tobacco and American Tobacco to L. E. Phillips. During the period 1957-60, securities of various corporations, including Vicks Chemical, Gillette, Hershey, and others, were traded with L. E. Phillips and his relatives.[47] In 1961, when Ford Motor Co. was seeking the acquisition of Philco, it needed one million shares of Ford stock to trade for four million shares of Philco Common stock. Ford Motor Co. acquired the shares from the Ford Foundation.[48] The Morton Fund (a tax-exempt foundation) acquired 300 shares of the Sodak Co. class B common stock by gift in 1953 from Sterling Morton, creator of the Morton Fund. On May 16, 1956, the Sodak Corporation purchased from the Morton Fund the 300 shares of the Sodak Co. class B common stock.[49]

In the Teich Foundation case,[50] Curt Teich, Sr. donated approximately $1.2 million worth of "blue chip" securities to the Teich Foundation in 1960. The foundation sold the shares and with the proceeds purchased almost all of the issued and outstanding common stock of the Teich family corporation. The court pointed out that there were no prohibitions against donor-foundation dealings and cited the Senate Report on the Revenue Act of 1950 which felt that the House provision prohibiting self-dealing was too harsh. The government appealed and lost; the Court of Appeals upheld the Tax Court completely.[51]

Since there was no prohibition against "self-dealing," creators of private foundations viewed the foundation as an integral part of their activities and used the foundation in all kinds of dealings. Since it was rarely necessary for a foundation and its creator or donors to engage in "self-dealing" in order for the foundation to carry out its charitable activities, all "self-dealing" could be viewed with suspicion. Furthermore, it was difficult to ascertain without an Internal Revenue Service examination whether the foundation had engaged in "self-dealing" (either permissible or prohibited) and if an examination did disclose "self-dealing," it was a difficult task to ascertain whether the transactions were at "arm's length" or not. If a foundation purchased assets from its founder, was the purchase consistent with the foundation's charitable objectives or was the founder deriving some private benefit that no investigation, no matter how extensive, would disclose?[52]

Unreasonable Accumulations

Under then-existing law,[53] an immediate deduction was permitted for contributions made to tax-exempt, private foundations, regardless of who controlled them. However, charity did not derive any benefit from private, nonoperating foundations until it received funds from them. The ability of foundation directors to withhold current charitable benefits from the public merely to build a larger fund for some future charitable giving was an abuse.[54] The usage of the term "unreasonable accumulation" in the law provided the private foundations with many avenues to circumvent the law. A term such as "unreasonable" did not provide the necessary guidelines for fair law enforcement. It also made the administration of the law difficult and the courts had to decide what "unreasonable" meant. In the Erie Endowment case,[55] a trust was created in 1936 and a trust provision provided that 90 percent of the net profits should be retained during the first five years; 80 percent during the second five years; 70 percent during the next ten years; and 50 percent during the succeeding ten years until a principal sum of ten million dollars was reached. The trust was created with an investment of $100,000 and by 1958, the trust had accumulated $389,000 of net income. The court said:

> Reasonableness, that hobgoblin of judicial minds, can only be devined on the basis of all relevant facts. The standard to be applied is whether the taxpayer can justify the total accumulation of income at the end of the taxable year, in terms of both time and amount, on the basis of a rational total program of charitable intent. The plan must be viewed in its entirety.

The court ruled that there was no program or project requiring the accumulation of income and hence the foundation was properly deprived of its tax exemption under Section 504.

Some foundations discovered a way to circumvent the law totally by first acquiring property subject to an indebtedness and then accumulating income to retire the indebtedness, claiming that the accumulation was necessary to liquidate the indebtedness and hence not unreasonable. In Tell Foundation v. Wood,[56] the creators conveyed property to the foundation subject to a first mortgage of $120,000 to an insurance company and a second mortgage to themselves of $50,000, making a total encumbrance of $170,000. The foundation owned the equity in the property and in order to preserve the property for the use and purpose for which it was created, made payments accruing under the mortgage. The court held that the foundation had not accumulated its income unreasonably or used it to a substantial degree for purposes other than those upon which its exemption was based.

The courts took a lenient attitude toward the unreasonable accumulations by private foundations. They were dealing with charitable work. The consequences to the foundation of a determination that an accumulation of income was unreasonable would have been the loss of its tax exemption.[57] There were no intermediary steps that the law permitted and, hence, there were no lesser penalties that a judge could prescribe in a particular case. Thus, unless the "unreasonable accumulation" was flagrant and the organization was involved in no charitable work, the courts would not remove its tax exemption.

Other Abuses

The use of the private foundation in estate planning permitted individuals, some of whom had accumulated tremendous wealth during their lives, to pass control of their wealth to their heirs or at least allow their heirs to enjoy the income from the wealth without the estate having to pay taxes.[58]

TAX REFORM ACT OF 1969

Tax on Foundations

In passing the Tax Reform Act of 1969, Congress finally recognized that granting special tax privileges to one group meant that some other sector was paying for the privilege. For the first time, Congress levied a tax on private foundations, thus removing a part of their tax exemption. The tax is an excise tax of 4 percent on net investment income.[59] The House Committee on Ways and Means stated:

> Your committee believes that since the benefits of government are available to all, the costs should be borne, at least to some extent, by all those able to pay. Your committee believes that this is as true for private foundations as it is for taxpayers generally. Also, it is clear that vigorous and extensive administration is needed in order to provide appropriate assurances that private foundations will promptly and properly use their funds for charitable purposes. This tax, then, may be viewed as being in part a user fee.[60]

Prohibited Transactions

The 1969 Act removed private foundations from the provisions of Section 503 of the I.R.C., which prohibited self-dealing not at arm's length between a foundation and its creator or substantial contributor.[61] In the Act of 1969, Congress recognized that a standard such as "arm's length" was difficult to enforce fairly and impartially.

> Arm's-length standards have proved to require dispro-
> portionately great enforcement efforts resulting in
> sporadic and uncertain effectiveness of the provisions.
> On occasion the sanctions are ineffective and tend to
> discourage the expenditures of enforcement effort.
> On the other hand, in many cases the sanctions are
> so great in comparison to the offense involved as to
> create reluctance in enforcement, especially in view
> of the element of subjectivity in applying arm's-length
> standards. Where the Internal Revenue Service does
> seek to apply sanctions in such circumstances, the same
> factors encourage extensive litigation and sometimes
> reluctance by the courts to uphold severe sanctions.[62]

Congress indicated that in many situations, current law did not adequately preserve the integrity of private foundations, even if the terms of law did apply.[63] Congress concluded that "even arm's-length standards often permit use of a private foundation to improperly benefit those who control the foundation."[64]

Finally, after many years, Congress recognized that higher standards were needed to guide the foundations. Foundations had engaged in all kinds of "self-dealing" activities due to a lack of standards. Congress decided to do away with the arm's-length standard and substituted something more appropriate for the type of institution involved.

> In order to minimize the need to apply subjective arm's-
> length standards, to avoid the temptation to misuse
> private foundations for noncharitable purposes, to
> provide a more rational relationship between sanctions
> and improper acts, and to make it more practical to
> properly enforce the law, your committee has determined
> to generally prohibit self-dealing transactions and to
> provide a variety and graduation of sanctions. . . .[65]

Section 4941[66] imposed a tax of 5 percent of the amount involved on each act of self-dealing between a disqualified person and a private foundation. The tax was imposed on the disqualified person and, in addition, a tax of 2.125 percent was imposed on the foundation manager if he knew it was an act of self-dealing. If the self-dealing was not corrected, then an additional tax of 200 percent of the amount involved was imposed on the disqualified person and 50 percent on the foundation manager.

Section 4941, which prohibits self-dealing, is a vast improvement over its predecessor Section 503 in that it removes the subjective criteria of "arm's length" and substitutes a flat prohibition against self-dealing. Thus, there are now objective criteria to guide a foundation and its managers as to which activities are expressly prohibited.

Involvement in Business

Prior law had no prohibition against a foundation's owning businesses directly or indirectly. The House Committee pointed out that:

> The use of foundations to maintain control of businesses, particularly small family corporations, appears to be increasing. It is unclear under present law at which point such non-charitable purposes become sufficiently great to disqualify the foundation from exempt status.[67]

The committee also noted that where the charitable purposes predominate, "the business may be run in a way which unfairly competes with other businesses whose owners must pay taxes on the income that they derive from the business."[68] Section 4943[69] imposed a tax of 5 percent on a private foundation's excess business holdings. If the foundation failed to dispose of the excess holdings within the correction period (90 days after receipt of a deficiency notice), an additional tax of 200 percent was imposed on the excess holdings. A foundation was permitted to hold 20 percent of the voting stock reduced by the percentage of voting stock owned by all disqualified persons.

Congress also dealt with the problem of the "sale and leaseback" and the "bootstrap sale." The remedy was to impose the unrelated business income tax on the income received by the exempt organization from the transaction in proportion to the debt existing on the income-producing property.[70] Thus, the Revenue Act of 1969 taxed the income received by the tax-exempt organization from debt-financed property. Congress recognized the related problem of the subsidiary corporation.

In certain cases exempt organizations do not engage in
business directly but do so through nominally taxable
subsidiary corporations. In many such instances the
subsidiary corporations pay interest, rents, or royalties
to the exempt parent in sufficient amount to eliminate
their entire income, which interest, rents, and royalties
are not taxed to the parent even though they may be derived from an active business.[71]

The Act removed the exemption from unrelated business tax
for passive income (interest, rents, royalties) if received from a
controlled corporation.[72]

Unreasonable Accumulations

Congress coped with the problem of foundations' unreasonable
accumulation of income. Congress recognized that while income is
being produced by the foundation-owned assets, the law did not
require its distribution until the accumulation became unreasonable.[73]
The law set no guidelines for "unreasonable accumulations" of income,
and the Committee on Ways and Means recognized the essential
problem by stating that "although a number of court cases have
begun to set guidelines as to the circumstances under which an
accumulation becomes unreasonable, in many cases the determination is essentially subjective."[74] The committee also noted that
"it frequently happens that the only available sanction (loss of exempt
status) either is largely ineffective or else unduly harsh."[75]
Section 504[76] was repealed by the Tax Reform Act of 1969,[77]
and Section 4942[78] was added to deal with "unreasonable accumulations." The new law imposed a tax on the undistributed income of
a foundation if such income has not been distributed in the year
earned or in the next year. The tax was 15 percent of the amount
undistributed and, if the foundation failed to take corrective action,
an additional tax of 10 percent was imposed on the amount undistributed.
The solution to a related problem in which a foundation received
as a contribution or purchased property that did not produce current
income (for example, jewelry, paintings), was to impose a minimum
income equivalent payout provision. The law required a foundation
to distribute all its income currently, but not less than 6 percent
of the fair market value of the foundation's investment assets.
Investment assets are all the assets of the foundation except those
used directly to carry out the foundation's exempt purpose.[79]

Congress, in approaching the problem through the minimum
income equivalent payout provision test, gave the enforcement
agency (Internal Revenue Service) objective criteria to utilize in
administering the law. It also gave the same criteria to the trustees
and administrators of foundations to consider when they decide on
the investments to be made by their foundations. It will impress
upon the administrators and trustees the fact that they must distribute
current income to charity. Since a current tax deduction was enjoyed
by the original donor of the property, the public is entitled to have
the foundation make an income distribution to charity on a current
basis.

Information Returns

Under prior law, private foundations were required to file annual
information tax returns (990-A). A portion of the private foundation's
tax return was considered a public document and hence available to
anyone who wished to examine it at the Internal Revenue Service.
The Tax Reform Act of 1969 continued that requirement.[80]
Congress recognized that the public was entitled to be informed
of the foundation's activities and financial situation.

The House and the Finance Committee concluded that
experience of the past two decades indicates that more
information is needed on a more current basis for more
organizations and that this information should be made
more readily available to the public. . . .[81]

Congress, in the Tax Reform Act of 1969, added a requirement that
an additional information return (990-AR) be filed and, in addition,
be made available for public inspection at the foundation's office
and that the foundation must publicize this fact in a local newspaper.
These new requirements apply to any private foundation having at
least $5,000 in assets at any time during a taxable year. In lieu of
the 990-AR, a private foundation may substitute an annual report
containing all the information specified on the 990-AR.[82]
A copy of the 990-AR or the equivalent annual report must be
furnished to the attorney general of the state in which the principal
office of the foundation is located, the state in which the foundation
was incorporated or created, and each state that the foundation is
required to list as an attachment to the Form 990 pursuant to Treasury
Regulations 1.6033-2(a) (iv).[83] In addition, the commissioner of the
Internal Revenue Service may designate one or more appropriate

libraries or depositories to which the foundation will be required to send copies of their annual reports.[84]

SUMMARY

Private philanthropic foundations have been misused in the past. Before 1950, they could engage in almost any activity as long as the proceeds ultimately went to charity. Congress, concerned with the effect of private foundations on competition, enacted the Revenue Act of 1950, designed to curb those abuses. However, the Revenue Act of 1950 did not deter the abusive practices as evidenced by the court cases and Treasury Department investigations of private foundations. To curb those abuses and, more importantly, to recognize that granting tax exemption to one group shifts the tax burden to other groups, Congress enacted the Tax Reform Act of 1969.

Presently, the federal tax statutes act as the major regulatory device of private foundations because tax exemption and related tax benefits have been a major incentive for the creation of many private foundations. Thus, federal taxation has and does play a vital role in the creation, organization, and operation of private foundations.

NOTES

1. J. S. Seidman, Seidman's Legislative History of Federal Income Tax Laws 1938-1861 (New York: Prentice-Hall, 1938), p. 1002.

2. Trinidad v. Sagrada Orden DePredicadores, 263 U.S. 578 (1924).

3. Sand Springs Home v. Commissioner of Internal Revenue, 6 B.T.A. 148 (1927).

4. Roche's Beach Inc. v. Commissioner of Internal Revenue, 38-1 USTC Para. 9302 (1938).

5. "The Macaroni Monopoly: The Developing Concept of Unrelated Business Income of Exempt Organizations," Harvard Law Review, April 1968.

6. C. F. Mueller Co. v. Commissioner of Internal Revenue, 51-1 USTC Para. 9360 (1951).

7. U.S. Congress, House, Revenue Act of 1950, 81st Cong., 2nd Sess., 1949, H. Rept. 2319, C.B., 1950-52, p. 410.

8. Ohio Furnace Co. v. Commissioner of Internal Revenue, 25 TC 179 (1959).

9. Law of Federal Income Taxation, Mertens, vol. 6 (Mandelein, Ill.: Callaghan & Co., 1968), pp. 97-109.

10. Ibid., p. 97.

11. Ibid.

12. U.S. Congress, House, Hearings before the Special Committee to Investigate Tax-Exempt Foundations and Comparable Organizations, 83rd Cong., 2nd Sess., 1954 (hereafter referred to as the Reece Hearings).

13. R. Wormser, Foundations: Their Power and Influence (New York: Devin-Adair, 1958), p. 11.

14. Norman Sugarman, "Current Issues in the Use of Tax-Exempt Organizations," Taxes, December 1956, p. 795.

15. U.S. Congress, House, Committee on Ways and Means, Treasury Department Report on Private Foundations, 89th Cong., 1st Sess., 1965, p. 9.

16. U.S. Congress, House, Revenue Act of 1950, 81st Cong., 2nd Sess., 1949, H. Rept. 2319, C.B. 1950-52, p. 408 (hereafter referred to as H.R., 1950).

17. I.R.C. (1954).

18. H. R., 1950, op. cit., p. 412.

19. Ibid.

20. U.S. Congress, Senate, Revenue Act of 1950, 81st Cong., 2nd Sess., 1950, Rept. 2375, C.B. 1950-52, p. 510 (hereafter referred to as S.R., 1950).

21. H.R., 1950, op. cit., p. 411.

22. U.S. Congress, House, Revenue Act of 1950, 81st Cong., 2nd Sess., 1950, H. Rept. 3124, C.B. 1950-52, p. 591.

23. H.R., 1950, op. cit., p. 408.

24. Section 511, I.R.C. (1954).

25. H.R., 1950, op. cit., p. 410.

26. Section 514, I.R.C. (1954).

27. Section 502, I.R.C. (1954).

28. Sico Foundation v. Commissioner of Internal Revenue, 61-2 USTC 9732 (1961).

29. Scripture Press Foundation v. Commissioner of Internal Revenue, 61-1 USTC Para. 9195 (1961), Sup. Ct. cert denied 368 U.S. 985, 1962.

30. Section 512(b), I.R.C. (1954).

31. New York Times, November 24, 1969, p. 1.

32. Ibid.

33. Section 514, I.R.C. (1954).

34. Section 511, I.R.C. (1954).

35. Section 502, I.R.C. (1954).

36. Anderson Dairy, Inc. v. Commissioner of Internal Revenue, 39 TC 1027 (1963).

37. U.S. Congress, House, Select Committee on Small Business, Tax-Exempt Foundations and Charitable Trusts: Their Impact on Our

Economy, 87th Cong., 2nd Sess., 1962 Chairman's Report to the
Select Committee on Small Business, 1st installment, p. 14.

38. Commissioner of Internal Revenue v. Clay Brown, 65-1
USTC Para. 9375 (1965).

39. University Hill Foundation v. Commissioner of Internal
Revenue, 71-1 USTC Para. 9440 (1971), reversing 51 TC 548 (1969).

40. Treasury Department Report on Private Foundations, op.
cit., p. 48.

41. Section 503, I.R.C. (1954).

42. Section 503(c) (1), I.R.C. (1954).

43. Patman Report, first installment, op. cit., p. 15.

44. Ibid., p. 79.

45. Ibid., p. 80.

46. Griswald v. Commissioner of Internal Revenue, 39 TC 620
(1962).

47. Patman Report, first installment, op. cit., p. 81.

48. Ibid., p. 82.

49. Ibid.

50. Teich Foundation v. Commissioner of Internal Revenue,
48 TC 963 (1967).

51. Commissioner of Internal Revenue v. Teich Foundation,
69-1 USTC Para. 9239 (1969).

52. Author's own experience as an Internal Revenue Agent in
the Tax-Exempt Group in the Manhattan District of the Internal
Revenue Service.

53. Section 170 for income tax purposes, section 2522 for gift
tax purposes, section 2055 for estate tax purposes, I.R.C. (1954).

54. Treasury Department Report on Private Foundations,
op. cit., p. 24.

55. Erie Endowment v. Commissioner of Internal Revenue,
63-1 USTC Para. 9373 (1963).

56. Tell Foundation v. Wood, 58-1 USTC Para. 9111 (1957).

57. Section 504, I.R.C. (1954).

58. T. Snee and L. Cusack, Principles and Practices of Estate
Planning (New York: Prentice-Hall, 1964), p. 250.

59. Section 4940, Tax Reform Act of 1969.

60. U.S. Congress, House, Tax Reform Act of 1969, 91st
Congress, 1st Sess., 1969, Report 91-413 (Part 1), (New York:
Commerce Clearing House, 1969), No. 35, p. 19.

61. Bill Section 101(j) (7), Tax Reform Act of 1969.

62. H.R., 1969, op. cit., p. 20.

63. Ibid.

64. Ibid., p. 21.

65. Ibid.

66. Section 4941, Tax Reform Act of 1969.

67. H.R., 1969, op. cit., p. 27.

68. Ibid.

69. Section 4943, Tax Reform Act of 1969.

70. Section 514, I.R.C. (1954), as amended by Tax Reform Act of 1969.

71. H.R., 1969, op. cit., p. 49.

72. Section 512(b) (15), I.R.C. (1954), as amended by the Tax Reform Act of 1969.

73. Section 504(a) (1), I.R.C. (1954).

74. H.R., 1969, op. cit., p. 25.

75. Ibid.

76. Section 504, I.R.C. (1954).

77. Bill Section 101(j) (15), Tax Reform Act of 1969.

78. Section 4942, Tax Reform Act of 1969.

79. Ibid.

80. Section 6056, Tax Reform Act of 1969.

81. U.S. Congress, Senate, Tax Reform Act of 1969, 91st Cong., 1st Sess., 1969, Report 91-552, (New York: Commerce Clearing House, 1969), No. 51, p. 52.

82. Section 6056 and Section 6104(d), Tax Reform Act of 1969.

83. Treas. Reg. 1.6056-1(b) (3).

84. Treas. Reg. 1.6056-1(b) (2).

3

OBJECTIVES OF FOUNDATION FINANCIAL REPORTING

USERS OF ANNUAL REPORTS

The question that must be answered before any critical analysis of current practices is undertaken is—Who uses the annual report of the private foundation and for what purpose? The objectives of foundation reporting can be determined only after determining who the user is. The private foundation presents information in its annual report to the interested reader. Is the type of information now presented useful to the reader for his objectives in connection with the private foundation?

Identification of the user of financial statements of private foundations is not an easy task. Even for profit-oriented enterprises, identity of the user remains uncertain and unresolved. Certainly the list would include present investors, prospective investors, financial analysts, creditors, and banks. However, of reports of the private foundations, none of the above would be a user because the foundation has no stockholders and does not rely on loans to carry out its objectives.

While nonprofit organizations do not have stockholders, some have reasonable equivalents. For example, churches have congregations, schools have student bodies, and governmental agencies have voters to act in the role of a direct constituency. However, private foundations do not have a congregation, student body, or a voting body; they lack a direct constituency.

Who, then, uses the annual report of the private foundations? I asked this question in interviews with representatives of both private foundations and certified public accounting firms that attested to their financial statements. The conclusion, while obviously not definitive, is that the general public is the ultimate user. In addition, there are also users who have a more direct interest in a particular foundation. One group indicated by the interviews was the board of directors or trustees of the foundation. This group is not an external user, but still a group that relies on the annual report for information.

Among external users, one group are grantees—those who are primarily interested in obtaining a grant from the foundation. Marianna O. Lewis, editor of the Foundation Center, indicated that the annual report is one source of many that potential grantees use in their efforts to obtain funds from a foundation for a particular project.[1] Other interviewees agreed. They also identified colleges and universities as users, either as potential grantees or as a reference source. Other users identified in the interviews are people interested in the same field of activity as the foundation. The Kress Foundation is interested in art and thus people interested in art might use that foundation's annual report to see what activities are being financed by the foundation. The interviews also indicated that private foundations are interested in the activities of each other and utilize annual reports as part of their effort to find out about other foundations. The information sought is the foundation's charitable activities, as well as such financial matters as investments, financial statement presentation, and accounting methods and standards.

The government is another user of annual reports. It acts as a representative of the general public to ascertain that a foundation is not violating any laws and, furthermore, that the private foundation is being truly utilized for charitable activities.

The general public is the ultimate user. It has granted the foundation valuable tax privileges under federal tax statutes and has the right to demand that the foundations carry out the objectives for which they were granted tax exemption. Chapter 2 demonstrated that the federal government has recognized its responsibility by passing a series of laws holding the private foundations much more accountable for their activities, both charitable and financial.

A picture emerges of users who are quite different from investors in profit-oriented enterprises and financial analysts, who are quite sophisticated financially.

OBJECTIVES OF THE FINANCIAL
STATEMENTS

In the past, private foundations have been somewhat secretive about their activities and finances. Writing on public accountability of private foundations, Eleanor Taylor complained that "a substantial number of foundations take the position that the predominantly private source of their funds frees them of any obligation to report their activities."[2] She also indicated that research workers have complained of this reticence.[3] Congressman Wright Patman also commented on the difficulty in obtaining information from some foundations:

Obtaining the information from the foundations has been a struggle. In many cases it has taken four or five letters and a reminder of the Committee's subpeona power to obtain the information needed for this study.[4]

The Commission on Foundations and Private Philanthropy expressed dismay over the tiny fraction of foundations issuing any annual report. It said that every foundation should publish some kind of report, even if only a few mimeographed pages.[5] The commission was aware of the harmful results caused by the lack of information and secretiveness on the part of private foundations when it said:

The sense of privatism which many foundations have displayed serves neither the public interest nor their own. One element underlying the current concern about foundations is a feeling of unease about activities behind the scenes; a suspicion nurtured by the paucity of available information.[6]

The annual report is a means of communicating information from the enterprise to those desiring the information. Certainly, then, one of the objectives of the financial statements in the annual report is or should be to give the user a view of the economic resources available and the use being made of them. It should answer the charge of critics that foundations surround themselves in a "cloak of secrecy." It may answer, in part, the following question asked by the Commission on Foundations and Private Philanthropy:

when the Congress was enacting the Tax Reform Act of 1969, philanthropy generally and the foundations specifically seemed to lack the active support of a broad based public constituency. The vocal part of the public seemed far more ready to decry the faults of some foundations than the silent part was ready to come to the support of what was worth preserving in others. Why?[7]

The commission concluded that full disclosure and public reporting of foundation activities serves the public's right to know and, in addition, "can serve as one of the most powerful ways of obtaining fuller accountability."[8]

Thus, when I asked in my interviews the question—"What should be the primary objective of the financial statements included in the annual report of the private foundations?", the responses indicated an awareness of the quasi-public nature of the private foundations and the nature of the users, with the public being the ultimate user. The interviews revealed a common thread in the answers to this question. Most interviewees responded that accountability for assets was the major objective. The foundation should reflect its stewardship of the assets entrusted to it. The foundation should describe clearly in monetary terms its activities. Is the foundation doing what it is supposed to be doing, and how well is it being operated? Is the foundation fulfilling its reason for existence?

The interviews revealed that the objectives of the financial statements should be to inform the reader of two things: the resources available to carry out foundation activity; and the activities of the foundations with those resources in the past.

Are the objectives of the financial statements different for a profit-oriented enterprise than for a nonprofit enterprise? The Study Group on the Objectives of Financial Statements said: "The basic objective of financial statements is to provide information useful for making economic decisions."[9] The group also recognized that one of the objectives of the financial statements is to serve users who have limited access, ability, resources, or authority to obtain information and thus rely on the financial statements as a primary source of information about the economic activities of the enterprise.[10] The group drew an analogy between investing in securities and investing in a hospital, university, or church and concluded that in many ways they are similar in that "making any of these decisions, a person contemplates making certain sacrifices in the hope of realizing particular benefits."[11]

The Committee on Accounting Concepts and Standards of the American Accounting Association said that the objectives of accounting are the same for profit as well as nonprofit organizations.

> The primary function of accounting is to accumulate and communicate information essential to an understanding of the activities of an enterprise, whether large or small, corporate or non-corporate, profit or non-profit, public or private.[12]

The committee concluded that the objectives of the financial statements should be to provide the users with information necessary to help them make decisions. The user, in making decisions, is hoping to obtain personal goals, whether financial or otherwise. The similarity between profit and nonprofit enterprises is that the user looks to both of them to achieve personal goals.[13]

The Study Group of the American Institute of Certified Public Accountants discussed accountability for performance and goal attainment and said that "reporting on such accountability is as important for not-for-profit organizations as it is for commercial enterprises."[14] The group specifically gave as an objective of financial statements for not-for-profit organizations the need to provide information useful for evaluating management effectiveness in the utilization of resources and in achieving goals.[15]

By definition, the objectives of a profit entity appear to be diametrically opposed to those of a nonprofit entity. Then how can the objectives of financial reporting be the same for both types of entities, a conclusion reached by both the Study Group of the American Institute of Certified Public Accountants and the Committee on Accounting Concepts and Standards of the American Accounting Association?

Both exist to satisfy needs of the user. In one case, the needs are economic and in the other, social. In both cases, a person makes sacrifices in order to derive benefits. Thus, the ultimate objective of financial reporting should be to provide information useful for evaluating management effectiveness in utilizing resources under its control to satisfy users' needs, whether economic or social.

However, to the extent of knowledge presently available, it is difficult, if not impossible, to achieve this objective for nonprofit entities, especially foundations. For example, if a foundation makes a grant to expand knowledge of some type of art, the evaluation of benefits received is extremely difficult, if not impossible, to measure, thus preventing any meaningful evaluation of management's effectiveness in utilizing resources under its control. This matter is extensively discussed in Chapter 7, "Measuring and Reporting Social Output."

The study group should have also set objectives for nonprofit reporting that are presently obtainable rather than just objectives that may never be realized. Thus, at the present time, intermediate objectives for private-foundation financial reporting are the only ones feasible. This does not mean that intermediate objectives are insignificant.

These intermediate objectives are not identical with the objectives of financial reporting of a profit entity. An individual may read the annual report of the Kress Foundation just to inform himself of the areas of art that the Kress Foundation is interested in; a reader may examine the annual report of the Rockefeller Foundation to see if they might possibly be interested in supporting his particular area of medical research.

I agree with the interviewees who concluded that the objectives
of private-foundation financial reporting should be to inform the
reader of two things: the resources available to carry out foundation
activities; and the activities of the foundation with those resources
in the past.

NEED FOR ACCOUNTING AND
REPORTING STANDARDS

Inherent in every decision-making process is the necessity to
compare, and one reason given by the study group for formulating
financial-statement objectives "is to guide the development of
accounting standards that will increase the ability to make comparisons."[16] Accounting standards are vital to make comparisons that
are inherent in any decision-making process. If the objectives of
financial statements are to permit a user to make decisions about
the enterprise under study, the user must be able to make comparisons; otherwise the whole decision process becomes mere guesswork.
To make valid comparisons, the objects being measured should be
measured with the same "yardstick." Accounting standards are as
important in nonprofit accounting as for profit-oriented enterprises.
However, accountants historically have devoted most of their efforts
to the profit-oriented segment of our economy, as was discussed
previously in Chapter 1.

The Commission on Foundations and Private Philanthropy was
dismayed by the absence of accounting standards for financial
reporting.[17] The commission said:

> Financial reports may be used for three purposes: to
> show the financial position and results of operations
> of a single foundation standing alone, to compare the
> results of several foundations, or to compile overall
> statistical data on foundations. Uniformity of definitions,
> bases of measurement, and reporting practices is essen-
> tial in order to permit comparisons between foundations
> or to compile meaningful statistical information.[18]

The commission recognized that accounting standards are vital
to prepare meaningful and comparative information.

The lack of standards has not received much attention from
accountants for various reasons. One is that the results of lack of
standards are not as visible as in the private sector, where investors
or creditors make financial decisions based on the data attested to
by accountants. The lack of standards in the profit-oriented sector

could cause, among other things, law suits directed at the public accountants for false or misleading information. This process is not at work for nonprofit organizations where the users generally have a more indirect relationship with the organization, and the lack of meaningful, comparable, and useful information will not result in lawsuits.

Misinformation may result in resources being misallocated, regardless of whether the organization is profit or nonprofit.

Users of the financial statements rely upon them as a source of information in the decision-making process. Investment decisions take place in the nonprofit area; the organizations do compete for resources and the resources should go to those organizations that will provide the services in the most efficient and economical manner. The only way it is at all possible to compare different entities providing similar services is to have them supply financial information on a comparable basis.

In addition, the general public subsidizes private foundations by granting them tax exemption. The general public is entitled to have useful information so that it too can make comparisons among different entities as to their efficiency in providing services.

NOTES

1. Interview with Mariana O. Lewis, Editor, Foundation Center, October 29, 1973.

2. Eleanor K. Taylor, Public Accountability of Foundations and Charitable Trusts (New York: Russell Sage Foundation, 1953), p. 114.

3. Ibid.

4. U.S. Congress, House, Select Committee on Small Business, Tax-Exempt Foundations and Charitable Trusts: Their Impact on Our Economy, 87th Cong., 2nd Sess., 1962 Chairman's Report to the Select Committee on Small Business, 1st installment, p. 2.

5. Commission on Foundations and Private Philanthropy, Foundations, Private Giving, and Public Policy (Chicago, Ill.: University of Chicago Press, 1970), p. 135.

6. Ibid., p. 154.

7. Ibid., p. 6.

8. Ibid., p. 124.

9. Report of the Study Group on the Objectives of Financial Statements, Objectives of Financial Statements (New York: AICPA, 1973), p. 13.

10. Ibid., p. 17.

11. Ibid., p. 49.

12. Committee on Accounting Concepts and Standards, American Accounting Association, Accounting and Reporting Standards for Corporate Financial Statements (Iowa City, Iowa: American Accounting Association, 1957), p. 1.

13. Ibid., p. 49.

14. Report of the Study Group, op. cit., p. 50.

15. Ibid., p. 51.

16. Ibid.

17. Commission on Foundations and Private Philanthropy, op. cit., p. 152.

18. Ibid.

4

REVIEW OF
THE LITERATURE

INTRODUCTION

The purpose of this chapter is to examine the literature on nonprofit organizations to determine the reasoning behind much of present-day accounting practices for private foundations. The chapter is presented without any attempt at analysis or evaluation; it serves to provide the rationale behind what exists today.

The literature does provide the logic or rationale behind many but not all of the present-day accounting practices of private foundations. For example, depreciation accounting for nonprofit organizations is dealt with adequately in the literature but accounting for grants paid is not covered.

Where gaps exist, I try to supply the rationale behind the accounting treatment relying on my own knowledge and experience in the nonprofit area. However, I do not necessarily agree or disagree with the rationale and logic that I provide to fill in the gaps.

CASH BASIS VERSUS ACCRUAL BASIS

Most advocates of the cash basis argue that the purpose of accrual accounting is to determine net income—a figure arrived at by a process of matching costs incurred against revenues earned. Since, by definition, a nonprofit organization's existence is to carry out charitable activities and not to earn a profit for the stockholders, then accrual accounting is unnecessary, more difficult to understand, and serves no useful purpose.

Louis Englander, a recognized authority on nonprofit organizations, wrote in 1957:

The purpose of matching costs with current revenues is to determine net income. In philanthropic organizations profits do not exist. There is no necessity for differentiating between the expired and deferred portion of any expenditures.[1]

One of the major reasons for the popularity of the cash basis is its simplicity. Laymen who are involved in nonprofit organizations more easily understand the cash basis. Many people who work for nonprofit organizations are on a voluntary, unpaid basis and often are not trained in accounting. Those individuals prefer the cash basis to keep records.

Another important reason for the cash basis is that accrual accounting is associated with measuring net income, and since by definition nonprofit organizations are not in business to earn a profit, the accrual basis would appear to be inappropriate.

Another reason for the popularity of the cash basis is the significance of stewardship over the assets in nonprofit organizations. The manager of a private foundation may feel obligated to account for the assets on a cash basis, to indicate the cash received and the cash disbursed in discharge of his stewardship. The gross income indicates the maximum amounts that can be paid for charitable activities. The accrual basis might suggest a disparity between income and cash available for charitable work.

The Committee on Accounting Practices for Not-for-Profit Organizations concluded that the current accounting and reporting practices of most not-for-profit organizations evolved from and focused upon legalistic dollar accountability on a year-by-year basis.[2]

It appears that since private foundations have been viewed as public trusts, and many private foundations have in fact been created by trusts rather than incorporation,[3] the principles of trust accounting have been applied with their emphasis on accounting for cash received and cash disbursed each year.

Additional evidence that the cash basis constitutes a generally accepted accounting principle for nonprofit organizations were the auditor's reports, which attested to the financial information whether on a cash basis (which sometimes was indicated) or on the accrual basis of accounting. I even found that the same auditor (Price Waterhouse & Co.) attested to the financial statements of the Kresge Foundation[4] on the accrual basis and the Samuel H. Kress Foundation[5] on the cash basis.

A search of the literature for accounting practices of nonprofit organizations reveals that, for the most part, the accrual method of accounting is the one recommended to reflect the stewardship and accountability for all the resources entrusted to the organization. The American Council on Education issued a guide for college administration. In this publication, they said that whether the institution is public or private, it is in the nature of a public trust, and thus the inherent obligations for stewardship and accountability require a system of accounting that will ensure full disclosure of operations and financial position.[6] The Committee on Health Care Institutions of the American Institute of Certified Public Accountants unanimously concluded that financial statements "should be prepared in accordance with generally accepted accounting principles."[7] The Committee of Voluntary Health and Welfare Organizations of the American Institute of Certified Public Accountants (AICPA) also concluded that "the accrual basis of accounting is required by generally accepted accounting principles for a fair presentation of financial position and results of operations."[8] The General Accounting Office, in a publication explaining accrual accounting in the federal government, said:

> The main reason for applying accrual techniques in
> government accounting is to produce more complete
> and accurate financial information on assets, liabilities,
> revenues, and costs than is obtainable from accounting
> systems that are concerned only with obligation and
> cash receipt and disbursement transactions.[9]

One writer, in formulating accounting postulates and principles for nonprofit organizations, wrote that since the fairness of presentation of the results of operations and financial position are vital in the determination of the availability of funds with which the nonprofit organization can carry out its programs, then the accrual basis should be used.[10] Another writer concluded that the financial statements "should be all-inclusive in scope and should embrace all activities of the organization."[11]

Emerson O. Henke concluded in his book on nonprofit accounting that the accrual method is superior to the cash-basis method for every nonprofit organization engaged in the management and conversion of economic resources.[12] "The accrual basis is desirable, for it provides for reflection of operational as well as dollar accountability in the financial statements."[13]

The Committee on Accounting Practices for Not-for-Profit Organizations recommended the accrual basis in order to determine total organizational expense, costs by function or activities, and unit cost of measurable units of output.[14] The Committee on Concepts of Accounting Applicable to the Public Sector stated that assigning expenses (applied costs) to time periods, or to programs receiving the benefits, is one of the principal objectives of accounting and that accrual accounting, including the recognition of both prepaid and accrual expenses, is necessary to achieve this objective.[15]

Peculiar problems arise in the recording of foundation grants. Basically, the problem is one of timing—when should the grant be recorded? Under the cash basis, the grant is recorded when paid. However, under the accrual basis, a timing problem still exists. Some foundations record the grants when appropriated, while others record the grant when the specific grantee is notified that his proposal has been accepted and will be funded by the foundation.[16] An appropriation is an internal designation of funds "for specific purposes, projects, or investment as an aid in the planning of expenditure and the conservation of assets."[17]

Some of the certified public accountants I interviewed indicated that, in their opinion, grants should be recorded when a specific grantee has been informed that he has been awarded a grant.[18]

In Standards of Accounting and Financial Reporting, it is noted that some nonprofit organizations have created general reserves or have made general appropriations from balances of unrestricted funds. The recommendation in this publication is that "no such reserves, appropriations, or contingencies should be included on an agency's balance sheet."[19] However, it is permissible to designate a portion of a fund balance for a particular purpose by a segregation in the fund balance.[20] In discussing accrual basis, the AICPA audit guide for voluntary health and welfare organizations states that financial statements prepared on this basis should conform to the practices of business organizations with respect to such items as accrual of liabilities.[21]

A related area discussed by Malvern Gross, Jr. is the situation wherein a private foundation makes a grant payable over several years. Usually, the subsequent payments depend upon satisfactory performance with the original grant. Thus, the foundation's liability is somewhat conditional.[22] Some foundations handle this type of grant on the cash basis while others record the grant on an "appropriation basis," and yet others record the full expense and liability at the time the grantee has received notification of approval.

Gross recommended that private foundations should

record both as an expense and a liability all amounts which grantee institutions have been informed they will receive. However, disclosure should be made of the various amounts of the total liability payable

in specific future years. While in some instances such
amounts will ultimately not be paid, these are usually
infrequent and the unpaid amounts should be restored
to income (as a reduction of expenses) in the year in
which it becomes apparent that the foundation will not
be making these payments.[23]

DEPRECIATION ACCOUNTING

Probably one of the most controversial areas in nonprofit organizations is accounting for fixed assets with proponents on both sides
supporting their position with theoretical arguments. Chapter 5
indicates that the immediate write-off of fixed assets is a popular
practice among private foundations and thus constitutes a generally
accepted accounting principle. The major arguments against
depreciation accounting to a certain extent are the same as for
cash-basis accounting.

Louis Englander advanced the following arguments against
capitalization and depreciation of fixed assets:

1. depreciation is an element of cost which affects net income in
   business enterprises but has no applicability to nonprofit entities.
2. contributors have already paid for the cost of assets and charging
   depreciation against current operations would, in effect, charge
   the contributors twice for the same expenditure.
3. the advantages of the immediate write-off of fixed assets out-
   weighs the disadvantages of understating the assets.[24]

Rosecrans Baldwin argued in a similar vein that since the
nonprofit organizations do not finance most of the fixed asset replacements from income, they need not charge income with depreciation.[25]
Others concurred in equating depreciation accounting and asset
replacement.

If it is the intent or policy to replace the plant or equipment used from general funds of the organization, an
amount equivalent to normal depreciation should be charged
to operations and credited to a replacement fund. A like
amount of cash or other liquid assets should be segregated
for the sole purpose of financial replacements . . . .[26]

Many other arguments are advanced to support the recording
of expenditures for fixed assets as current expenses rather than as
assets. Many accountants are of the opinion that since nonprofit

organizations operate under an appropriation type of budgeting control showing proposed receipts and disbursements, accounting must disclose this data.[27] They contend that the outlay section of an operating statement should agree with assets disbursed.[28] Budgets usually are prepared on the basis of receipts and disbursements or revenues and disbursements basis; thus, disbursements are considered the criteria for accounting and not accrual-type expenses.[29]

Other accountants simply believe that depreciation accounting serves no useful purpose in nonprofit entities. Since fixed assets in nonprofit organizations do not generate revenue in the same sense that revenue-producing assets do in commercial enterprises, charging current operations with depreciation introduces a distorted net income; revenues are charged with costs that do not generate revenue.[30] Still others question the value of taking last year's expenditures for fixed assets, or expenditures of many years ago, and depreciating them so that they will be reflected in the current year's budget. They have been paid for.

Rosecrans Baldwin asked: "Why cloud what is essentially a simple picture of receiving money and spending it?"[31] He gave the following arguments against depreciation accounting:

1. Depreciation expense would inevitably cause the nonprofit organization to show a large annual deficit, and the Board of Directors may well be tempted to reduce expenditures in order to reduce the deficit.
2. The deficit produced would be meaningless.
3. Boards ordinarily do not understand the concept of depreciation accounting but do understand receipts and expenditures.
4. If the organization shows a profit because of capitalization of items, how will the Board explain that there is no money?
5. In theory, the revenues and expenditures for each year should exactly balance, and nothing at all should appear on the bottom line of the income statement.

The National Committee on Governmental Accounting opposed depreciation accounting and gave major arguments against depreciation accounting:

The Committee recommends that depreciation of general fixed assets not be recorded as an expense in governmental accounting because no constructive purpose would be achieved by doing so . . . . In Commercial accounting, depreciation charges must be recorded as an expense because they must be related to the revenue produced by the fixed assets in determining

accurately the net profit or loss for a stated period of
time . . . With the exception of self-supporting Enterprise Funds, governmental units are not faced with the
same requirements for profit and loss determination as
privately-owned enterprises. Governments exist to
provide public services and regulatory activities on a
continuing basis, and the general expenditures incurred
therefore have no causative relationship with and do
not generate any general revenues. Governments do
not pay taxes based on income; their general fixed assets
are not directly related to their general credit and debt-
incurring capacity; governmental units are not traded
or sold as are private businesses; and any excess of
revenues over expenditures—for a single year or
cumulatively—is not available for distribution to
citizens and taxpayers in the manner that corporate
profits are available for distribution to stockholders.
Under these operating characteristics so devoid of
profitability considerations, any recording of depreciation on general fixed assets in the formal books of
account would not only fail to serve any essential
informational purpose in the financial statements
and reports, but could actually be misleading to the
users of such statements and reports. The latter
can result because the charging of current operations
with depreciation indicates a matching of costs with
directly related revenues in the generally accepted
commercial sense when, in fact, no causative relationship between revenues and expenditures exists for
most general governmental operations.[32]

The authoritative bodies of accounting all support depreciation
accounting. The American Accounting Association's Committee on
Not-for-Profit Organizations recommended depreciation accounting:

The accounting records and related reports of a not-for-
profit organization should disclose the cost of use or
consumption of the assets allocated to services and/or
time periods . . . by an acceptable depreciation technique.[33]

The Committee on Voluntary Health and Welfare Organizations
of the American Institute of Certified Public Accountants discussed
depreciation accounting and concluded that most arguments against
depreciation accounting are based on replacement accounting.[34]

The committee said "the means of replacing such assets and the degree to which replacement should be currently funded . . . are financing decisions to be made by the governing board and do not directly offset the cost of providing program or supporting services."[35] The committee concluded that if it is necessary to measure costs of providing services, depreciation accounting is an element of such measurement and is not optional or discretionary.[36] "Where depreciation is omitted, the cost of performing the organization's services is understated."[37] The National Health Council, in its exposure draft on accounting for voluntary health and welfare organizations, took the same position as the American Institute of Certified Public Accountants on depreciation accounting.[38]

ACCOUNTING FOR GRANTS PAID AND CONTRIBUTIONS RECEIVED

For the most part, accountants have remained silent about measurements of income and expense for nonprofit organizations. Thus, as Chapter 5 reveals, grants paid are treated as a deduction in the determination of net income by a majority of private foundations, yet the alternative of deducting grants paid from principal also constitutes a generally accepted accounting principle, since 34 percent of the foundations surveyed used this method.

Since most foundations are self-sustaining and do not rely on contributions, income is the primary source of funds for paying grants and indicates the ability to pay grants. Therefore, the majority of foundations deduct the grants from income, since the purpose of the income is to pay grants.

Including contributions received as income does not accord with the accountants' definition of income; however, that definition is designed for profit-oriented enterprises. A search of the literature dealing with nonprofit organizations reveals that income, receipts, and revenues are defined loosely and quite often are used interchangeably. Thus, Louis Englander stated that "the operating statement may be either a statement of cash receipts and disbursements, or a statement of income and expenses."[39] The National Health Council recommends that pledges should be included in "support" or "other revenue" when the pledge is made.[40] Even the American Institute of Certified Public Accountants, in its audit guide for Voluntary Health and Welfare Organizations, failed to discuss or explain this matter.[41]

Since the objective of the private foundation is to make grants, many foundation managers view the source of the receipts as an immaterial factor and lump together all receipts under one term called "income." To them, it is immaterial whether the receipt was from a contributor directly or from income generated from investments, which at one time were also contributed to the foundation, perhaps by the same contributor. To them, the amount of funds available for the payment of grants is important. Finally, if the objective of the nonprofit organization is to raise funds for charitable work, are not those receipts its income, since this is what it is in business to do?

The type of contributions received by foundations that included contributions received as part of principal may have differed from those of foundations that included contributions received as income. Some contributions are given to pay the current expenses or grants of the foundation, while others are given to provide the foundation with future revenues. Quite often, the contributor will specifically state that only the income from his or her gift can be used for current operations. That kind of restriction often explains why a foundation includes the contributions received as principal. The accounting follows trust accounting with the separation of the income and the principal. Other foundations that do not include contributions received as income may be guided by generally accepted accounting principles for profit-oriented enterprises, whose principles narrowly define income.

ACCOUNTING FOR CAPITAL GAINS AND LOSSES

Chapter 5 reveals that 73 percent of all foundations having capital gains or losses included them as part of principal, as opposed to the generally accepted accounting principle of including capital gains or losses as part of income. Why, then, do most private foundations treat capital gains as principal and not income? The answer is that trust accounting has had much more of an influence on private foundations than commercial accounting. In a typical trust, the trustee is charged with protecting the interests of two divergent groups, the income beneficiaries and the remaindermen. The income beneficiaries receive all income from the trust for a specified time period and then the principal is distributed to the remaindermen. Gains or losses on the disposal of principal assets increase or decrease the amount of the trust principal.[42] Private foundations follow the principles of trust accounting in separating income into two parts; one to be paid out and another part to be retained because it constitutes gains or losses on the sale of principal and is recorded directly with the principal. As a result private foundations are not concerned so much with the measurement of income as they are with the management of net income. The income figure represents the amounts that will be distributed, as far as private foundations are concerned.

The Ford Foundation commissioned Cary and Bright to study the law of endowment funds with the objective of gaining additional usable income for the private colleges. The result was the publication of The Law and the Lure of Endowment Funds.[43] The authors pointed out that the suggestion has been made to college administrators that capital gains as well as dividends and interest be taken into account in considering overall return to be used by the colleges for their operations; however, college administrators claimed that as a matter of law, capital gains may not be spent, because the capital gains are part of the principal of the endowment funds, which principal must be maintained intact.[44]

FUND ACCOUNTING

Fund accounting is popular with all types of nonprofit organizations, such as government, churches, educational institutions, voluntary health and welfare organizations, hospitals, and so on. The emphasis in fund accounting is to "disclose how the organization's resources have been acquired and used to accomplish the objectives of the organization."[45]

Whether created by incorporation or by a trust, most foundations are required to maintain the principal intact and disburse the income for charitable purposes. In a trust, the income is often paid to one recipient and the principal is eventually paid to another recipient. So a strict separation is required of amounts to be included in income from amounts to be included in principal. Foundation fund accounting closely follows trust accounting in this respect, and most foundations that use fund accounting use an income fund and a principal fund.

Twenty years ago, Delmer Hylton wrote on the difficulties of understanding governmental financial statements. He said: "Few accountants can draw basic conclusions from those statements without intense study, and to the typical nonaccountant, this type of report is so much 'gibberish.' "[46]

Others, such as Henke, writing on fund accounting, reached the same conclusion: "The use of too many fund entities may result in fragmentation of the accounting data and in hindering the preparation of useful financial reports for the organization as a whole."[47] The American Accounting Association's Committee on Accounting Practices for Not-for-Profit Organizations discussed the problem of fund accounting, and it said that the segregation of funds results in financial statements that are not statements for the entity as a whole

but are statements expressing separate bits of financial information
relative to "dollar accountability" of individual funds or groups.
The financial reports "become mere summaries of transactions
within subsets and not expressions of the activities, achievements,
and position of the overall operational entity."[48] C. W. Bastable,
in discussing fund accounting's role in responsible stewardship,
said that he was "not willing to concede that responsible stewardship
cannot be achieved except by the fragmentation, or compartmentaliza-
tion, that is fund accounting."[49]

Malvern J. Gross wrote that the financial statements should
tell clearly what has happened during the period. "They should be
easily comprehensible so that any person taking the time to study
them will understand the financial picture."[50] The unresolved issue
in accounting principles for nonprofit institutions was stated 25 years
ago:

> None of the techniques of compressing and simplifying
> data which have been successfully used in reporting on
> far-flung industrial organizations has been applied to
> nonprofit institution reports. Intricate detailed reports
> showing interrelations between various elements of
> the organization are necessary for management control
> but are of no real significance to the public. A compre-
> hensive activity report that transcends the fund struc-
> ture, thus giving the reader an overall view of the
> activities of the organization, would much more nearly
> fulfill the social responsibility of accounting.[51]

Recently, the Committee on Voluntary Health and Welfare
Organizations of the American Institute of Certified Public Accountants recommended that the balance sheet and the other financial
statements should show the revenue, expenses, and changes in fund
balances to reflect the activity within each fund where "the various
types of restricted funds . . . have been established in response to
donor or grantor restrictions."[52]

The Committee on Not-for-Profit Organizations of the American
Accounting Association concluded that:

> Current accounting and reporting practices of Not-
> for-Profit organizations are overly focused on the
> individual fund aspects to the exclusion of considera-
> tions relative to the operating entity as a whole.[53]

The committee recommended that attention be given to development
of supplementary statements that combine or consolidate fund informa-

tion to provide information relative to the entity as a whole. Statements on a fund basis can be prepared if necessary for special reasons, but they should be considered special reports rather than general reports. Consolidated statements provide a more meaningful and understandable overview for users resulting in better-informed users.[54]

The Accounting Advisory Committee concluded that financial statements are often difficult to understand because of adherence to the concepts of fund accounting.[55] The committee said:

> The financial statements of many philanthropic organizations are difficult to understand for the reader not familiar with the specialized accounting principles and reporting practices followed by such organizations. This difficulty results largely from the historic "stewardship" approach to accounting for funds given to such organizations for designated purposes. This stewardship approach is usually referred to as "fund accounting", a system of accounting in which separate records are kept for funds given to an organization for a specific purpose . . . . This can result in a proliferation of financial statements, often without any summary for the entity as a whole.[56]

ACCOUNTING ADVISORY COMMITTEE'S
RECOMMENDATIONS

The Commission on Private Philanthropy and Public Needs was formed in November 1973, as a privately funded group to study the role of philanthropic giving in the United States and to make recommendations for its improvement.[57] An Accounting Advisory Committee, a private group not affiliated with the American Institute of Certified Public Accountants, was formed consisting of four certified public accountants in public practice. The committee's purpose was to make recommendations to the Commission on Private Philanthropy and Public Needs.

The Accounting Advisory Committee issued a report to the Commission on Private Philanthropy and Public Needs in October 1974.[58] The report dealt with the following four points: the adequacy of present accounting principles and reporting practices of eight major types of philanthropic organizations; the desirability and practicability of establishing a single set of accounting principles and reporting practices for all philanthropic organizations; a survey of present federal and state regulatory financial reporting requirements and the extent to which uniform reporting exists; and a study of the financial information appropriate for regulatory agencies.[59]

The committee reached four conclusions and made two recommendations. The committee concluded that present reporting practices require substantial improvement; too many alternative accounting principles exist from which the philanthropic organizations can choose. (Furthermore, the three nonprofit audit guides of the American Institute of Certified Public Accountants do not uniformly prescribe accounting principles and reporting practices for the nonprofit organization to follow); the differing federal, state, and other municipalities' regulatory reporting requirements have caused a needless expense for philanthropic organizations in preparing the different reports; and the basic information required by the various regulatory agencies could be improved in regard to fairness of presentation, clarity, and uniformity.[60]

The Accounting Advisory Committee recommended that a single, uniform set of accounting principles be adopted by all philanthropic organizations. Furthermore, a uniform Standard Accounting Report (SAR) be adopted by each regulatory agency that now requires annual financial information from philanthropic organizations.[61] The Accounting Advisory Committee addressed itself to 16 issues, giving the significance of each issue, arguments in favor of each alternative, and the committee's conclusions. Some of the conclusions were: the accrual basis of accounting should be followed; total all funds information is appropriate provided the separate funds are also presented; all gifts and bequests should be reported in one statement as support, revenue, and other additions, all capital gains and losses should be reported in one statement as support, revenue and other additions; fixed assets should be capitalized; fixed assets should be depreciated; investments, exclusive of fixed assets held for use in the organization's program, should be carried at market-fair value; and expenses should be reported on a functional basis in the financial statements.

NOTES

1. Louis Englander, Accounting Principles and Procedures of Philanthropic Institutions (New York: New York Community Trust, 1957), p. 13.

2. American Accounting Association, Report of the Committee on Accounting for Not-for-Profit Organizations, Supplement to Vol. 46 of the Accounting Review, 1971, p. 86.

3. Foundation Directory, 3rd ed. (New York: Russell Sage Foundation for the Foundation Library Center, 1967), p. 13.

4. Kresge Foundation, Annual Report, 1972.

5. Samuel H. Kress Foundation, Annual Report, 1973.

6. College and University Administration (Washington, D.C.: American Council on Education, 1968), p. 141.

7. Committee on Health Care Institutions of the American Institute of Certified Public Accountants, Hospital Audit Guide (New York: American Institute of Certified Public Accountants, 1972), p. 3.

8. Committee of Voluntary Health and Welfare Organizations, Audits of Voluntary Health and Welfare Organizations (New York: American Institute of Certified Public Accountants, 1974), p. 33.

9. Frequently Asked Questions About Accrual Accounting in the Federal Government (Washington, D.C.: U.S. General Accounting Office, 1970), p. 9.

10. John C. Overhiser, "Accounting Postulates and Principles for Non-Profit Organizations," New York Certified Public Accountant, May 1962, p. 309.

11. Gross, op. cit., p. 5.

12. Emerson O. Henke, Accounting for Non-Profit Organizations (Belmont, Calif.: Wadsworth Publishing Co., 1966), p. 123.

13. Ibid.

14. Committee on Accounting Practices for Not-for-Profit Organizations, 1971, op. cit., p. 93.

15. American Accounting Association, Report of the Committee on Concepts of Accounting Applicable to the Public Sector, Supplement to Vol. 47 of the Accounting Review (1972), p. 101.

16. This problem was disclosed to me during my interviews with the certified public accountants, specifically during my interviews with Malvern Gross, Jr., June 18, 1974, and Howard Ray, June 26, 1974. It should be noted that the interviewees were indicating to me problems not specifically covered by my questions and thus my failure to cite other interviewees does not indicate agreement or disagreement on their part with the proposed solution since the issue was not raised by me during the interview.

17. Committee on Voluntary Health and Welfare Organizations of the AICPA, op. cit., p. 2.

18. See note 16.

19. Standards of Accounting and Financial Reporting for Voluntary Health and Welfare Organizations (Exposure Draft) (New York: National Health Council, 1974), p. 162.

20. Ibid.

21. Audits of Voluntary Health and Welfare Organizations, op. cit., p. 32.

22. Malvern Gross, Jr., Financial and Accounting Guide for Nonprofit Organizations, 2nd ed. (New York: Ronald Press, 1974), p. 276.

23. Ibid.

24. Englander, op. cit., pp. 13-14, 16.

25. Rosecrans Baldwin, "Depreciation for Non-Profit Organiza-tions—An Opposing View," New York Certified Public Accountant, August 1963, p. 552.

26. Overhiser, op. cit., p. 311.

27. Henke, op. cit., p. 124.

28. Ibid.

29. Committee on Accounting for Not-for-Profit Organizations, 1971, op. cit., p. 112.

30. Ibid.

31. Baldwin, op. cit., p. 550.

32. National Committee on Governmental Accounting, Govern-mental Accounting, Auditing and Financial Reporting (Chicago: Municipal Finance Officers Association, 1968), p. 11.

33. Committee on Accounting Practices for Not-for-Profit Organizations, 1971, op. cit., p. 119.

34. Committee on Voluntary Health and Welfare Organizations of the AICPA, op. cit., p. 11.

35. Ibid.

36. Ibid., p. 12.

37. Ibid.

38. Standards of Accounting and Financial Reporting for Voluntary Health and Welfare Organizations, op. cit., p. 31.

39. Englander, op. cit., p. 32.

40. National Health Council, op. cit., p. 18.

41. Committee on Voluntary Health and Welfare Organizations of the AICPA, op. cit.

42. W. Karrenbrock and H. Simons, Advanced Accounting, Comprehensive Volume, 3rd ed. (Cincinnati, Ohio: South-Western Publishing Co., 1961), p. 743.

43. W. L. Cary and C. B. Bright, Law and the Lore of Endow-ment Funds (New York: Ford Foundation, 1974).

44. Ibid., p. 5.

45. Committee on Voluntary Health and Welfare Organizations of the AICPA, op. cit., p. 1.

46. Delmer Hylton, "Needed: More Informative and Under-standable Financial Statements for Governmental Units," The Accounting Review, January 1957, p. 51.

47. Henke, op. cit., p. 5.

48. Committee on Accounting Practices for Not-for-Profit Organizations, 1971, op. cit., p. 99.

49. C. W. Bastable, "Collegiate Accounting Needs Re-evaluation," The Journal of Accountancy, December 1973, p. 53.

50. Gross, Financial Reporting Guide for Non-Profit Organiza-tions, op. cit., p. 5.

51. Robert Dickens, "Formulation of Accounting Principles for Non-Profit Institutions," New York Certified Public Accountant, June 1958, p. 410.

52. Committee on Voluntary Health and Welfare Organizations of the AICPA, op. cit., p. 4.

53. Committee on Not-for-Profit Organizations, 1971, op. cit., p. 87.

54. Ibid.

55. Accounting Advisory Committee, Report to the Commission on Private Philanthropy and Public Needs, October 1974, p. 13.

56. Ibid., p. 7.

57. Report of the Commission on Private Philanthropy and Public Needs, Giving in America (Washington, D.C.: Commission on Private Philanthropy and Public Needs, 1975), p. 1.

58. Accounting Advisory Committee, op. cit.

59. Ibid., p. 4.

60. Ibid.

61. Ibid.

5

CURRENT ACCOUNTING AND REPORTING PRACTICES OF PRIVATE FOUNDATIONS: AN EMPIRICAL STUDY

INTRODUCTION

Approximately 250 foundations currently publish annual reports.[1] I decided to examine all 250 of these reports in order to determine present accounting and reporting practices. However, I did not do them all because the Foundation Center[2] had only 198 annual reports available and 39 of those were reports of foundations that did not meet the criteria of being private foundations. That left 159 relevant annual reports for this study. Nine annual reports included no financial statements, leaving 150 foundations with usable annual reports.

The foundations were categorized by asset value[3] as follows:

Very large—Over $100 million in assets*
Large—$10 to $100 million
Intermediate—$1 to $10 million
Small—Less than $1 million

In each case, the latest annual report available was used for the study and most of the reports were for a fiscal year that ended in 1972, with the total time range being from 1970 to 1973. Data concerning the size of the foundations examined are summarized in Table 5.1, which reveals that 88 percent of the foundations which prepared an annual report had assets in excess of one million dollars, and 58 percent had assets in excess of $10 million. There are

---

*I used the Foundation Center's classification except that I added the "very large" category.

TABLE 5.1

Foundations Classified by Asset Size

Classification	Assets	Number of Foundations	Percent of Total
Very large	Over $100 million	21	14
Large	$10 to $100 million	66	44
Intermediate	$1 to $10 million	45	30
Small	Less than $1 million	18	12
Totals		150	100

Source: All tables in this chapter have been compiled by the author.

approximately 30,000 private foundations in the United States.[4] Most of these foundations are small and do not publish annual reports and they are not required to do so.

CASH BASIS VERSUS ACCRUAL BASIS

Table 5.2 reveals that the full cash basis is prevalent among private foundations: 42 percent of all foundations use that basis. Seventeen percent use some modified form of cash basis. Full cash basis means that investment income and expenses, operating expenses, and grants are all reported on a cash basis. The most prevalent type of modified cash basis used is one in which investment income and expenses, and operating expenses, are reported on the cash basis but grants are reported on the accrual basis. Fifteen percent of all foundations used this type of modified cash basis.

Even among very large foundations, which have assets in excess of $100 million, 48 percent are on some type of cash basis.

CAPITALIZING FIXED ASSETS VERSUS
EXPENSE OF PERIOD OF ACQUISITION

An examination of financial statements showed that some foundations capitalized fixed assets and then depreciated them; other foundations listed as an accounting practice the immediate write-off of fixed assets; still other foundations listed no fixed assets and mentioned no accounting treatment of them. This last group was

TABLE 5.2

Cash Basis Versus Accrual Basis

Basis	Very Large Number	Very Large Percent	Large Number	Large Percent	Intermediate Number	Intermediate Percent	Small Number	Small Percent	Totals Number	Totals Percent
Full cash basis	4	19	31	47	16	35	12	67	63	42
Modified cash basis[a]	5	24	12	18	4	9	2	11	23	15
Modified cash basis[b]	1	5	0	–	0	–	0	–	1	1
Modified cash basis[c]	0	–	1	2	0	–	0	–	1	1
Subtotals	10	48	44	67	20	44	14	78	88	59
Full accrual basis	11	52	22	33	25	56	4	22	62	41
Totals	21	100	66	100	45	100	18	100	150	100

[a]Investment income and expenses on cash basis, operating expenses on cash basis, grants on accrual basis.
[b]Investment income and expenses on cash basis, operating expenses on accrual basis, grants on accrual basis.
[c]Investment income and expenses on accrual basis, operating expenses on accrual basis, grants on cash basis.

TABLE 5.3

Capitalizing Fixed Assets Versus Expense of Period of Acquisition

	Very Large Number	Very Large Percent	Large Number	Large Percent	Intermediate Number	Intermediate Percent	Small Number	Small Percent	Totals Number	Totals Percent
Capitalized fixed assets	7	33	18	27	7	16	1	6	33	22
Expense of period of acquisition	6	29	11	17	5	11	0	0	22	15
Could not determine	8	38	37	56	33	73	17	94	95	63
Totals	21	100	66	100	45	100	18	100	150	100

classified as "could not determine" in Table 5.3. However, most of them probably belong in the same category as "expense of period of acquisition," since most private foundations have some fixed assets, such as furniture, equipment, typewriters, and so on, and none appears in their financial statements.

Table 5.3 reveals that recording fixed assets as an expense of the period of acquisition is a prevalent practice for private foundations and also constitutes a generally accepted accounting principle in contrast to profit-oriented enterprises, where depreciation accounting is the standard.

BASIS FOR VALUING INVESTMENT ASSETS

Table 5.4 reveals that most foundations value their investment assets at cost: very large foundations use market value to a greater extent than any other size category. These foundations follow generally accepted accounting principles for valuing long-term investments of profit-oriented enterprises. Most foundations (88 percent) that use cost also disclose the market value of their investments, a practice also widely accepted for profit-oriented enterprises.

One foundation used the lower of cost or market for valuing its investment assets. Twenty-four percent of the very large foundations used the market method of valuing their investments. This does not constitute a generally accepted accounting principle for most profit-oriented enterprises at the present time. However, recently, the American Institute of Certified Public Accountants sanctioned it as an alternative to the cost method for nonprofit organizations.[5]

DEDUCTING GRANTS PAID FROM NET
INCOME VERSUS DEDUCTING THEM
FROM PRINCIPAL

Grants paid by a foundation might be deducted in determining net income or might be deducted directly from principal after net income is determined. Table 5.5 reveals that foundations, regardless of asset size, favor deducting grants paid as an item to determine net income.

Presently, both methods constitute generally accepted accounting principles for nonprofit organizations because both are widely used and accepted. Since the purpose of the earning of income is the payment of grants, then a majority (66 percent) of foundations surveyed indicated that the grants paid are a logical deduction from net

TABLE 5.4

Valuing Investment Assets

	Very Large		Large		Intermediate		Small		Totals	
	Number	Percent	Number	Percent	Number	Percent	Number	Percent	Number	Percent
Cost	16	76	61	72	44	98	16	88	137	91
Lower of cost or market	0	–	0	–	1	2	0	–	1	1
Market	5	24	5	8	0	–	2	12	12	8
Totals	21	100	66	100	45	100	18	100	150	100
Cost-Market*	14	88	58	95	36	82	13	81	121	88

*Foundations valuing assets at cost, disclosing market values either by footnote or parentheses.

TABLE 5.5

Deducting Grants Paid

	Very Large		Large		Intermediate		Small		Totals	
	Number	Percent	Number	Percent	Number	Percent	Number	Percent	Number	Percent
Deducting grants paid from principal	6	29	20	30	17	38	8	44	51	34
Deducting grants paid from income	15	71	46	70	28	62	10	56	99	66
Totals	21	100	66	100	45	100	18	100	150	100

TABLE 5.6

Inclusion of Contributions Received

	Very Large		Large		Intermediate		Small		Totals	
	Number	Percent	Number	Percent	Number	Percent	Number	Percent	Number	Percent
Contributions included in principal	5	56	10	63	9	43	8	53	32	52
Contributions included in income	4	44	6	37	12	57	7	47	29	48
Totals	9	100	16	100	21	100	15	100	61	100
No contributions received	12	57	50	76	24	53	3	17	89	59
Totals	21	–	66	–	45	–	18	–	150	–

income because the final net income figure is viewed as the indicator of the amounts that the private foundation has available for the payment of grants.

Foundations deducting grants paid after the determination of net income, while in a minority (34 percent), are probably using the more conventional definition of net income of profit-oriented enterprises and are treating the grants paid as the equivalent of a distribution of profits. Since that certainly constitutes a generally accepted accounting principle for profit-oriented enterprises, it would by extension apply to nonprofit organizations.

INCLUDING CONTRIBUTIONS RECEIVED AS INCOME VERSUS INCLUDING THEM IN PRINCIPAL

By definition, a private foundation is self-funded and does not rely on contributions on a year-by-year basis. Table 5.6 reveals that 59 percent of all foundations received no contributions during the year examined. Of the foundations receiving contributions during the year, approximately one-half included the contributions directly in principal, while the other one-half included the contributions received as part of income or revenue.

EXTENT OF FUND ACCOUNTING

A fund is defined as a:

sum of money or other resources segregated for the purpose of carrying on specific activities or attaining certain objectives in accordance with special regulations, restrictions or limitations, and constituting an independent fiscal and accounting entity.[6]

Table 5.7 reveals the extent to which private foundations use fund accounting. I determined whether fund accounting was being used by the terminology in the financial statements. A reference to a principal fund, income fund, or any other usage of the word "fund" resulted in my classifying the foundation as using fund accounting. Thirty-two percent of all foundations used some form of fund accounting—the larger the foundation, the greater the extent of fund accounting. Forty-three percent of very large foundations used some form of fund accounting but of small foundations, only 6 percent used fund accounting. Fund accounting is complex and requires a substantial amount of assets to warrant its usage. That explains its greater use by the largest foundations and its declining use as the foundations become smaller.

The funds created by most foundations using fund accounting were of two types—an income fund and a principal fund. However, some foundations had other types of funds. For example, the Turrell Fund listed three types: current fund, memorial fund, and scholarship fund.[7]

In comparison, voluntary health and welfare organizations generally use a current fund, land, building and equipment fund, and an endowment fund. Since by definition private foundations are primarily grant-making organizations that do not rely on current contributions to carry out their objectives, the types of funds used by the voluntary health and welfare organizations would be inappropriate and I found these types of funds were not generally used by the private foundations.

ACCOUNTING FOR CAPITAL GAINS AND LOSSES

The treatment of capital gains and losses by nonprofit organizations differs greatly from that of commercial enterprises. In a commercial enterprise, the capital gain is part of income; in nonprofit organizations, capital gains are sometimes considered income and sometimes they are not.

Table 5.8 reveals that 73 percent of all foundations treated capital gains as part of principal rather than income. Very large, large, and small foundations treated capital gains as part of principal to the same degree (approximately 80 percent). However, there was a variation even among foundations that included capital gains in principal. Logic dictates that foundations including capital gains as part of principal should uniformly include the capital gains in the changes in principal statement, yet Table 5.9 reveals that several did not. Of the 74 foundations that treated capital gains as principal, 11 (15 percent) included the capital gains directly in the statement of financial position.

REPORTING PRACTICES

The annual report of the private foundation is generally presented in two parts. The president or secretary reports in the first part on the activities, accomplishments, programs, and other activities and objectives of the foundation. The second part is financial, usually

TABLE 5.7

Extent of Fund Accounting

	Very Large		Large		Intermediate		Small		Totals	
	Number	Percent	Number	Percent	Number	Percent	Number	Percent	Number	Percent
Fund accounting: yes	9	43	26	39	13	29	1	6	49	32
Fund accounting: no	12	57	40	61	32	71	17	94	101	68
Totals	21	100	66	100	45	100	18	100	150	100

TABLE 5.8

Accounting for Capital Gains and Losses

	Very Large		Large		Intermediate		Small		Totals	
	Number	Percent	Number	Percent	Number	Percent	Number	Percent	Number	Percent
Capital gains included in income	4	19	9	14	13	29	2	11	28	19
Capital gains included in principal	16	76	36	55	15	33	7	39	74	49
Subtotals	20	95	45	69	28	62	9	50	102	68
No capital gains or losses	1	5	21	31	17	38	9	50	48	32
Totals	21	100	66	100	45	100	18	100	150	100

TABLE 5.9

Accounting for Capital Gains and Losses in Principal

	Very Large		Large		Intermediate		Small		Totals	
	Number	Percent	Number	Percent	Number	Percent	Number	Percent	Number	Percent
Capital gains included in changes in principal statement	14	88	31	86	12	80	6	86	63	85
Capital gains included in balance sheet	2	12	5	14	3	20	1	14	11	15
Totals	16	100	36	100	15	100	7	100	74	100

including financial statements, a list of grantees and amounts received, and a summary of investments.

Unlike large, publicly held corporations, private foundations are not required to have their statements audited annually, yet as Table 5.10 reveals, all very large foundations are audited. As the foundations decline in asset size, the proportion that have their financial statements audited also declines. Twenty-four percent of intermediate foundations (assets $1 million to $10 million) did not have their financial statements audited, and the number of unaudited statements approaches 50 percent for small foundations.

The wording in the report of the independent accountants is similar to the standard short-form report used by independent accountants for profit-oriented enterprises. Differences were usually because of reference to cash-basis accounting.[8] However, there were some quite unusual types of audit reports. The Louis and Maud Hill Family Foundation financial statements were attested to by the First Trust Co. of St. Paul.[9] The financial statements of the Jessie Smith Noyes Foundation had a statement attached stating that "the accounts are audited annually by McGrath, Doyle & Phan, Certified Public Accountants, New York."[10] A similar type of statement was included in the Charles and Joy Pettinos Foundation.[11] The Lilia Babbitt Hyde Foundation included a statement in its annual report that "the financial data presented on this page [sic] was obtained from the annual report of the independent certified public accountants."[12]

It appears from Table 5.11 that an accepted practice on the part of foundations is to disclose their investment portfolios. The very large and large foundations disclose that information to a much greater extent than intermediate and small foundations.

Foundations disclose their investment policies or objectives to a much lesser extent than investments themselves. Only 3 percent of all foundations disclosed their policies, as indicated in Table 5.11. The best example of disclosure was the Ford Foundation,[13] which specifically outlined what it hoped to accomplish as well as the type of investments needed to carry out its investment objectives.

Table 5.12 reveals that almost all private foundations disclosed the recipients and amounts of the grants paid. All of the very large foundations and at least 91 percent of the other foundations indicated that this information is vital and should be included in the annual report. That point appears to be the one on which more foundations agree than any other.

A majority of all foundations indicated in the annual reports the procedure and forms necessary to apply for a grant. A typical example of the disclosure of the application procedure is the McGregor Fund, which informs the potential grantee that its letter of request "should state clearly and briefly the specific purpose and what it will

TABLE 5.10

Extent of Audited Financial Statements

	Very Large		Large		Intermediate		Small		Totals	
	Number	Percent	Number	Percent	Number	Percent	Number	Percent	Number	Percent
Audited financial statements: yes	21	100	56	85	34	76	10	56	121	81
Audited financial statements: no	0	–	10	15	11	24	8	44	29	19
Totals	21	100	66	100	45	100	18	100	150	100

TABLE 5.11

Disclosure of Investments

	Very Large		Large		Intermediate		Small		Totals	
	Number	Percent	Number	Percent	Number	Percent	Number	Percent	Number	Percent
Disclosed investments: yes	18	86	49	74	20	44	8	44	95	63
Disclosed investments: no	3	14	17	26	25	56	10	56	55	37
Totals	21	100	66	100	45	100	18	100	150	100
Disclosed investment policy: yes	2	10	2	3	0	–	0	–	4	3
Disclosed investment policy: no	19	90	64	97	45	100	18	100	146	97
Totals	21	100	66	100	45	100	18	100	150	100

accomplish,"14 and then lists five requirements that must be complied with in the grant application.

Only 22 percent of all foundations disclosed the criteria used by the foundation to determine which grants to make and which to reject. There was no uniformity in this area, with some foundations disclosing the criteria quite specifically, while others disclosed them in more general terms. The vast majority of foundations (78 percent) did not disclose any criteria at all in their annual reports.

Do the foundations disclose their success and failure in carrying out their mission? The answer to this question is: No, they do not. I found only one foundation that mentioned in its annual report any failures in its activities and programs, the Edwin Gould Foundation for Children: "Not all investment was productive, but if the programs we have supported were without risk, there would have been no need to seek Foundation help."15

NUMBER OF FINANCIAL STATEMENTS USED

The financial statements for profit-oriented businesses in general use at the present time are an income statement, a retained earnings statement, a balance sheet, and a statement of changes in financial position. Those four statements are articulated and deemed the minimum for disclosure of economic activity.16

The starting point in analyzing the types of financial statements included by the private foundations in their annual reports was to count the number of financial statements presented. Table 5.13 reveals that the number of financial statements included in the annual report range from one to seven. Thirty-eight percent of small foundations used one financial statement to convey their economic activity to the reader; however, 5 percent of large foundations and 4 percent of intermediate foundations also relied on one financial statement to convey financial information. The most prevalent number of financial statements used by a foundation was two, with 60 percent of all foundations using two financial statements, and 25 percent of all foundations using three financial statements to transmit their financial information to the reader. One large foundation used seven financial statements to satisfy the same objectives.

It cannot be assumed, however, that foundations using the same number of financial statements included the same kinds of financial statements. The next step was to analyze the types of financial statements included in the annual report. Financial statements were classified into three types:

1. Income Statement—statements summarizing receipts, revenue, income, expenses, expenditures

TABLE 5.12

Disclosure of Grant Information

	Very Large		Large		Intermediate		Small		Totals	
	Number	Percent	Number	Percent	Number	Percent	Number	Percent	Number	Percent
Disclosed grants paid: yes	21	100	64	97	41	91	17	94	143	95
Disclosed grants paid: no	0	–	2	3	4	9	1	6	7	5
Totals	21	100	66	100	45	100	18	100	150	100
Disclosed application criteria; yes	12	57	42	64	21	47	9	50	84	56
Disclosed application criteria; no	9	43	24	36	24	53	9	50	66	46
Totals	21	100	66	100	45	100	18	100	150	100
Disclosed selection criteria; yes	4	19	17	26	9	20	3	17	33	22
Disclosed selection criteria; no	17	81	49	74	36	80	15	83	117	78
Totals	21	100	66	100	45	100	18	100	150	100

TABLE 5.13

Number of Financial Statements Included in Annual Report

Number of Financial Statements	Very Large		Large		Intermediate		Small		Totals	
	Number	Percent	Number	Percent	Number	Percent	Number	Percent	Number	Percent
One	0	–	3	5	2	4	7	38	12	8
Two	8	38	40	61	33	74	9	50	90	60
Three	9	42	18	27	9	20	1	6	37	25
Four	2	10	1	1	1	2	1	6	5	3
Five	2	10	3	5	0	–	0	–	5	3
Seven	0	–	1	1	0	–	0	–	1	1
Totals	21	100	66	100	45	100	18	100	150	100

2. Balance Sheet—financial statements showing position
3. Financial statements showing changes in position of principal, funds, or assets

   Among the 12 foundations that relied on one financial statement to summarize their economic activity, the most popular statement was the balance sheet. Five foundations (43 percent) out of the 12 presented only a balance sheet. Two out of the five were large foundations with assets in excess of ten million dollars. Another two submitted income statements as their only financial statement, and the balance submitted financial reports combining various types of information in one statement. (See Table 5.14.)

   Of the 90 foundations that relied on two financial statements to convey information, the most prevalent pairing was an income statement and balance sheet. Thirty-nine used those two financial statements. Twenty-four submitted a balance sheet and a statement of changes in fund balances, which is akin to a statement of changes in retained earnings for a profit-oriented enterprise. Another 24 presented a combined income statement and changes in fund balances, as well as a balance sheet. Three presented a balance sheet and a statement of changes in financial position.

   Of the 37 foundations that relied on three financial statements, the most prevalent was an income statement, balance sheet, and changes in fund balances. Twenty-five used these three financial statements. Table 5.14 indicates that of the remaining 12, each foundation had its own unique set of financial statements.

   Of the five foundations which relied on four financial statements to convey economic activity, each had a set of unique financial statements. The same was true of the foundations with five financial statements and seven financial statements, neither being presented in Table 5.14 because of their uniqueness.

INCOME STATEMENT

   The statement measuring the net gains or losses for an accounting period is almost universally referred to as an income or earnings statement by profit-oriented businesses. Table 5.15 reveals that among the 75 foundations which chose to present the statement separately, 30 different titles were used. The various titles show that to a large extent foundations are on a cash basis and use fund accounting. Some of the titles differ greatly but provide the same financial information, such as income statement, statement of excess of revenues over expenses, and income account.

TABLE 5.14

Types of Financial Statements Included in Annual Reports

	Very Large		Large		Intermediate		Small		Totals	
	Number	Percent	Number	Percent	Number	Percent	Number	Percent	Number	Percent
One financial statement										
Financial report	0	–	1	33	0	–	0	–	1	8
Balance sheet	0	–	2	67	1	50	2	29	5	43
Income statement	0	–	0	–	0	–	2	29	2	17
Trustee's report	0	–	0	–	0	–	1	14	1	8
Transactions and asset balances	0	–	0	–	1	50	1	14	2	16
Revenues and appropriations	0	–	0	–	0	–	1	14	1	8
Totals	0	–	3	100	2	100	7	100	12	100
Two financial statements										
Income statement and balance sheet	1	13	19	48	14	43	5	56	39	43
Balance sheet and statement of changes in fund balances	2	25	10	25	10	30	2	22	24	27
Combined statement of income and changes in fund balances, and balance sheet	5	62	11	27	7	21	1	11	24	27
Balance sheet and statement of changes in financial position	0	–	0	–	2	6	1	11	3	3
Totals	8	100	40	100	33	100	9	100	90	100
Three financial statements										
Income, balance sheet, changes in fund balances	5	56	12	64	7	78	1	100	25	66
Income, balance sheet, commitments, and commitment reserves	0	–	1	6	0	–	0	–	1	3
Balance sheet, statement of changes in current funds, statement of changes in endowment and similar funds	0	–	1	6	0	–	0	–	1	3
Income, balance sheet, changes in financial position	1	11	0	–	0	–	0	–	1	3
Income, balance sheet, appropriations and payments	0	–	1	6	2	22	0	–	3	8

(continued)

(Table 5.14 continued)

	Very Large		Large		Intermediate		Small		Totals	
	Number	Percent	Number	Percent	Number	Percent	Number	Percent	Number	Percent
Income, balance sheet, gains and losses on sale of trust investments	0	–	1	6	0	–	0	–	1	3
Combined statement of income and changes in fund balances, balance sheet, sources and uses of cash	2	22	0	–	0	–	0	–	2	5
Income, balance sheet, net income and grants paid from inception through current year	0	–	1	6	0	–	0	–	1	3
Balance sheet, changes in funds, marketable securities–principal fund	1	11	0	–	0	–	0	–	1	3
Balance sheet, combined statement of income and changes in fund balances, investments and other assets	0	–	1	6	0	–	0	–	1	3
Totals	9	100	18	100	9	100	1	100	37	100
Four financial statements										
Balance sheet, income, changes in funds, sources and uses of cash	1	50	0	–	0	–	0	–	1	20
Balance sheet, income, changes in funds, changes in financial position	1	50	0	–	0	–	0	–	1	20
Balance sheet, income, expenses, changes in principal	0	–	0	–	0	–	1	100	1	20
Balance sheet, income, changes in funds, summary of operations from inception	0	–	1	100	0	–	0	–	1	20
Balance sheet, changes in funds, changes in reserve balances, changes in endowment and similar funds	0	–	0	–	1	100	0	–	1	20
Totals	2	100	1	100	1	100	1	100	5	100

78

TABLE 5.15

Financial Statements of Private Foundations Summarizing Receipts, Revenues, Income, Expenses, Expenditures

	Very Large		Large		Intermediate		Small		Totals	
	Number	Percent	Number	Percent	Number	Percent	Number	Percent	Number	Percent
Income statement	2	22	11	30	5	23	0	–	18	25
Statement of income and disbursements	0	–	2	5	2	10	1	12.5	5	8
Statement of revenues collected and expenditures disbursed	0	–	1	3	0	–	0	–	1	1
Statement of receipts and disbursements	0	–	2	5	3	14	2	25.0	7	10
Income and expenditures	0	–	2	5	0	–	0	–	2	3
Statement of excess of revenues over expenses	0	–	1	3	0	–	0	–	1	1
Statement of contributions, income and expenditures	0	–	0	–	1	5	0	–	1	1
Statement of income, expenses, and grants paid	0	–	2	5	2	10	0	–	4	6
Revenue, disbursements, and income available for grants	0	–	0	–	1	5	1	12.5	2	3
Statement of gains and losses on sale of trust investments	0	–	1	3	0	–	0	–	1	1
Statement of income and contributions received and contributions and grants made	0	–	0	–	0	–	1	12.5	1	1
Summary of operations	0	–	1	3	0	–	0	–	1	1
Statement of income collected and expenses disbursed	1	11	0	–	0	–	0	–	1	1

(continued)

(Table 5.15 continued)

	Very Large		Large		Intermediate		Small		Totals	
	Number	Percent	Number	Percent	Number	Percent	Number	Percent	Number	Percent
Statement of income, appropriations, and expenses	0	—	2	5	0	—	0	—	2	3
Statement of administrative and other expenses, principal fund	1	11	0	—	0	—	0	—	1	1
Income account	1	11	0	—	1	5	1	12.5	3	4
Expenses	0	—	0	—	0	—	1	12.5	1	1
Consolidated operating statement	0	—	0	—	1	5	0	—	1	1
Statement of receipts and disbursements of income fund	0	—	0	—	1	5	0	—	1	1
Statement of revenues and expenses	0	—	1	3	0	—	0	—	1	1
Revenues and expenditures	0	—	1	3	0	—	0	—	1	1
Statement of cash receipts and disbursements of current fund	0	—	1	3	0	—	0	—	1	1
Statement of cash receipts and disbursements of memorial fund	0	—	1	3	0	—	0	—	1	1
Statement of cash receipts and disbursements of scholarship fund	0	—	1	3	0	—	0	—	1	1
Statement of income fund	3	34	4	10	4	18	0	—	11	16
Summary of appropriations and payments	0	—	2	5	0	—	0	—	2	3
Statement of allocation and appropriation of income	1	11	0	—	0	—	0	—	1	1
Statement of appropriations account	0	—	1	3	0	—	0	—	1	1
No title	0	—	0	—	0	—	1	12.5	1	1
Totals	9	100	37	100	21	100	8	100	75	100

In another vein, some of the titles are almost identical but were different enough for me to classify them separately. For example, an income statement is not the same as a Statement of Income Fund. The latter indicates that there is a principal fund which may also have gains or losses. Receipts are not the same as revenues and expenditures or disbursements are not the same as expenses. Therefore, these were classified separately. A statement of income and disbursements is not the same as a statement of receipts and disbursements. Similarly, a statement of revenues and expenditures is not the same as a statement of revenues and expenses nor is it the same as a statement of income and disbursements. To further complicate matters, 67 percent of the private foundations using the term "income statement" (or "income and expense" which I treated the same as an income statement) were on the cash basis and in reality their statements are more a statement of receipts and disbursements. (See Table 5.16.) Table 5.15 reveals that "income statement" is the most popular terminology, with 25 percent of all private foundations which presented this type of statement separately using it. Another 16 percent used the title "statement of income fund" or similar terminology. After those two, the percentages become very small, indicating that each term is almost unique to a particular foundation.

Many of the titles are descriptive of what is included in the financial statement, such as "statement of income and contributions received and contributions and grants made." Some of the titles used give little clue to what is included in the financial statement; for example, "Summary of Appropriations and Payments" or "Statement of Allocation and Appropriation of Income."

BALANCE SHEET

Table 5.17 reveals that 29 differently titled financial statements were presented by private foundations to show their financial position. However, although bearing different titles, many of the statements are in reality the same, conveying similar information as to the status of the assets, liabilities, and capital of the foundation. Different titles with essentially similar information are:

Balance Sheet
Statement of financial position
Statement of net assets
Statement of assets, liabilities, and fund balances
Statement of assets, liabilities, and foundation principal
Statement of assets, obligations, and principal fund
Statement of net assets and fund balances

TABLE 5.16

Income Statement on Cash Versus Accrual Basis

	Very Large		Large		Intermediate		Small		Totals	
	Number	Percent	Number	Percent	Number	Percent	Number	Percent	Number	Percent
Cash basis	0	–	8	73	4	80	0	–	12	67
Accrual basis	2	100	3	27	1	20	0	–	6	33
Totals	2	100	11	100	5	100	0	–	18	100

TABLE 5.17

Financial Statements of Private Foundations Showing Position

	Very Large		Large		Intermediate		Small		Totals	
	Number	Percent	Number	Percent	Number	Percent	Number	Percent	Number	Percent
Balance sheet	11	46	33	47	24	59	7	52	75	50
Statement of financial position	3	13	2	3	3	7	0	–	8	6
Statement of net assets	1	4	2	3	2	5	1	8	6	4
Statement of assets, liabilities, and fund balances	3	13	7	11	4	10	1	8	15	11
Statement of assets, liabilities, and foundation principal	1	4	0	–	0	–	0	–	1	1
Statement of assets and principal resulting from cash transactions	1	4	0	–	0	–	0	–	1	1
Statement of assets, obligations, and principal fund	1	4	0	–	0	–	0	–	1	1
Statement of net assets and fund balances	0	–	6	9	4	10	0	–	10	7
Statement of assets, liabilities, and net worth	0	–	1	1	0	–	0	–	1	1
Statement of assets and liabilities	0	–	7	11	3	7	0	–	10	7
Statement of condition	0	–	1	1	1	2	1	8	3	2
Statement of assets and undistributed fund balances	0	–	0	–	0	–	1	8	1	1

Statement	(1)	(%)	(2)	(%)	(3)	(%)	(4)	(%)	Total	(%)
Statement of assets and trust principal resulting from cash transactions	0	—	1	1	0	—	0	—	1	1
Statement of assets and fund balances resulting from cash transactions	0	—	1	1	0	—	0	—	1	1
Condensed financial report	0	—	1	1	0	—	0	—	1	1
Statement of marketable securities, principal fund	2	8	0	—	0	—	0	—	2	1
Statement of corporate notes and other investments, principal fund	1	4	0	0	0	—	0	1	1	1
Statement of position	0	—	0	0	0	—	1	8	1	1
Statement of investments and other assets	0	—	1	1	0	—	0	—	1	1
Balance sheet of current assets and liabilities	0	—	1	1	0	—	0	—	1	1
Statement of assets, liabilities, and equity	0	—	1	1	0	—	0	—	1	1
Statement of assets, liabilities, income fund balance, and principal resulting from cash transactions	0	—	1	1	0	—	0	—	1	1
Statement of assets except cash	0	—	1	1	0	—	0	—	1	1
Statement of resources and appropriations	0	—	0	—	0	—	1	8	1	1
Statement of assets and unexpended income	0	—	1	1	0	—	0	—	1	1
Statement of assets, liabilities, and funds	0	—	1	1	0	—	0	—	1	1
Statement of commitments approved	0	—	1	1	0	—	0	—	1	1
Statement of reserves for unpaid commitments on grants in progress	0	—	1	1	0	—	0	—	1	1
Statement of commitments against future income	0	—	1	1	0	—	0	—	1	1
Statement of commitments and commitment reserves	0	—	1	1	0	—	0	—	1	1
Totals	24	100	73	100	41	100	13	100	151	100

Statement of assets, liabilities, and net worth
Statement of condition
Statement of assets and undistributed fund balances
Statement of position
Statement of assets, liabilities, and equity
Statement of assets, liabilities, and funds
Statement of assets and liabilities

Some of the financial statements reveal in their title that the
cash method of accounting is used in determining their balances,
such as, "statement of assets and fund balances resulting from cash
transactions." Since many foundations are on the cash basis, in
reality they would be included with the above list in showing position.
Some of the financial statements deal with only part of the overall
position of the foundation, with the "statement of investments and
other assets" being an example.

Of the foundations presenting a financial statement to show
financial position, 50 percent preferred the title "Balance Sheet"
for the statement summarizing assets, liabilities, and capital. An
examination by asset size reveals that the same percent holds for
all class sizes from very large to small foundations. After "balance
sheet," there are no other titles with substantial usage by the foundations. The titles "net assets and fund balances" and "assets and
liabilities" both were used by only 7 percent of all foundations, and
"statement of financial position" was used by 6 percent of all foundations. Table 5.17 reveals that almost all the remaining titles are
unique for one particular foundation.

CAPITAL STATEMENT

The capital of a private foundation is usually called principal
or fund balance. In a commercial enterprise, changes in capital
due to the generation and distribution of profits are summarized in
the statement of retained earnings. Other changes in financial
position are summarized in the statement of changes in financial
position. Seventy-eight foundations presented a separate statement
of changes in principal, funds, or assets, and 32 differently titled
statements were used. The distinction between changes in principal
and assets was a bit muddled and will be discussed in Chapter 6.
The most popular title was "statement of changes in funds," with
35 percent of all foundations using that title (Table 5.18). An examination of the usage by asset size reveals that title was most popular
from very large to small, the same is true with 30 percent of very
large, 29 percent of large, 40 percent of intermediate, and 32 percent of small using this title.

TABLE 5.18

Financial Statements of Private Foundations Showing Changes in Assets, Principal, or Funds

	Very Large		Large		Intermediate		Small		Totals	
	Number	Percent	Number	Percent	Number	Percent	Number	Percent	Number	Percent
Statement of changes in funds	6	30	9	29	9	40	2	32	26	35
Statement of balances in funds	1	5	2	6	0	–	0	–	3	5
Statement of principal fund	4	20	5	16	4	17	1	17	14	19
Statement of changes in fund balances—current funds	0	–	1	3.5	0	–	0	–	1	1
Statement of changes in fund balances—endowment and similar funds	0	–	1	3.5	0	–	0	–	1	1
Statement of changes in net assets	0	–	0	–	3	13	1	17	4	6
Sources of funds	0	–	0	–	1	5	0	–	1	1
Statement of sources and uses of cash	2	10	0	–	0	–	0	–	2	3
Statement of changes in financial position	2	10	0	–	1	5	0	–	3	5
Summary of cash	0	–	1	3.5	0	–	0	–	1	1
Statement of changes in principal fund balance and income fund deficiency	0	–	1	3.5	0	–	0	–	1	1
Statement of fund activity	0	–	0	–	1	5	0	–	1	1
Statement of changes in reserve balances	0	–	0	–	1	5	0	–	1	1
Statement of changes in endowment and similar funds—principal and income	0	–	0	–	1	5	0	–	1	1
Statement of changes in foundation principal and pension fund	0	–	1	3.5	0	–	0	–	1	1
Statement of accumulated net fund	0	–	1	3.5	0	–	0	–	1	1
Statement of funds	0	–	1	3.5	1	5	0	–	2	3
Statement of changes in income fund balances	0	–	1	3.5	0	–	0	–	1	1
Statement of changes in trust principal	0	–	1	3.5	0	–	0	–	1	1
Statement of changes in principal	1	5	0	–	0	–	0	–	1	1
Statement of changes in general fund	0	–	1	3.5	0	–	0	–	1	1
Foundation fund statement	1	5	0	–	0	–	0	–	1	1
Statement of changes in reserve for insurance and annuities	1	5	0	–	0	–	0	–	1	1
Recapitulation of principal account	0	–	0	–	0	–	1	17	1	1
Statement of changes in cash	1	5	0	–	0	–	0	–	1	1
Statement of capital	0	–	0	–	0	–	1	17	1	1
Statement of changes during the year	0	–	1	3.5	0	–	0	–	1	1
Statement of changes in special funds	1	5	0	–	0	–	0	–	1	1
Statement of current fund	0	–	1	3.5	0	–	0	–	1	1
Statement of memorial fund	0	–	1	3.5	0	–	0	–	1	1
Statement of scholarship fund	0	–	1	3.5	0	–	0	–	1	1
Totals	20	100	30	100	22	100	6	100	78	100

TABLE 5.19

Financial Statements Combining Income and Changes in Principal or Funds

	Very Large		Large		Intermediate		Small		Totals	
	Number	Percent	Number	Percent	Number	Percent	Number	Percent	Number	Percent
Statement of income, expenses, and changes in fund balances	3	37.5	4	17	0	—	0	—	7	18
Statement of income and accumulated net income in excess of grants	0	—	1	5	0	—	0	—	1	2
Statement of income and fund equities	0	—	0	—	1	8	0	—	1	2
Statement of operations and fund balances	0	—	0	—	1	8	0	—	1	2
Statement of income, expenditures, and unexpended income balances	0	—	1	5	0	—	0	—	1	2
Statement of revenues collected, expenditures, and changes in fund balances	0	—	1	5	1	8	0	—	2	5
Income and principal fund statement	0	—	2	8	0	—	0	—	2	5
Trustee's report	0	—	0	—	0	—	1	25	1	2
Statement of revenues, expenditures, and income, and principal fund balances	0	—	1	5	0	—	0	—	1	2
Statement of operations and fund principal	0	—	0	—	1	8	0	—	1	2
Statement of income, appropriations, and cumulative excess of appropriations over income	0	—	1	5	0	—	0	—	1	2
Statement of revenues, expenditures, and general fund balance	0	—	1	5	0	—	0	—	1	2
Statement of income and principal	0	—	1	5	1	8	0	—	2	5
Statement of transactions and asset balances	0	—	0	—	1	8	0	—	1	2
Statement of changes in income and principal funds	0	—	0	—	2	18	0	—	2	5
Statement of income, expenses, and appropriation fund	0	—	1	5	2	18	1	25	4	10
Statement of income, expenses, fellowship grants, and general surplus	0	—	1	5	0	—	0	—	1	2

Statement	No.	%	No.	%	No.	%	No.	%	No.	%
Statement of current income, expenditures, appropriations, and fund balances	0	–	0	–	1	8	0	–	1	2
Statement of investment income, expenses, grants, and changes in foundation principal	0	–	1	5	0	–	0	–	1	2
Statement of revenues, expenses, appropriations, and uncommitted income fund	1	12.5	0	–	0	–	0	–	1	2
Statement of operations and cumulative excess of grants and expenses over income	1	12.5	0	–	0	–	0	–	1	2
Statement of receipts and disbursements and changes in undistributed fund balance	0	–	0	–	0	–	1	25	1	2
Statement of income fund receipts, expenses, appropriations, and surplus	0	–	1	5	0	–	0	–	1	2
Statement of income, appropriations, and changes in principal fund	1	12.5	0	–	1	8	0	–	1	2
Statement of revenues, gifts, and expenditures, and principal fund balance	0	–	0	–	1	8	0	–	1	2
Statement of income, expenses, and income fund balance	0	–	1	5	0	–	0	–	1	2
Statement of income and funds	1	12.5	0	–	0	–	0	–	1	2
Statement of income, expenses, grants, and projects and income fund	0	–	1	5	0	–	0	–	1	2
Statement of operations and accumulated deficit	0	–	1	5	0	–	0	–	1	2
Statement of cash receipts of income, disbursement of expenses, distribution, and changes in income fund balances	0	–	1	5	0	–	0	–	1	2
Statement of income, transfer, appropriations, and changes in income funds	1	12.5	0	–	0	–	0	–	1	2
Statement of income received, expenses, distributions disbursed, and fund balances resulting from cash transactions	0	–	0	–	0	–	1	25	1	2
Totals	8	100	21	100	12	100	4	100	45	100

The next most popular title was "statement of principal fund," with 19 percent of all foundations using that title. The title indicates the use of fund accounting for both the income fund, revealing the assets generated and spent by the foundation, and the principal fund, revealing the changes in its balance due to the operation of the income fund.

The remaining statements are all used in a very small percentage of cases. Some of the titles indicate that the private foundation was created by trust instruments—for example, "Statement of Changes in Trust Principal." Some of the financial statements deal with changes in a certain aspect of the foundation's financial picture, such as the "Statement of Changes in Reserve for Insurance and Annuities." Some foundations that have different funds presented statements showing changes in each fund separately, such as:

Statement of Current Fund
Statement of Memorial Fund
Statement of Scholarship Fund

An overall scrutiny of the titles used reveals that a major factor responsible for the different titles is the use of fund accounting, and the different titles indicate the foundations' solution to the problem of presenting the changes in the funds.

Forty-five foundations chose to combine income and changes in principal or fund balances in one financial statement. Thirty-four differently titled statements resulted. The most popular title is a "Statement of Income, Expenses, and Changes in Fund Balances," with 18 percent of the total. Table 5.19 reveals that again most other titles have a very small percentage of total use, indicating a uniqueness to one particular foundation.

NOTES

1. Guide to Foundation Annual Reports on Film, 1970 (New York: The Foundation Center, 1972), preface.

2. Ibid.

3. Foundation Directory, Edition 3 (New York: Foundation Library Center, 1967), p. 22.

4. The Foundation Grants Index 1972 (New York: The Foundation Center, 1972).

5. Committee of Voluntary Health and Welfare Organizations, Audits of Voluntary Health and Welfare Organizations (New York: American Institute of Certified Public Accountants, 1974), p. 6.

6. Emerson O. Henke, Accounting for Non-Profit Organizations (Belmont, Calif.: Wadsworth Publishing Co., Inc., 1966), p. 5.

7. Turrell Fund, Annual Report, 1971.

8. Samuel Kress Foundation, Annual Report, 1973, p. 17.

9. Louis and Maud Hill Family Foundation, Annual Report, 1972.

10. Jessie Smith Noyes Foundation, Annual Report, 1970.

11. Charles and Joy Pettinos Foundation, Annual Report, 1972.

12. Lilia Babbitt Hyde Foundation, Annual Report, 1970.

13. Ford Foundation, Annual Report, 1972.

14. McGregor Fund, Annual Report, 1973, p. 6.

15. Edwin Gould Foundation for Children, Annual Report, 1972.

16. Accounting Principles Board, "APB Accounting Principles," Current Text as of June 30, 1973 (New York: American Institute of Certified Public Accountants, 1973), Sec. 1022, 02-07.

CHAPTER

6

EVALUATION OF
CURRENT PRACTICES AND
RECOMMENDATIONS

CASH BASIS VERSUS ACCRUAL BASIS

The argument that accrual accounting is the universal standard for profit-oriented enterprises by itself does not justify its use in nonprofit entities; accrual accounting must be justified as useful for nonprofit accounting. Private foundations are engaged in two activities: one is raising funds to carry out charitable activities, the other is the charitable activity itself. Foundations rely on their own income-generating principal, rather than contributions; hence the measurement of their income-producing activities should be on the accrual basis, the same as any other entity generating income. There is no justification for measuring their income on a cash basis except for simplicity, which cannot be used as a theoretical argument against accrual accounting, which has the weight of the body of accounting theory to support it. Thus all its income-generating activities should be measured on the accrual basis.

One of the principal objectives of the financial statements is to permit comparisons among organizations, whether profit or non-profit; comparison is one of the principal means of evaluating an organization. Under the accrual basis, assets are recognized when goods or services that will benefit future periods are acquired, and expenses are recognized when the future service potential expires. Liabilities are recognized when the organization becomes obligated for goods or services received. Therefore, emphasis in the measurement of revenues and expenses under the accrual method is on the concepts of earning and using respectively, rather than on receiving and paying.

A profit-making enterprise measures its accomplishments (revenue) against its efforts (expenses) to determine its income.

Since profit is not an objective of the nonprofit entity, it is not concerned with matching costs against revenues but is concerned with matching efforts against accomplishments. (The problem of measuring accomplishments will be discussed separately.) The measurement of effort requires accrual accounting. How much a program costs in a particular year can be answered only by accrual accounting, since it is the matching of the costs incurred against a time period that will reveal the total costs of the program for a particular year.

In Chapter 4, I discussed the alternative methods of accounting for grants. Under proper accrual accounting, the expense and liability for grants should be recorded when the grantee is notified that he or she has been awarded the grant. Recording grants at the time of appropriation is not warranted. The financial statements should reflect transactions with outsiders and not mere internal designations. Appropriations do not represent expenditures nor are they actual obligations on the part of the foundation. Until the grantee has been notified of a grant award, the foundation has the authority to change, modify, or reverse its appropriations. The foundation at the time of appropriation is merely indicating areas of interest that it intends to fund. The foundation has not committed itself to any specific grantee, nor has any specific grantee taken any action because of the appropriation. The commitment takes place at the time the grantee is notified of the award, and at that time the grantee will start carrying out the requirements of the grant proposal.

I see no reason for private foundations not to follow as closely as possible current business practice in regard to the recording of liabilities. Thus the appropriate time to record grant liabilities is when a commitment is made to the grantee. At this point, the foundation has committed funds and the grantee assumes an obligation to carry out the grant in accordance with the grant proposal. The cash basis of accounting for grants is unacceptable because financial statements prepared on this basis do not reflect economic reality. The failure to record liabilities makes the financial statements on the cash basis misleading because financial statements prepared on this basis do not reflect a full picture of the foundation's resources and obligations.

In the situation in which a foundation makes a grant payable over several years, contingent upon satisfactory performance, the full grant liability should be recorded. The recommendation of Malvern Gross, Jr., that all of the facts be disclosed in the financial statements and in the event the grant is not fully paid, the unpaid amounts should be restored to income, should be followed in this type of situation.

DEPRECIATION ACCOUNTING

The primary criteria should be usefulness in deciding whether or not to depreciate. Which would be more useful to the user of the annual report?

I conclude that depreciation accounting is more useful for various reasons. The private foundation must be held accountable for all resources entrusted to the organization, and furthermore, it should be held accountable for all resources used during the period regardless of the period in which the resources were acquired. Although the fixed assets do not generate revenue, they generate services provided and depreciation is an element in the measurement of the effort (cost) required to produce the services.

Assets used in providing services are both valuable and exhaustible. Accordingly, there is a cost expiration associated with the use of depreciable assets, whether they are owned or rented, whether acquired by gift or by purchase, and whether they are used by a profit-seeking or by a not-for-profit organization.[1]

If one private foundation purchased its building, while another rents its quarters, failure to record depreciation would make it difficult to compare the costs of the services which these two foundations are providing, negate the usefulness of the statistical information about the costs of services provided, and make comparisons between different accounting periods meaningless.

ACCOUNTING FOR GRANTS INCURRED AND CONTRIBUTIONS RECEIVED

The Accounting Principles Board of the American Institute of Certified Public Accountants defined revenue, expense and net income as follows:

Revenue—gross increases in assets or gross decreases in liabilities recognized and measured in conformity with generally accepted accounting principles that result from those types of profit-directed activities of an enterprise that can change owners' equity.
    Expenses—gross decreases in assets or gross increases in liabilities recognized and measured in conformity with generally accepted accounting principles that result from those types of profit-directed activities of an enterprise that can change owners' equity.

> Net income—the excess (deficit) of revenue over
> expenses for an accounting period . . . of an enter-
> prise for an accounting period from profit-directed
> activities that is recognized and measured in conformity
> with generally accepted accounting principles.[2]

Since the concept of net income has a quite specific meaning to
accountants, the definition should not be changed by the nonprofit
organizations because to do so would leave the readers unsure of the
meaning of the figure called "net income" if it is measured differently
by nonprofit organizations and profit-oriented enterprises.

I conclude that since net income has a specific definition and
that definition is universally accepted in the business sector, it would
be in the best interests of the user of the financial statements in the
annual report to maintain the same definition as for profit-oriented
enterprises.

Grants incurred do not meet the American Institute of Certified
Public Accountants' definition of an expense since it is not a decrease
in assets due to some "profit-directed" activity of the enterprise.
Grants incurred have no counterpart in profit enterprises. They
are not expenditures made for the purpose of deriving income—the
objective of business enterprises but not foundations—but they are
expenditures for meeting the organizations' objectives. Grants
incurred should not be included as a deduction from income in measuring net income.

Contributions received do not play a significant role in private
foundations, since by definition foundations are self-supporting,
relying on their principal to derive additional funds for activities.
Generally, contributions received are principal, not income, and
therefore should be treated as such. If the contributions received
are to be used for current activities, they should not be treated as
income but should be shown as another source of funds in the financial
statements, a matter that will be discussed later in this chapter.

CAPITAL GAINS AND LOSSES

Private foundations follow the trust laws in treating capital gains
as other than income to accommodate the divergent interests of
income beneficiaries and remaindermen.[3] Under trust law, capital
gains and losses are identified with principal rather than income.

It was pointed out earlier that many foundations have been created
by trust instruments rather than by corporations and hence are using
the concepts of trust law in their accounting for capital gains.

Messrs. Cary and Bright made two interesting points: 1) their
study revealed that only a small percentage of instruments specifically

stated that the principal of the fund was to remain intact or that only the income from the investments could be expended, and 2) if only income can be expended, the question remains whether capital gains constitute income or principal.[4] New York is the exemplar of the doctrine of absolute ownership, consisting of jurisdictions which hold that:

> Educational institutions are the absolute owners of their endowment funds. Even specific words of trust in donative instruments are often brushed aside in these jurisdictions as excess verbiage. All formal trusts involve a separation of the legal and equitable titles to the trust property, and no person can be trustee for himself; therefore, courts in these jurisdictions say, it follows that educational institutions cannot be trustees of their own endowment funds.[5]

Furthermore, the courts have shown a marked tendency to apply corporate principles rather than trust principles when the issue involved investment of funds, accounting for their use, or other aspects of administration. The purpose was to "accord charitable corporations a maximum degree of flexibility in their operations."[6]

Commercial accounting treats capital gains as part of income, and the federal government taxes capital gains as part of the income of private foundations. The only possible justification for treating capital gains as part of principal is a legal one and Cary and Bright responded by saying:

> We are thus led to the conclusion that there is no substantial authority under existing law to support the widely held view that the realized gains of endowment funds . . . must be treated as principal. No case has been found which holds that such an institution does not have the legal right to determine for itself whether to retain all such gains or to expend a prudent part.[7]

Malvern Gross, Jr., partner in Price Waterhouse & Co., and a recognized authority on nonprofit organizations, reached the same conclusion as Cary and Bright. He wrote that "the historical belief that only dividends and interest could be considered income usable for current operations has now been challenged and many believe that capital gains, at least in part, may also be considered 'income.' "[8]

Furthermore, the New York State nonprofit corporation law was amended in 1969 and 1971 to specifically permit most nonprofit organizations to include capital gains in usable income.[9]

Congress, in the Tax Reform Act of 1969, levied an excise tax on the net investment income of private foundations, with net investment income defined to include capital gains.[10] Congress treated capital gains as part of the income of private foundations by levying an excise tax on it.

If a commercial enterprise places restrictions on the use of its income, whether voluntarily for plant expansion or involuntarily for retirement of bonds, the measurement of its net income would be the same as if there were no restrictions. It would be improper accounting to exclude from net income the amounts required to satisfy the restrictions. Income measurement should not be confused with income management. Foundations transferring capital gains directly to principal are involved in income management and the resultant net income figure is misleading because it is not a true indicator of the asset inflows generated by the investment assets.

VALUING INVESTMENT ASSETS

Moral Issues in Investment Policy

In recent years, a movement has started to hold corporations responsible for acts that may be damaging environmentally, economically, or socially.

At an annual meeting of Kennecott Copper Company, a number of shareholders led by the Episcopal Church requested that Kennecott indemnify those on whom its mining projects have imposed environmental damage.[11] Honeywell Corporation, at an annual meeting, was asked by some stockholders to terminate manufacture of anti-personnel bombs because of "the death and dismemberment which its grotesquely efficient anti-personnel bombs have visited on many thousands of South Vietnamese civilians whom we are said to be assisting."[12]

At a Gulf Oil Corporation meeting, a small minority of stockholders asked that the company stop supporting what they termed the Portuguese repression of Africans in the colony of Angola.[13]

Portfolio managers, especially those of nonprofit organizations, have been asked to deploy their funds specially with political, social, moral, and environmental objectives. The basic question is should the portfolio manager be guided by nonfinancial considerations in acquiring, selling, and voting shares owned in various corporations.

John G. Simon, of the Taconic Foundation, responded by saying:

I believe that, as a shareholder, a foundation has the responsibility to make sure that it does what it reasonably can to avoid acquiescing in, or reinforcing or encouraging,

the imposition of social injury by the corporations in
which the foundation holds shares.[14]

Roger Kennedy, of the Ford Foundation, wrote:

An increasing number of investors are behaving as
if they believed that the possession of assets carries
with it the responsibility to understand as much as possible
about the effects those assets, in motion, produce upon
the fragile structure of civil order.[15]

He indicated that the trustees of the Ford Foundation set forth
an affirmative action policy toward Ford's social responsibility.
"That is, it should not have as the sole criterion for investment the
production of maximum financial return."[16]
      It is not my purpose to debate the philosophical and moral issues
raised in this section. I do not think that, in principle, anyone would
seriously disagree with the concept of supporting what is good and
not supporting what is bad. The problem is—how does one decide
which companies should be favored for investment and which companies should not? Xerox Corporation has been cited as an example
of a good company to invest in because of its socially useful product;
however, others have cited it as a bad company because it does
business in South Africa.[17]
      A professional investor writing on the subject of social responsi-
bility said: "To my knowledge, no one has yet developed standards
by which a corporation's social behavior can be defined and measured."[18] Was a corporation that manufactured napalm for use by
the United States military during the Vietnam War guilty of some
evil and not to be invested in, or was it performing a necessary
patriotic act and should have been invested in? No objective standards
exist to make such a decision.
      Milton Friedman has spoken and written on the question of whether
business has a social responsibility.

I have called it a fundamentally subversive doctrine
in a free society, and have said that in such a society
there is one and only one social responsibility of
business—to use its resources and engage in activities
designed to increase its profits so long as it stays
within the rules of the game, which is to say, engages
in open and free competition without deception or
fraud.[19]

Need for Evaluation

Private foundations, unlike many other types of charitable organizations, are self-sustaining. Once created, they basically rely on their principal to generate funds for the charitable operations of the foundation. Thus the performance and yield of the principal is a vital element in the generation of funds with which to operate.

Performance in the private sector is constantly evaluated by management, creditors, stockholders, and investors. For example, performance of a mutual fund is evaluated by the investors who, in effect, vote on good or poor performance by buying and selling the fund shares.

A foundation in certain aspects is similar to a mutual fund in that the principal of both is invested in stocks and bonds rather than in commercial activities, and the yields in both are the returns on investment. The return in one goes to stockholders, while in the other it supports charitable activities. Mutual funds are monitored, evaluated, and rated based on information supplied by accounting. The accountant does not actually evaluate but provides the necessary information so that others may evaluate. Historically, that has been the accountant's role in the private sector of our economy.

However, a private foundation has no creditors, stockholders, or investors to evaluate its performance. Should the foundations be evaluated on their performance in investing their assets? And to what extent should the accountant become involved in the evaluation? Those are the areas to which I will direct my inquiries in this section.

One of the questions asked on the interviews was: Should the foundation be evaluated on its performance in investing its assets? The response of the public accountants was almost unanimously "Yes!" However, the response by the foundations to the same question was different. Some foundations' officials, such as Jack Gould, financial vice president of the Edna McConnell Clark Foundation, and David Freeman, president of the Council on Foundations, agreed with the public accountants on the need for evaluation. Others, such as Stewart Campbell, treasurer of Duke Endowment, and Leo Kirschner, controller of the Rockefeller Foundation, said that foundations were already being evaluated by the minimum payment provisions of the Tax Reform Act of 1969. Finally, the balance of the interviewees affiliated with the private foundations said that it would serve no useful purpose, it would be misunderstood, or, that while foundations should answer to society on their investments, it would be practically impossible to do so.

Everyone agrees that the foundation must be held accountable for its resources. Would accountability be satisfied by the founda-

tion's burying its assets in the ground to be dug up whenever necessary to show that they still exist and are in the foundation's control?
Accountability means more than just safeguarding the assets. Part
of accountability is that the resources are invested efficiently. Jack
Gould said that the "funds are invested, and the foundation should be
accountable for its investment."[20]

One of the identified areas of tax abuse engaged in by private
foundations has been their performance in investing their assets.
The abuse was that some foundations were investing in assets that
gave very little or no current yield. Quite often, it was stock of
some enterprise that the creator of the foundation had some interest
in. As was discussed in Chapter 2, Congress imposed a minimum
payout rate on investment assets to cope with this abuse. A foundation, invested in low-yielding securities, would be forced to sell
them in order to meet the minimum payout provisions.

Some of the interviewees indicated that the minimum payout rate
constituted an evaluation of investment performance. None could
really clarify how the minimum payout rate constituted an evaluation
of investment performance. Setting a floor does not indicate the
height of the ceiling in a building, and the same is true of private
foundations. Congress set a floor to deal with the problem of foundation investment in unproductive assets. Private foundations are
required to distribute their entire net income on a current basis,
the minimum being 6 percent of their investment assets (minimum
payout rate). Congress recognized the fact that foundation rate of
return on investment assets may be higher than 6 percent by requiring
foundations to distribute their entire net income currently, not just
6 percent. So in no sense does the minimum payout rate constitute
an evaluation on foundation performance.

No organization has unlimited resources. To the extent of the
resources available, there is need for analysis, control, and evaluation to ensure efficient and appropriate use of resources.

> Efficiency as a desirable goal is accepted without question
> because a lack of efficiency means less can be accom-
> plished by the use of society's limited funds. Lack of
> efficiency is basically incompatible with the concept of
> scarce resources.[21]

To the extent of inefficiencies by the foundation in investing its
assets, charity will receive less, and ultimately the general public
suffers. It is a vital part of accountability that some kind of evaluation take place to ensure that the assets are not being invested
inefficiently.

The Commission on Foundations and Private Philanthropy criticized the private foundations for their performance in investment performance. The commission, addressing the foundation managers and trustees, said: "They must recognize the importance of their responsibility to invest the foundation's assets productively. Too often this responsibility has had a low priority."[22] The commission also noted that, while lacking all the evidence needed concerning investment performance on the part of the foundations, "everything we have seen points strongly in the direction of a need for great improvement."[23]

Historically, there has never been pressure on the trustees of the private foundation to perform adequately in the investment area, since the incentives to do well were lacking. Authors Cary and Bright, discussing the managers of the endowment funds of colleges, described them as conservative "and some of them have insisted that their only duty is to safeguard the original dollar value of the funds entrusted to their care."[24] Most likely, some of the managers of the investment portfolios of the private foundations have a similar attitude.

I conclude that evaluation of the investment performance by the private foundation is vital for various reasons:

1. There is no market mechanism at work to evaluate performance.
2. To the extent that inefficiencies exist, charity suffers.
3. Knowledge that performance is being evaluated will provide motivation for the managers to do a better job of portfolio management.

Valuing Securities at Market

Chapter 5 revealed that almost all the foundations surveyed valued their investment portfolios at cost. Valuation of long-term investments at market does not constitute a generally accepted accounting principle for most businesses. Accountants' reluctance to depart from cost is understandable because cost possesses two desirable attributes—verifiability and objectivity. In addition, valuing securities at market implies the recognition of unrealized gains and losses on the appreciation or depreciation in value of the securities. Presently, accountants record gains and losses only when a sale takes place, yet a search of the accounting literature reveals few advocates of historical cost for the valuation of investments.

A whole research study could be devoted to this vexing problem of the valuation of securities; however, I will attempt to deal with this problem in private foundations by drawing on research and discussion in the overall sector of security valuation. Basically, the answer to this question is that whatever is more useful should be the method adopted.

The need for an evaluation of the performance of the foundation in investing its assets exists, regardless of who performs the evaluation. The economic data supplied should be useful for evaluation and accountability purposes. Reporting the securities at cost is misleading if a private foundation was started by a contribution of $30 million in securities 40 years ago, and today the same securities are worth $300 million. Furthermore, it would make an evaluation impossible, because all evaluations involve comparisons and not measuring on a common basis produces results that are not comparable. To illustrate that point, if another foundation had, either by sales or current contributions, assets with a value of $300 million and earned 30 million dollars in interest and dividends, while the first foundation earned $18 million in interest and dividends, which foundation performed better in its portfolio management? If historical cost is used, the first foundation performed better because its rate of return is 60 percent, while the latter's rate of return is 10 percent. However, any rational comparison requires that the comparison be made on the basis of current value, since that is the amount of economic resources each manager had at his disposal to produce income, and that current basis should be the one utilized. Using current value, the latter foundation performed better since its rate of return is 10 percent, while the former's rate of return is 6 percent.

In reality, any investor, creditor or investment analyst would use current value as a basis for comparisons and evaluations. Chambers described the current value of the assets as the missing link in the supervision of the securities market.

> It is the one piece of information which pins all expectations and opinions to the facts of the marketplace, where buyers and sellers, issuers and brokers, borrowers and lenders make their play and their profits and losses. It is linked to every interest and is essential to the informed judgment of every party at interest.[25]

The valuation at current market price will result in the foundation's being held accountable for the current worth of the economic resources at its disposal.

It is difficult to defend historical cost in the area of security valuation and, as the Study Group on the Objectives of Financial Statements pointed out, "standards and practices that do not fulfill objectives are aimless and difficult to modify, or control."[26] Further-more, the study group gives as an objective of financial statements the ability to supply information that will be useful in evaluating the ability of management "to utilize enterprise resources effectively in achieving the primary enterprise goal."[27] The study group emphasized the importance of useful information: "information that does not bear on the problem for which it is intended simply is not useful, regardless of its other qualities."[28] Economic reality must become the basis for the accounting, not the legal or technical form.[29]

Howard Ross has advocated for years that the balance sheet should become what it appears to be—a statement of values of the enterprise, calculated by using current values, thus answering his own question— Is it better to be precisely wrong than vaguely right?[30] The Study Group also discussed the question of accuracy and they said that "the requirement that accounting information should be reliable does not imply that the information can possibly approach 100 percent accuracy."[31]

Morton Backer, in discussing current values and the balance sheet, concluded that the closer the accounting system comes to achieving current values and changes in value, the more meaningful would be the output.[32] Marvin Stone wrote that the number of people needing and wanting understandable means of security evaluation is increasing and present financial statements are not meeting those needs.[33] He suggested that a better goal for accountants would be to expend efforts toward "providing useful information for people who rely on us,"[34] and current value financial statements are what the consumers need.

In addition to making the balance sheet more of a statement of current values, recording at market gives recognition to unrealized appreciation and depreciation in the value of the securities. This is another departure from the generally accepted accounting principles which provide that gains and losses be recognized only when a sale takes place. Cary and Bright discussed this point and they said:

> It is not the sale and buy-back which increase or decrease its purchasing power, but the gradual appreciation or diminution of the market value of its portfolio which preceded these transactions. For this reason a growing number of people disregard realization and look instead to changes in market value to measure income or loss.[35]

If a foundation sells a security that it had held for five years, recording the gain or loss at the point of sale ignores the increases or decreases in value during prior years and bunches the aggregate gain or loss in the year of sale. However, the economic activity that gave rise to the gain or loss happened over the five-year period, not just at the point of sale. The sale is merely a conversion of one asset into another; the gains or losses were caused by the increased or decreased values in the securities of the enterprises in which the foundation had invested; the actual selling in no way creates economic gains or losses.

The Accounting Principles Board also felt that reporting of investments in common stocks at market would meet most closely the objective of reporting the economic consequences of holding the investment in some situations; however, it concluded that further study was necessary before the market-value method was extended beyond current practice.[36] Recently, the American Institute of Certified Public Accountants sanctioned the use of market as an acceptable alternative to cost. In 1973, the industry audit guide for colleges and universities stated that, as a permissible alternative, investments could be reported at current value.[37] In 1974, in its industry audit guide for voluntary health and welfare organizations, the AICPA sanctioned the use of market as an acceptable method of valuing investments, and if this method is used, the unrealized appreciation or depreciation should be included in income.[38] The National Health Council adopted the AICPA's position on valuing investments for voluntary health and welfare organizations.[39] Arthur Andersen & Co. proposed as an accounting standard for business enterprises throughout the world that marketable securities should be carried at quoted market prices.[40]

The problem of valuing securities was covered in the interviews as part of the question of evaluating the foundation on its performance in investing its assets. Of the seven certified public accountants interviewed, only one did not favor market. The responses indicated that cost had no significance; market was the only way to evaluate performance and the proper basis for reporting is market. Of the eight foundations interviewed, four favored market and three favored cost. Two officers were interviewed in the remaining foundation and one favored cost and the other favored market. The responses of those favoring market indicated that market was more meaningful, market relates earning assets to foundation activities, and that use of market would avoid the charge that foundations are hiding their assets. Those favoring cost indicated that market would not be understood, market has no worthwhile purpose, and that cost is the only proper basis. The foundations seemed to be aware, however, of the limitations of using cost.

The interviews indicate that the time has come to value securities at market. The interviews indicated an awareness of the need for recording economic realities and a willingness to depart from the traditional methods toward a method that is in the best interests of the user to whom the information is being communicated.

FUND ACCOUNTING

If management deems it desirable for internal management, budgeting, and planning to use fund accounting, no one would seriously question their right to do so; however, serious problems occur if financial statements are prepared from the accounts in the same amount and in the same structure as in the accounts. The main problem is a reader difficulty in understanding the results.

There can be only two justifications for the use of fund accounting in financial reporting by private foundations. One, that it is legally required and/or two, the information presented in that fashion is more useful than if it were presented in another fashion. In Chapter 4, it was pointed out that foundations are following legal concepts with emphasis on charge and discharge of accountability in the stewardship of the assets. The accounting closely resembles trust accounting in which various funds must be segregated by law. In a school district in which a constituency votes on budgets and the budget allocates funds for various activities, fund accounting may be justified to show that the school board has discharged its stewardship properly, the funds voted for the plant were spent on the plant, the funds voted for salaries were spent on salaries, the funds voted for maintenance were spent on maintenance, and so on. The same may be said for a governmental agency, but even there writers question the usefulness of fund accounting.[41]

Fund accounting is not legally required for private foundations because they own the principal of all their funds. They do not submit a budget to a constituency to vote on, committing the board to the budget. The managers of the foundation are free to use their judgment about the activities and expenditures within the constraints of the foundation's charter. Appropriating funds for various activities is a management-planning decision and is not legally required to be revealed in the financial statements. The principles of trust accounting do not govern the preparation of the financial statements and, as Cary and Bright pointed out, under the doctrine of absolute ownership, all formal trusts involve a separation of the legal and equitable titles to the trust property, and no person can be trustee for himself.[42] Private foundations are the absolute owners of their property; while there may be restrictions on the use of the property, it does not warrant the use of fund accounting. No enterprise, whether profit or nonprofit, receives funds without any restrictions on it, whether the restrictions are placed by the contributor, taxpayer, stockholder, or the government, as a matter of law. Fund accounting is justified if the paramount consideration is dollar accountability for the funds as in a formal trust. I conclude that there is no legal requirement that the financial statements of private foundations be prepared on a fund basis.

Are financial statements prepared on a fund basis more useful than if they were prepared on some other basis? The answer depends upon who the user is. In my interview with John Harrigan he indicated that boards of directors have a strong sense of stewardship and are afraid of their principal being consumed. Being conscious of maintaining and protecting principal into perpetuity, boards lean toward isolating their principal to see clearly what is happening to it.[43]

While the boards of directors may desire to use fund accounting to protect the principal, as Harrigan so aptly perceived, the board is ultimately held accountable, and thus other users' needs must take priority over the needs of the board, which anyhow can be satisfied with internal reports. External users—including the general public, the ultimate user—are not sophisticated financial analysts who can manipulate and interpret a mass of data.

Chapter 4 indicated that the AICPA's Committee on Voluntary Health and Welfare Organizations recommended fund accounting where restricted funds have been established in response to donor or grantor restrictions.[44] I do not wish to dispute the recommendations of the AICPA, but perhaps this recommendation was made without full consideration of the problems involved in understanding reports prepared on a fund basis. The AICPA's committee recommended fund accounting for funds that "have been established in response to donor or grantor restrictions." The committee remained silent about the situation where there are no such restrictions; presumably fund accounting would not be mandated in those circumstances.

The role of the accountant is to process a mass of data and present the results in a comprehensible fashion. In commercial accounting, for a corporation that has many subsidiaries, consolidated financial statements are presented, although legally each subsidiary is a separate corporation. The accountant does not present a mass of data taken from the books of account. He decides what information is useful and summarizes the data so that the reader sees the overall picture of the entity under study. Reports that are useful for management are not necessarily useful or significant to the general public.

My interviews revealed divergent views on fund accounting. The responses from the private foundations themselves were almost a unanimous "no" to fund accounting for the following reasons: they are very difficult to comprehend, they serve no useful purpose, and they are unrealistic in the financial statements and should just be for internal accounting.

The response of the public accountants was more favorable toward fund accounting; they expressed concern for legalities. They said that fund accounting in the financial statements would be appropriate under the following circumstances: restricted funds exist, principal is to be maintained and not spent, and legal restrictions on the principal exist. If those circumstances do not exist, then fund accounting in the financial statements should not be used. One interviewee said that the proliferation of funds is unwarranted and sometimes intentional to make the financial statements difficult to understand.

Only Quentin Squires of Main Lafrentz & Co. disagreed in principle with limiting the use of fund accounting when he said that fund accounting is essential because each fund has a different purpose and to combine them would be misleading. The readers are presumably knowledgeable and can interpret the various funds but if they are combined, the reader may conclude that all the assets are available for unrestricted use.

FINANCIAL STATEMENTS AND TERMINOLOGY

Income Statement

Louis Englander, who in his book approved many alternative accounting treatments, said "there is a definite need for the creation of a uniform terminology in this field, and a refinement of the concepts applicable to the terminology established."[45]

Chapter 5 revealed the popularity of the "income statement" or "statement of income and expenses" to report revenues, receipts, income, expenses, and expenditures. In a profit-oriented enterprise, an income statement reveals the revenues generated by business activities less all the necessary expenses incurred to produce the revenue. In a private foundation, the income statement becomes a mixture of income and income-producing expenses and non-income receipts and non-income-producing expenses. Any reference to revenue, expense, or net income should meet the definition of revenue, expense, or net income of a profit-oriented enterprise. Net income has a specific meaning—revenue minus expenses. It is a measure of the success of the enterprise. An examination of the income statements of private foundations reveals many expenditures which are not expenses for the production of income, yet are included in an income statement. Grants paid was discussed previously, but other expenses such as rents, and salaries paid in connection with carrying on foundation activities, are not income-producing expenses. Therefore, the usage of the term "income statement" should be restricted to a true income statement which purports to measure net income.

Some foundations have attempted to deal with this situation by using descriptive titles; for example, the Robert Wood Johnson Foundation titled its statement "Statement of Investment Income,

ILLUSTRATION 6.1

Rockefeller Foundation: Statement of Operations
and Changes in Principal Fund, Year Ending
December 31, 1973

Investment income:	
Dividends	$ 25,407,843
Interest	4,071,748
Royalties on investment received by bequest	107,219
	29,586,810
Less: investment expenses	913,588
Investment income before federal excise tax	28,673,222
Less: provision for federal excise tax	1,109,365
Net investment income	27,563,857
Grant appropriations announced and program costs incurred during the year	40,271,699
General administrative expenses	3,869,182
	44,140,881
Excess of grant appropriations announced, program costs, and general administrative expenses incurred over income	(16,577,024)
Principal fund at beginning of year as restated	914,326,844
Increase (decrease) in unrealized appreciation on marketable securities net of deferred federal excise tax (1973: reduction ($6,030,000); 1972: provision $3,950,000)	(204,693,139)
Realized gain on sale of marketable securities less provision for federal excise tax (1973: $1,498,469; 1972: $974,011)	93,242,842
Contributions to the Foundation	76,012
Net increase (decrease) in property account	15,272
Principal fund at end of year	$786,390,807

Source: Rockefeller Foundation, Annual Report, 1973.

Expenses, Grants and Changes in Foundation Principal."[46] The
Rockefeller Foundation called the same statement a "Statement of
Operations and Changes in Principal Fund" (See Illustration 6.1).
Both foundations have combined investment income and operational
expenditures in one financial statement.

I believe that a true income statement should be a primary
financial statement of private foundations, because for most foundations income is the primary source of funds. The income statement
should carry the same significance which it does for a profit-making
enterprise, where the goal of economic activity is profit; hence, the
income statement becomes a vital part of the information supplied
by that enterprise.

In a private foundation, net income indicates the productivity
of the investment assets. The income statement should reveal the
types of income and the expenses incurred to produce income.
Illustration 6.2, a fictitious foundation, shows my recommended
income statement. It starts with gross investment income and
includes realized capital gains and losses which are income and,
in addition, includes unrealized gains as losses which should also
be included as discussed in this chapter.

To make the income statement as useful and as revealing as
possible, I believe that the investment expenses should be broken
down between direct and indirect. The direct expenses include all
the directly related and incurred expenses for the production of
income. Subtracting the direct expenses and the excise tax from
the gross income results in a subtotal called contribution margin.
The contribution margin approach is extremely useful for decision
making. Horngren emphasizes that advocates of the contribution
approach "do not maintain that fixed costs are unimportant or irrele-
vant; but they do stress that the distinctions between behaviors of
variable and fixed costs are crucial for certain decisions."[47]

Not distinguishing between the direct and indirect investment
expenses can result in misleading conclusions, as is demonstrated
by the following example. A private foundation whose total investment assets is $1 million has two alternative investment choices:
use an investment service which would yield 7 percent or $70,000,
or invest themselves with the following results: gross investment
income, $85,000; direct investment expense, $10,000; allocated
portion of overhead (rent, salaries, and so on), $8,000. If the
decision maker includes the overhead expenses in the second alternative, the net investment income totals $67,000, which would
indicate that first alternative is the better choice. However, since
the $8,000 in expenses are indirect and would be incurred regardless
of the decision on hand—that is, rent would still be paid and the
salaries would still be paid to the secretaries and officers—the
second alternative is the better choice because its contribution to
the overall profits would be greater. Thus, not distinguishing
between direct and indirect expenses can lead to misleading conclusions for decision making; therefore, only the direct investment

ILLUSTRATION 6.2

Hypothetical Foundation: Income Statement
and Changes in Principal, Year Ending
December 31, 1975

Investment income		
Dividends		$ 30,000.00
Interest		60,000.00
Realized capital gain		40,000.00
Unrealized capital gain		30,000.00
		160,000.00
Less direct expenses		
Direct investment expenses	$20,000.00	
Federal income tax	4,000.00	24,000.00
Contribution margin		136,000.00
Less: indirect investment expenses		10,000.00
Net investment income		126,000.00
Less: income used for current activities		
(Exhibit B)		56,000.00
Income transferred to principal		70,000.00
Principal balance beginning of year		1,000,000.00
Principal balance end of year		$1,070,000.00

Source: Compiled by the author.

expenses and excise tax should be subtracted from the investment
income in determining a contribution margin.

The private foundation may also incur indirect investment
expenses for the production of income. Part of the treasurer's
time may be involved, part of the secretaries' time, and part of
the office, which would mean part of the rent and utilities. Part
of these expenses should be allocated to investment expense since
they are a part of the investment process, and in order for the
foundation to reveal the full and complete extent of the investment
cost, these indirect investment expenses should be subtracted from
the contribution margin to arrive at net investment income.

The income statement then tells the reader the portion of
income used for current activities and the portion of income transferred to principal. The income statement in Illustration 6.2 is
prepared in accordance with my recommendations in this chapter
regarding capital gains. Thus, even though the capital gains are
used to increase the principal of the private foundation, they are

included in the income statement. The reader is shown the income used for current activities and the income used to increase principal. A statement of changes in principal may either be presented as a separate statement or, alternatively, combined with the income statement with the combined statement titled "Income Statement and Changes in Principal." Table 5.18 in Chapter 5 revealed the extent and variety of financial statements showing changes in principal or fund balances. Since there is no clear delineation between income and other sources of funds, expenses and other distributions of funds, the variety of titles and types of financial statements used to report on changes in principal is bewildering and totally confusing. The "Statement of Changes in Funds", which is popular, may merely be a reconciliation of the opening and ending principal, a summary of the income and expenses that accounted for the changes in funds, or other changes in the fund principal not reflected through the income statement. The point is that the title of the financial statement served as little clue to contents since almost every foundation felt free to determine for itself the contents and format of its financial statements.

I prefer the combined statement because the principal section for most foundations will merely reveal the equity of the foundation at the beginning of the year, plus or minus the income transfers to or from principal and the equity at the end of the year. Additional principal contributions received would be added directly to principal. Combining the two financial statements would be more meaningful to the reader because the changes in principal usually derive from the income of the foundation during the year.

Preparing an income statement and changes in principal following my approach would provide useful information as well as an overall picture of the private foundation's investment activities and would serve a variety of users' needs.

Statement of Financial Activities

In Illustration 6.3, I present a "Statement of Financial Activities." This statement summarizes two things: first, what the foundation did with its funds and, second, where the funds came from. I have followed the recommendation of the AICPA audit guide for voluntary health and welfare organizations in which functional reporting of expenses is recommended.[48] The audit guide describes the variety of persons and groups interested in the activities of voluntary health and welfare organizations and the guide concludes:

Although each of these groups may be interested in information about particular types of expenses, the

ILLUSTRATION 6.3

Hypothetical Foundation: Statement of
Financial Activities, Year Ending
December 31, 1975

What we did with our funds		
Grants		
Education		$17,000.00
Community action		3,000.00
Religion		6,000.00
Science		4,000.00
Conservation		13,000.00
Vocational training		17,000.00
Housing		5,000.00
Cultural institutions		1,000.00
Total grants		66,000.00
Management expenses		10,000.00
Total expenses		$76,000.00
Sources of our funds		
Income (Exhibit A)	$56,000.00	
Contributions received for		
current activities	20,000.00	
Total funds used for current activities		$76,000.00

Source: Compiled by the author.

cost of providing various services or other activities is
of greater importance and becomes apparent only when
the expenditures are summarized on a "functional"
basis.[49]

My first section captioned "what we did with our funds" presents
the expenses of the private foundation by function. Foundations
traditionally have reported expenses by type rather than by function.
And some foundations have been accused of having administrative
expenses too high in comparison to other foundations.[50] This problem
clearly demonstrates the need for standards in the measurement and
reporting process. Before any comparisons can be made, there
must be assurance that "apples are being compared to apples and
not oranges." The critics can not be faulted since they are dealing
with the information presented to them by the foundations, and a
lack of standards is preventing meaningful comparisons.

If one foundation makes a grant in which the grantee incurs the entire cost of the program using its own staff, while another foundation makes a grant in which part of its own staff supplies necessary expertise but the staff is considered part of the administrative expense of the latter foundation, a comparison of the administrative expenses between these two foundations would be misleading, since we are not comparing the same thing. The functions performed by a foundation should be subdivided into two major categories. Sustentation expenses should be included in the first category and in the second service implementation expenses.[51] Sustentation expenses are expenses incurred to keep the organization alive. All expenses incurred to maintain the organization should be so classified, and expenses incurred for programs should be identified with the programs. This breakdown will inform the reader of the program costs and the costs of managing the foundation. It will also permit comparisons to be made of different foundations.

Direct expenses in each category present no problems in identifying the expense with the category. Therefore, staff salaries paid to employees who are involved with a particular grant would be classified with that grant. Expenses that can be directly identified with a particular grant should be assigned to it. The problem arises with expenses incurred that pertain to more than one functional purpose. In order to obtain full and complete functional reporting, it is necessary to allocate these costs among different functions. Examples of this type of expense include employees' salaries, rent, and utilities. Horngren states that "given a total-cost pool and a cost object, the most important criteria for selecting a cost allocation base is to relate the total cost to its most causal factor."[52]

The audit guide for voluntary health and welfare organizations provides guidelines for allocation that will ordinarily result in a reasonable allocation of the indirect expenses:

1. Daily time records may be kept to allocate employee salaries to various programs.
2. Automobile and travel costs may be allocated on the basis of the expense or time reports of the employees involved.
3. Telephone expenses may be allocated based on the salary allocation of the employee using the telephone.
4. Stationery, supplies, and postage costs may be allocated based on a study of their use.
5. Rental and similar occupancy costs may be allocated on the basis of a factor determined from a study of the function of the personnel using the space involved.[53]

Functional reporting of expenses will tell the reader of the financial statements the areas of activity being financed by the foundation and the amounts expended. Private foundations are in business to further religious, scientific, educational, or other philanthropic activities. It is important to tell the reader how much the foundation has spent in furthering philanthropic objectives by areas of interest. Information of this nature is more useful to the reader than information which tells how much was spent on salaries, rent, telephone, travel, and similar expenses.

The second part of my recommended financial statement (Illustration 6.3) tells the reader the source of the funds being spent to carry out the foundation's philanthropic mission. It indicates that income was the primary source and contributions the secondary source of funds. Many private foundations do not receive any contributions (Table 5.6) and thus income would constitute their only source of funds.

Statement of Changes in Financial Position

Some foundations submitted a statement of changes in financial position or similar title in addition to the changes in funds or principal, and others submitted a statement of changes in cash. The Accounting Principles Board of the American Institute of Certified Public Accountants made the statement of changes in financial position a basic financial statement to be included for each period for which an income statement is presented.[54] This requirement pertains, however, to a business enterprise and not nonprofit entities.[55]

The purposes of the statement of changes in financial position are: "(1) to summarize the financing and investing of the entity . . . (2) to complete the disclosure of changes in financial position during the period."[56] For a business enterprise, profits are one source of funds and it is necessary to disclose the results of financing and investing activities such as borrowing, capital investments, sales and purchases of investments, acquisitions and dispositions of plant and equipment, increases and decreases in receivables, in payables, and in inventories.

The private foundation does not generally borrow funds, does not have inventories or receivables, and does not usually have much in the way of plant and equipment. Thus, the statement of changes in financial position is superfluous since income is generally the only source of funds and its disposition is dealt with adequately in the statement of operation. An examination of the annual report of the Alfred P. Sloan Foundation revealed the following financial statements:

Balance sheet
Statement of income and funds
Statement of changes in financial position [57]

The statement of changes in financial position did not reveal much information not already revealed in the first two financial statements, because it was essentially a rearranging of the information presented in the balance sheet and statement of income and funds.

A statement of changes in financial position prepared on a cash receipts and cash disbursements basis would be useful especially if the financial statements are prepared on the accrual basis. Changes in financial position prepared on a cash receipts and disbursements basis would act as a supplement to the accrual-based financial statements for planning purposes and show the availability of and disposition of funds in the past. Table 5.18 in Chapter 5 revealed that statements showing changes in cash were being used with titles such as "Statement of Sources and Uses of Cash." However, the "Statement of Changes in Financial Position," as used by the Rockefeller Foundation, was a statement of cash receipts and disbursements.[58] Since the concept of the statement of changes in financial position as used by the Accounting Principles Board[59] is much broader than cash, I recommend that private foundations do not use the title "Statement of Changes in Financial Position" if such a statement is prepared on a cash receipts and disbursements basis; more appropriate terminology should be used such as "Statement of Cash Receipts and Disbursements."

Balance Sheet and Related Information

Either title "Balance Sheet" or "Statement of Financial Position" is well understood and appropriate and should be continued under its usual format. All the accounting principles applicable to the presentation of a balance sheet for a commercial enterprise should be used by the private foundation to prepare its balance sheet since both show the same thing—the financial status of the enterprise at a particular point in time.

Private foundations should also provide a summary and reconciliation of grants by function. Illustration 6.4 acts as a summary and reconciliation of grants by function. The first column of this schedule reveals the liability for unpaid grants on January 1, 1975. Column two shows the grants approved during 1975 and this column agrees with the "Statement of Financial Activities" (Illustration 6.3). Column three tells the reader the actual cash expenditures during 1975 for grants and the last column indicates the liability on Decem-

ILLUSTRATION 6.4

Hypothetical Foundation: Schedule of Grant
Information, Year Ending
December 31, 1975

	Grants Unpaid, Jan. 1, 1975	Grants Approved, 1975	Grants Paid, 1975	Grants Unpaid, Dec. 31, 1975
Education	$ 9,000	$17,000	$19,000	$ 7,000
Comunity action	1,000	3,000	4,000	–
Religion	5,000	6,000	8,000	3,000
Science	2,000	4,000	3,000	3,000
Conservation	15,000	13,000	12,000	16,000
Vocational training	3,000	17,000	15,000	5,000
Housing	5,000	5,000	7,000	3,000
Cultural institutions	–	1,000	1,000	–
Totals	$40,000	$66,000	$69,000	$37,000

Source: Compiled by the author.

ber 31, 1975 for grants approved but not yet paid. The last column
would agree with the grant liability on the balance sheet at the end
of the year.

In addition, the private foundations should reveal the specific
grantee and general purpose of each grant approved. Illustration 6.5
reveals the format for this type of information.

One of the questions I asked foundation officials in my interviews
was—Who uses the annual report? The response was that one of the
users were other foundations. It is not surprising that when faced
with a problem, or a need for certain information, foundations turn
to other foundations for information.

Investments are the primary source of funds for private foundations and foundation officials are concerned with investment performance. Society, also, has a legitimate interest in knowing how much
was produced for society by the foundations and if they are managing
their own investments in ways that could produce the best possible
investment return for the greatest possible payout to charity. The
greater the investment return, the more that can be spent for charity.
Foundation managers need information on interest, dividends, capital
gains.

Chapter 5 revealed that a majority of all foundations (63 percent)
disclose their investment portfolios. The very large foundations
(86 percent) and the large foundations (74 percent) disclose that

information to a much greater extent than intermediate (44 percent) and small foundations (44 percent).

The Kress Foundation's "Statement of Investments" (see Illustration 6.6) is fairly typical. The common stock section reveals the number of shares, the cost, and the current value. All foundations should provide this information and, in addition, should provide

ILLUSTRATION 6.5

Hypothetical Foundation: Grants Awarded,
Year Ending December 31, 1975

Education	
Baruch College: Scholarships to be awarded to four accounting students with the highest overall academic averages	$17,000
Community Action	
Lower East Side Civic Association: Support of program to set up a senior citizens park	3,000
Religion	
Rabbi Jacob David Hebrew School: Support of religious programs for Jewish religious education	6,000
Science	
Rockefeller University: To provide funds in support of selected teachers and researchers working in the basic medical sciences	4,000
Conservation	
National Audubon Society: General support of its activities in the conservation field	5,000
Smithsonian Institution: Support of its land acquisition program at Chesapeake Bay	8,000
Vocational Training	
Manhattan Community College: Support of program for the training and placement of Russian immigrants	17,000
Housing	
Educational Alliance of New York: Support of program for the training of "disadvantaged people" in apartment furnishing and decoration	5,000
Cultural Institutions	
South Street Seaport Museum: Toward restoration of the dock	1,000

Source: Compiled by the author.

ILLUSTRATION 6.6

Samuel H. Kress Foundation: Statement of
Investments, August 31, 1973

Industrial Common Stocks	Number of Shares	Cost or Carrying Value	Value Based on Market Quotations
American Home Products Corporation	21,000	258,021	921,000
Caterpillar Tractor Company	10,000	502,202	642,000
Corning Glass Works	11,750	1,115,480	1,304,000
Eastman Kodak Company	8,000	1,140,124	1,088,000
Ford Motor Company	6,000	326,902	332,000
General Electric Company	22,000	1,524,534	1,301,000
General Foods Corporation	20,000	730,364	498,000
General Motors Corporation	4,200	175,073	270,000
Gillette Company	32,400	1,585,507	1,940,000
Great Lakes Chemical Corporation	10,000	90,925	93,000
International Business Machines Corporation	6,375	1,196,426	1,919,000
Ingersoll-Rand Company	22,500	1,469,668	1,491,000
Kellogg Company	18,200	219,269	266,000
Kraftco Corporation	29,000	1,118,367	1,243,000
Merck & Company	10,000	492,440	814,000
Nabisco Incorporated	17,200	874,835	669,000
Pandick Press Incorporated	23,300	461,677	99,000
RCA Corporation	9,078	210,417	216,000
Sears, Roebuck & Company	14,000	1,265,754	1,347,000
Zale Corporation	16,400	620,182	295,000
		15,378,167	16,748,000

Source: Samuel H. Kress Foundation, Annual Report, 1973.
This illustration is only a partial schedule of the investments owned
by the Kress Foundation.

information on effective yields. Illustration 6.7, a hypothetical
foundation, shows my recommended schedule of investments.

My recommended schedule of investments incorporates reporting
of the number of shares owned, cost, and current value, but adds
two additional items: effective rate of return for the current year,
and effective rate of return for the total period of owning the investment. For a common stock, the effective rate of return for the

current year would be obtained by adding the dividends received for the year plus or minus appreciation or depreciation in value during the current year. For example, assume that a private foundation owns 1,000 shares of X Corporation, for which it paid $50 per share on January 1, 1970. On January 1, 1975, the stock is worth $55 per share and on December 31, 1975, the stock is worth $60 per share. In addition, the X Corporation paid quarterly dividends of 25 cents a share since it was acquired by the foundation.

Total dividend received during 1975	$1,000
Appreciation in value during 1975	5,000
Total gain	$6,000

Dividing the total gain by the current value of the investment at the beginning of 1975 ($55,000) gives an effective rate of return for 1975 of 10.9 percent.

The next column of my recommended "Schedule of Investments" reveals the effective return for the total time period that the investment is owned by the foundation. The effective rate of return on the investment is determined by using discounted cash flow techniques to determine the time adjusted rate of return. To obtain a rate of return, the income generated by the investment (dividends plus or minus capital appreciation or depreciation) is compared with the original cost of the investment. To allow for the time factor, the income must be discounted. For this purpose, in the discounted

ILLUSTRATION 6.7

Hypothetical Foundation: Schedule of
Investments, December 31, 1975

Common Stock	Date Acquired	Number of Shares	Cost	Current Value	Effective Rate for 1975	Effective Rate for Time Period Owned
X Corporation	1/1/70	1,000	50,000	60,000	10.9%	4.9%
Y Corporation	1/1/72	5,000	150,000	125,000	35	2.7
Z Corporation	1/1/73	500	50,000	40,000	2.2	5.7
Totals			250,000	225,000		

Bonds	Date Acquired	Principal Amount	Cost	Current Value	Life of Bonds	Effective Rate
B Corporation	1/1/75	100,000	92,500	92,300	10 years	6.1%

Source: Compiled by the author.

cash flow method, the rate is ascertained which would cause the present value of the dividends received from the investment plus the current market value of the investment to equal the initial cost of the investment.

To summarize the facts of the first example:

Original investment—1/1/70	$50,000
Dividends per year	1,000
Value of investment—12/31/75	$60,000

Using trial and error, a 5 percent interest factor produces the following:

P.V. of an annuity of $1 for 6 years at 5%	=	5.076
P.V. of $1 for 6 years at 5%	=	.746
5.076 x $ 1,000	=	$ 5,076
.746 x $60,000	=	44,760
Total P.V.		$49,836
Original investment		$50,000

Interpolating gives a rate of return of 4.9 percent.

Example Two: Investment in Y Corporation	
Original investment—1/1/72	$150,000
Dividends per year	10,000
Value of investment—1/1/75	100,000
Value of investment—12/31/75	125,000
Dividends received during 1975	10,000
Appreciation in value during 1975	25,000
Total	$ 35,000

$\frac{35,000}{100,000}$ = 35 percent return for 1975

P.V. of an annuity of $1 for 4 years at 2.5%	=	3.762
P.V. of $1 for 4 years at 2.5%	=	.906
3.762 x $ 10,000	=	$ 37,620
.906 x $125,000	=	113,250
Total present value		$150,870
Original investment		$150,000

Interpolating gives a rate of return of 2.7 percent.

Example Three: Investment in Z Corporation

Original investment—1/1/73	$50,000
Dividends per year	6,000
Value of investment—1/1/75	45,000
Value of investment—12/31/75	40,000
Dividends received during 1975	6,000
Depreciation in value during 1975	(5,000)
Total	$ 1,000

$\frac{1,000}{45,000}$ = 2.2 percent return for 1975

P.V. of an annuity of $1 for 3 years at 5.5%	=	2.698
P.V. of $1 for 3 years at 5.5%	=	.851
2.698 x $ 6,000	=	$16,188
.851 x $40,000		34,040
Total Present Value		$50,228

Original investment	$50,000

Interpolating gives a rate of return of 5.7 percent.

Example Four: Investment in B Corporation Bonds

Original investment—1/1/75 (cost)	$ 92,500
Face Value	100,000
Nominal interest rate	5%
Life to maturity	10 years

P.V. of an annuity of $1 for 10 years at 6%	=	7.360
P.V. of $1 for 10 years at 6%	=	.558
7.360 x $5,000 (interest per year)	=	$36,800
.558 x $100,000		55,800
Total Present Value		$92,600

Interpolating gives an effective yield of 6.1 percent.

Recommendations of AICPA and Other Groups

In the industry audit guide for voluntary health and welfare organizations, a set of articulated financial statements are illustrated.

The "Statement of Support, Revenue, and Expenses and Changes in Fund Balance" is prepared on a columnar basis, each column representing a different fund and a column for a "total all funds." The funds shown in the industry audit guide are a current fund, land, building and equipment fund, and an endowment fund. The Accounting Advisory Committee's Report contains a set of recommended financial statements to be used by eight different types of philanthropic organizations, including private foundations, to satisfy regulatory reporting requirements. The format of the recommended financial report (SAR) is similar to the recommendations of the AICPA audit guide for voluntary health and welfare organizations.[60]

I have already discussed the problems of fund accounting and my recommendation to curtail its use. I cannot comment on the merits of the Accounting Advisory Committee's recommendation of using one SAR to satisfy the regulatory reporting requirements of eight different charitable organizations since my study deals just with private foundations. I agree with the concept of having one report to satisfy various regulatory agencies since it would avoid a duplication of work.

A set of articulated financial statements geared for private foundations would be more comprehensible and useful to users of foundations' annual reports than financial statements that cover many different types of charitable organizations. Both voluntary health and welfare organizations and private foundations are in business to carry out philanthropic work; however, voluntary health and welfare organizations generally are directly engaged in charitable work, i.e., the Red Cross. These organizations are engaged in the direct operation of their own programs. Private foundations, by definition, are primarily grant-making and not engaged in the direct carrying on of charitable activities. Many sources of funds for voluntary health and welfare organizations such as contributions from fund raising, monies received from other fund-raising agencies, program-related income, and membership dues, are not usually applicable to private foundations. Expenses incurred to operate various programs would also not be applicable.

990-AR

In Chapter 2, I discussed the Tax Reform Act of 1969 and its new requirement that an additional information return (990-AR) be filed and, in addition, be made available for public inspection at the foundation's office and that the foundation must publicize this fact in a local newspaper. These new requirements apply to any private foundation having at least $5,000 of assets at any time during the

current year. In lieu of the 990-AR, a private foundation may substitute an annual report containing the same information. The 990-AR
devotes one line to each of the following items:

1. Amount of gifts, grants, bequests, and contributions received
   for the year.
2. Gross income for the year.
3. Total.
4. Disbursements for the year for the purpose for which exempt
   (including administrative expenses).
5. Expenses attributable to gross income.

The 990-AR then devotes a section each for information pertain-
ing to foundation managers: balance sheet at the beginning of the
year, itemized statement of securities and all other assets held at
the close of the taxable year, and grants and contributions paid or
approved for future payment during the year.

The 990-AR[61] is deficient for the following reasons. The amount
of gifts, grants, bequests received are one line rather than listed
individually. Gross income is combined to arrive at a total. Thus,
income sources of funds are being combined with non-income sources
of funds. Disbursements for the year, including administrative
expenses, are listed on one line. There is no breakdown of grants
and other program costs from administrative expenses of running
the foundation. In addition, the grants are not classified on a functional basis, as is recommended in the AICPA audit guide for voluntary
health and welfare organizations. Expenses attributable to gross
income are listed on a separate line. These expenses are not deducted
from gross income to arrive at a net income figure. The cash or
accrual basis may be used except for contributions and grants which
must be on the cash basis. Capital gains realized and unrealized
are not included in the income. The balance sheet to be supplied
is at the beginning of the year, rather than at the end of the year.
I do not understand why the government requires a balance sheet
at the beginning rather than at the end of the year.

The 990-AR does not present a complete and total picture of
the foundation's financial activities. It does not tell the reader the
full story of the foundation's endeavors.

AUDITED FINANCIAL STATEMENTS

Since the relationship between a private foundation and its
constituency is indirect and remote, some assurance about the
accuracy, fairness, and reliability of the financial statements is

vital. The reader must rely on the CPA to attest that the financial statements are being prepared on some logical basis with standards that will tell the story in financial terms of the resources that were available to the foundation and what it did with those resources in carrying out its programs, activities, and services.

The standard accountant's opinion states that the financial statements were prepared in accordance with generally accepted accounting principles, but as Chapter 5 established, the accounting for foundations is varied with every conceivable alternative being utilized and attested to. Statements prepared on a cash basis were attested to as income statements. Different treatment of expenses, grants, capital gains, and contributions were all attested to as conforming to generally accepted accounting principles. The terminology used varied from foundation to foundation and was used loosely without the level of preciseness found in the profit area.

Some foundations indicated that their records were audited by banks, while other foundations indicated that a certified public accountant was involved in the foundation's accounting. Neither alternative is an acceptable substitute for an independent audit by a certified public accountant. The private foundation, as a quasi-public institution, has an obligation to its public. The obligation is as great as that of a corporation to its stockholders that its financial statements accurately, fairly, and fully disclose the financial endeavors of the organization under review, and, in addition, that the financial statements can be compared with other like organizations. Each foundation, whether small or very large, should be audited annually to give credence and creditability to its financial affairs. This matter is discussed in Chapter 10, which deals with my recommendations to the government.

NOTES

1. Committee of Voluntary Health and Welfare Organizations, Audits of Voluntary Health and Welfare Organizations (New York: American Institute of Certified Public Accountants, 1974), p. 12.

2. APB Accounting Principles, Current Text, As of June 30, 1973, Vol. 1 (New York: AICPA, 1973), Sec. 1025.21.

3. W. L. Cary and C. B. Bright, Law and the Lore of Endowment Funds (New York: Ford Foundation, 1974), p. 30.

4. Ibid., pp. 11-12.

5. Ibid., p. 15.

6. Ibid., p. 26.

7. Ibid.

8. Malvern J. Gross, Jr., "An Accountant Looks at the 'Total Return' Approach for Endowment Funds," CPA Journal, November 1973, p. 977.

9. Ibid., p. 981.

10. Sec. 4940, Tax Reform Act of 1969.

11. John G. Simon, "Foundations as Stockholders: Corporate Responsibility," Conference on Charitable Foundations, Tenth Biennial New York University 1971 Proceedings (New York: Matthew Bender & Co., 1971), p. 41.

12. Ibid.

13. Ibid.

14. Ibid.

15. Roger Kennedy, "Shareholder Responsibility in Institutional Investment," Trusts and Estates, April 1975, p. 214.

16. Ibid., p. 216.

17. Burton G. Malkiel and Richard E. Quandt, "Moral Issues in Investment Policy," Harvard Business Review, March–April 1971, p. 41.

18. J. Parker Hall III, "The Professional Investor's View of Social Responsibility," Financial Analysts Journal, September/October 1971, p. 33.

19. Milton Friedman, "Does Business Have a Social Responsibility?" Magazine of Bank Administration, April 1971, p. 16.

20. Interview with Jack Gould, Financial Vice President of the Edna McConnell Clark Foundation June 11, 1974.

21. American Accounting Association, Report of the Committee on Accounting for Not-for-Profit Organizations, Supplement to Vol. 46 of the Accounting Review, (1971), p. 125.

22. Commission on Foundations and Private Philanthropy, Foundations, Private Giving, and Public Policy (Chicago, Ill.: University of Chicago Press, 1970), p. 137.

23. Ibid.

24. Cary and Bright, op. cit., p. 5.

25. R. J. Chambers, "The Missing Link in Supervision of the Securities Market," Abacus, September 1969, p. 36.

26. Report of the Study Group on the Objectives of Financial Statements, Objectives of Financial Statements (New York: AICPA, 1973), p. 15.

27. Ibid., p. 26.

28. Ibid., p. 57.

29. Ibid.

30. Howard Ross, "Is It Better to Be Precisely Wrong Than Vaguely Right?" Financial Executive, June 1971, p. 10.

31. Study Group on the Objectives of Financial Statements, op. cit., p. 58.

32. Morton Backer, "A Model for Current Value Reporting," CPA Journal, February 1974, p. 27.

33. Marvin Stone, "The Age of Aquarius—Even for Accounting," Journal of Accountancy, August 1971, p. 69.

34. Ibid., p. 67.

35. Cary and Bright, op. cit., p. 34.

36. Accounting Principles Board, "The Equity Method of Accounting for Investments in Common Stock," APB No. 18 (New York: American Institute of Certified Public Accountants, March 1971), p. 352.

37. Committee on College and University Accounting and Auditing of the American Institute of Certified Public Accountants, Audits of Colleges and Universities (New York: American Institute of Certified Public Accountants, 1973), p. 8.

38. Audits of Voluntary Health and Welfare Organizations, op. cit., p. 6.

39. Standards of Accounting and Financial Reporting for Voluntary Health and Welfare Organizations (Exposure Draft) (New York: National Health Council, 1974), p. 157.

40 Accounting Standards for Business Enterprises Throughout the World (New York: Arthur Andersen & Co., 1974), p. 43.

41. Randle R. King and C. David Baron, "An Integrated Account Structure for Governmental Accounting and Financial Reporting," The Accounting Review, January 1974, p. 77.

42. Cary and Bright, op. cit., p. 15.

43. Interview with John Harrigan, Manager in Peat, Marwick & Mitchell, May 22, 1974.

44. Committee on Voluntary Health and Welfare Organizations of the AICPA, op. cit., p. 4.

45. Louis Englander, Accounting Principles and Procedures of Philanthropic Institutions (New York: New York Community Trust, 1957), p. 43.

46. Robert Wood Johnson Foundation, Annual Report, 1972.

47. Charles T. Horngren, Cost Accounting: A Managerial Emphasis, 3rd ed. (Englewood Cliffs, N.J.: Prentice-Hall, 1972), p. 309.

48. Committee on Voluntary Health and Welfare Organizations of the AICPA, op. cit., p. 24.

49. Ibid.

50. Interviews with Kenneth J. Herr, Treasurer of the Andrew W. Mellon Foundation, May 28, 1974 and Leo Kirschner, Controller of the Rockefeller Foundation, May 16, 1974.

51. Committee on Accounting Practices for Not-for-Profit Organizations, 1971, op. cit., p. 141.

52. Horngren, op. cit., p. 397.

53. Committee on Voluntary Health and Welfare Organizations of the AICPA, op. cit., p. 28.

54. Accounting Principles Board, "Reporting Changes in Financial Position," APB No. 19 (New York: American Institute of Certified Public Accountants, March, 1971), p. 373.

55. Ibid.

56. Ibid., p. 372.

57. Alfred P. Sloan Foundation, Annual Report, 1973.

58. Rockefeller Foundation, op. cit.

59. APB No. 19, op. cit., p. 373.

60. Accounting Advisory Committee, Report to the Commission on Private Philanthropy and Public Needs, October 1974, p. 36.

61. 990-AR, 1975.

CHAPTER 7

MEASURING AND REPORTING SOCIAL OUTPUT

INTRODUCTION

Every organization is committed to accomplishing something. The output of a business in the form of goods and services is measurable because the marketplace places a measurable value on them. However, while the output of nonprofit entities is also goods and services, they presently are extremely difficult to measure quantitatively, since they require value judgments of their worth.

The starting point is to first decide whether the social output of foundations should be measured at all. If the conclusion to this basic question is "no," there is no need to consider how or who will do it.

The Commission on Foundations and Private Philanthropy criticized foundations for spending too little time and resources in evaluating their grants or their overall programs.[1] Resources available to every organization are scarce, regardless of how received, and there is a definite need to ensure an appropriate use of its available resources.[2] In a democracy, agencies entrusted with public resources have a responsibility to render a full accounting of their activities, and auditing standards for these agencies should include "not only financial and compliance auditing but also auditing for economy, efficiency, and achievement of desired results."[3] Furthermore, if those agencies are not made aware of relative efficiencies or inefficiencies, they may go on indefinitely allocating resources for inefficient purposes, since no one project can break the agency.[4] David Linowes, in an article, compared a profit enterprise with a nonprofit enterprise. If the profit enterprise invests in the wrong endeavor, it is hurt and, at worst, goes under. The same is not true of the social agency, whose dubious programs are too often perpetuated; blatant failures are discontinued and new ones

are set up. Rarely does the social agency go out of business regardless of the number of failures. However, the business press is full
of stories about businesses spun off, plants shut down, top executives
replaced.[5]

Linowes pointed out that the only purpose for which any social
agency is created is to satisfy human needs:

> The reason these needs so often remain unfulfilled is
> that institutions have never been required to justify
> their existence by "showing a profit." A social organi-
> zation can increase in size, in unwieldiness, in ineffi-
> ciency, and still remain in business.[6]

Linowes concluded that when huge amounts of public funds are invested
in social programs, the public has the right to a qualitative evaluation
of how the funds were spent.[7]

Elmer Staats, comptroller general of the United States, addressed
the accounting profession and said that the development of effective
methods for the measuring and reporting of social impacts of government is an urgent need of our nation. Furthermore, the General
Accounting Office is committed to help the accounting profession find
solutions to the extremely difficult problems of social measurement.[8]
Without social measurement, it is doubtful that desired goals can be
reached, yet,

> most areas of social concern and public policy suffer
> from lack of even the most elementary information,
> leaving the field wide open for guessing, emotion,
> low-grade politics, and waste, while the problems
> remain.[9]

The United States Department of Health, Education, and Welfare
recognized the significance and importance of social measurements
and expressed its concern that the citizens and policy makers who
are concerned with the state of the American society lack the necessary information to decide what should be done about it. "Nor are
they able to choose confidently between alternative solutions to
these problems or decide how much money should be allocated to
any given program."[10]

The American Accounting Association's Committee on Measures
of Effectiveness for Social Programs defined social programs as
experiments, and "as such, these programs are more often than
not poorly planned experiments with vague purposes and shoddy
implementation . . . . Goals are poorly defined and controls are
lacking . . . ."[11]

The profit mechanism serves as the allocator of resources in the United States. Profits serve as the basis for capital allocation decisions. The role of the accountant is to provide reliable, accurate, and useful information so that the marketplace can function properly. Capital is also allocated to the nonprofit areas, not for profit purposes, but to satisfy other basic needs of the society. In order for the marketplace, whether it be government or individuals in a private capacity, to function, it too should have information so that intelligent decisions can be made rather than mere guessing or "hunches" becoming the basis for decision making.

The interviews revealed that the interviewees were acutely aware and concerned with the measurement of the foundations' output. I specifically asked the individuals interviewed whether foundations should be evaluated on their effectiveness in carrying out their social programs. Of the certified public accountants interviewed, most indicated that foundations should be evaluated on their effectiveness in carrying out their social programs. However, they qualified their responses by asking how will it be done and by whom? They indicated concern with a lack of meaningful and realistic yardsticks. One certified public accountant said "No" because he could see no way of measuring effectiveness of social programs. Malvern Gross, Jr. also said "No" but gave different reasons, such as: foundations can innovate and respond to the needs of the time; once measurements are started, the private foundation's reason for being will be destroyed; it is difficult to evaluate different foundations—how would one foundation be compared to another?; and the measurements are difficult to make and ultimately it would lead to government regulation. Gross said that private foundations are basically doing a good job in the United States, and measurements would be self-defeating, since they would encourage the foundations to do well in the measurement process without considering the merits of the program.

Joseph Dodwell of Coopers and Lybrand, a recognized expert in the field of operational auditing, said the following about measuring the social output of private foundations:

1. There is no inherent need for the foundation to be efficient and productive, and there is lacking a demand on the part of the directors of the foundation that it be measured.
2. Very little research has been done in the public sector in the area of social measurements in contrast to the private sectors in which much research has been done for at least 50 years.
3. This research project defines a tremendous need, but few answers will be forthcoming.
4. The public should demand more measures of effectiveness.
5. Lack of measurements and standards may prod Congress to force foundations to set means of measurements.

The foundation officials were more evenly divided on the question of evaluating foundation performance. Jack Gould, of the Edna McConnell Clark Foundation, said that it was imperative for the foundation to measure performance to avoid inefficiencies and the frittering away of assets, even though the measurements are difficult both conceptually and in implementation. Approximately one-half of the foundation officials concurred with this view.

Other foundation officials interviewed said "No" to evaluations basically for the same reasons—there are no standards for measurement, and as a practical matter, it would be difficult, if not impossible, to do. The complexity of cultural, economic, and social activities is such that how would one go about measuring the effect of a grant? William Mebane, of the Sloan Foundation, expressed somewhat different thoughts when he responded that the U.S. government, to some extent, has forced the foundations to be evaluators with the trustees doing the evaluation of the programs. Reporting on the effectiveness of the programs would be misunderstood by the public and Congress. He felt that the public probably doesn't care and he recognized the difficulty in setting standards and getting those involved to agree on the standards set.

The General Accounting Office, in describing audit standards for governmental programs, said that public officials, legislators and the general public want to know that public monies were handled properly and that programs were conducted efficiently, effectively, and economically. These groups "also want to have this information provided, or at least concurred in, by someone who is not an advocate of the program but is independent and objective."[12]

The certified public accountant exists to perform one major function—the attesting to of financial statements. That public interest exists in this function is evidenced by regulation and licensing requirements. The public interest exists in two ways: first, the need of the individual investor or creditor to receive accurate, reliable, and truthful information about the entity under consideration; and second, the ultimate interest in the attesting function is that profits act as the allocator of resources in our economy. To the extent of any inaccuracies or misleading measurements, resources are misallocated. The lack of any measurement of output on the part of private foundations can, and does, cause misallocations of scarce resources.

I conclude that, if possible, the social output of foundations should be measured for various reasons. First, it would help the foundations themselves to better utilize the limited resources available to them. "The most efficient utilization of resources will maximize the accomplishment of the greatest number of desirable goals."[13] Second, the interests of society are involved in these quasi-public institutions. The lack of the profit mechanism as a regulatory device and the lack of a direct constituency, such as stockholders or even a congregation, to continually evaluate performance can cause a misallocation of the foundations' scarce resources.

WHO WILL MEASURE OUTPUT?

A need exists to measure foundation output. Who should be the one to measure and report on that output? Social measurement is outside the usual scope of accountants' activities. There is no agreement as to the extent and degree of involvement that accountants should assume in this area.

A study of the literature revealed the conflicting views on the subject of accountants' involvement in social measurements and reporting. Sybil Mobley wrote that accountants are in the measurement business "and the only way that accountants can perform a useful service is to measure what needs to be measured."[14] Robert Beyer asked: "Who is more qualified by tradition, training, and experience than accountants?"[15] Robert Elliot criticized the accounting profession for ignoring social measurements when he wrote the following:

> Consider an important decision which must be made;
> it depends on two facts: one is of major importance
> but difficult to measure, the other is of minor importance
> but easily measured. No sane person would advocate
> ignoring the important fact just because it is difficult
> to measure, yet this is precisely what accountants do
> when they report easily quantified financial data and
> ignore the difficult social and environmental data.[16]

However, M. E. Frances responded with the opposite conclusion. She said that since accountants would be called upon to audit the work of biostaticians, econometricians, demographers, social scientists, and so on, accountants would have to receive at least the same training or better than them. "Does the accountant possess the training or experience to qualify him over others to audit in the social area? The evidence seems to indicate that the answer to this question is negative."[17] Others, such as C. West Churchman, said that accountants who become involved in social accounting "have the responsibility to go the entire way—to understand why the numbers make a difference and why the difference they make is the right difference."[18]

If accountants have to acquire the same skills as those they are measuring and reporting on, social measurement would be impossible because no accountant can be expected to have the necessary knowledg of his own discipline and, in addition, have the same knowledge as

those he is auditing. Accountants presently audit areas in which
they are not as expert as those being audited. They are not as expert
as marketing people, production people, management people, or the
research and development scientist personnel in those areas. That
does not prevent accountants from measuring in those areas, and I
do not see why it should be necessary in the social area.

No one suggests that the accountant take on this task alone.
Knowledgeable accountants, such as Robert Beyer, recognized that
economists, social scientists, and environmentalists would be involved.[19] The American Accounting Association's Committee on
Not-for-Profit Organizations stressed "that accounting does not
purport to establish the qualitative standards. . . ."[20] David Linowes,
who coined the term "socio-economic accounting," wrote that "socio-
economic accounting is within the accounting discipline."[21] "Recognition of the difficulties, however, ought not deter accounting and other
disciplines from collaborating to evalue appropriate methodologies."[22]
He stressed that the accountant's expertise must be coordinated with
that of other disciplines.[23]

It must be emphasized that the mainstream of accounting thought
in the area of social measurement recognizes the limitations of
accountants and that any measurements must be done on an interdisciplinary basis. Robert Beyer cautions that "it is the accountant's
job to handle the data; not to decide what data to handle. That task
is turned over to the sociologists, psychologists, and other staff of
the program."[24] The American Accounting Association's Committee
on Non-Financial Measures of Effectiveness described the accountants' role as one "that might perform routine data gathering, attesting,
and reporting measures whose design and specification are obtained
from experts in other disciplines."[25] Arthur Toan, at a seminar
for social measurement conducted under the auspices of the AICPA
involving representatives of various disciplines, spoke on the
accountants' role in the measurement process. He said that accountants do not claim to have the ability to identify what ought to be
measured and in many cases the ability to interpret results.[26]

> Accountants believe that it will, in most instances,
> be the function of other disciplines to decide what should
> be measured and, once measured, reported, and inter-
> preted, but that they can contribute to developing measure-
> ment systems that are valuable to the user and yet
> practical from the standpoint of the producer.[27]

If a foundation undertakes a program to improve education of
minority children, the accountant certainly does not have the expertise
to decide on the criteria for evaluating success or the skills to decide

on the measurement process. "Success" as a goal would have to
be clearly defined by the social scientists and the measurement techniques would also have to be designed by others. The role of the
accountant would involve the attesting to the performance and control
of the system.

A need exists for social measurement not only of private foundations but many other social institutions. Presently, no group is
satisfying this need and some are suggesting that accountants appear
to be the most logical profession to satisfy this need by expanding
their role to include social measurements and reports.

METHODOLOGY OF MEASUREMENT

Basic Problem

Many of those interviewed expressed agreement with the concept
of measurement in principle, but felt as a practical matter it would
be both difficult in concept and in implementation. It may turn out
that at the present state of the art, measurements are limited; however, that does not negate the concept in principle that foundations
should be evaluated on their performance in utilizing their resources.

A review of the literature and numerous interviews revealed to
me that some types of measurement can be implemented easily,
while others may be extremely difficult to implement. The basic
problem is the lack of measurement standards. Some accountants
and social scientists believe that it will be impossible to set standards.
In fact, some accountants questioned whether social measurements
are "accounting."[28]

In the business sector, no one measurement is used to evaluate
the performance of an organization. There are numerous types of
measurements, depending on the purpose of the evaluation. Thus,
as a starting point, there is no need to search for any one measurement that will permit a total evaluation of the foundation. The
measurement process used to evaluate the performance of a foundation in investing its portfolio will certainly not be the same as the
process to be used to measure its social performance. In the business world, the accountant provides the necessary information so
that others may perform the evaluation, and that should also be true
in the nonprofit area. There is a fine line between providing the
information and performing an evaluation. The accountant should
be aware of how the information provided will be utilized, otherwise
he will not know what information to provide. The accountant will
be involved in the evaluation process if he supplies the information
used for evaluations. I want to emphasize, however, that I am not

suggesting the accountant be the chief evaluator or even the primary evaluator.

In the private sector, efforts are translated into costs, and accomplishments are translated into revenues; both are combined to arrive at a net income. That is possible because both use a common scale of dollars. The efforts of the private foundation can be measured using the appropriate accounting techniques, but to measure a net difference would be impossible unless the accomplishments can be placed on the same scale. If present knowledge permitted that, the performance of a foundation could be reduced to a net income or loss measurement, the same as for the private sector. That, if possible, would constitute the ultimate measurement; however, it is presently impossible to place dollar values on social programs. How much is it worth to save one person from starving? While the cost of feeding the person can be measured, the accomplishment (revenue) cannot be measured in terms of dollars, a measurement necessary in order for the two to be combined in a common income statement. Even though that type of income statement cannot be prepared presently, it does not mean that nothing can be done in the measurement of performance. The discussion to follow progresses from measurements that are certainly within the accountant's capabilities to the boundaries of the state of the art and perhaps a little beyond his present horizon.

Planning Programming Budgeting System

A tool that may be useful to private foundations in helping them achieve their objectives is a Planning Programming Budgeting System (PPBS). This system goes by several names such as Planning Programming Budgeting, Program Budgeting, Cost Effectiveness, Program Analysis, or simply the McNamara Method.[29]

The system was developed by the Rand Corporation and was adopted by the Defense Department in 1961 under Secretary of Defense McNamara.[30]

The principal components of a PPBS system are the program budget and the technique of cost-benefit analysis, or cost-effectiveness analysis.[31]

As described by David Novick of Rand Corporation, the method of a PPBS system

is to set forth certain major objectives, to define programs essential to these goals, to identify resources to the specific types of objectives and to systematically analyze the alternatives available.[32]

The traditional budget approach of government and other nonprofit entities is one prepared on a departmental object-by-object basis and adopted on a line-item basis.[33] The emphasis is on input, not output. The program budget shifts the emphasis to output. The budget is prepared on a program basis. The programs are the desired output of the organization. The programs are the reason for the organization's existence. Thus, costs are expressed in terms of desired ends or programs. The program budget is prepared by costing the activities that will produce the end product. "Each activity is the program by which an objective is sought."[34]

Expenditures are related to the objectives of the organization rather than to the organization itself. For example, salaries of counselors would not be budgeted on a line basis as salaries of counselors, but would be budgeted in the program or programs that the counselors are working in.

Thus, a PPBS system starts with objectives or plans and then a determination of what it will cost to achieve them. Cost analysis and cost effectiveness are the main tools used by the decision maker to measure the effectiveness of the different alternatives available to achieve the desired goals.[35] Program budgeting encourages the use of cost-effectiveness analysis because it tries to relate the benefits to be received from the costs committed. The relationship between the program costs and program goals can be viewed as a problem of discovering the best cost/benefit ratio possible, under assumed standards of quality of performance.[36]

Roderick K. Maclead, in an article in the Harvard Business Review, described the application of Program Budgeting to a mental health clinic. Approximately thirty different programs were identified as being conducted by the clinic. Maclead then described the benefits derived, as follows:

1. The conceptual discipline for defining what the institution is doing
2. The process of sorting out expenditures so as to identify the direct and indirect costs
3. The process of matching funding to the intended purpose
4. The means for estimating with confidence the cost consequences of expanding or contracting any program and the impact on other programs.
5. The means for examining the financial implications of a program over a span of time.[37]

The significance of program costs was emphasized in this article when the author concluded: "I must again emphasize that even a rough idea of the cost of a program is so useful that arguments about precision are reduced to the level of quibbles."[38]

Some of the concepts of a PPBS system such as program costs and cost-effectiveness analysis have specific applicability to the private foundation and will be discussed in the next two sections.

Cost of Programs

The starting point in any evaluation process is the inputs. Efficiency is measured by a comparison of output to the cost of input. Chapter 6 discussed the need for reporting costs by function which for foundations would be programs or grants. The use of cost accounting can be an extremely useful tool in the evaluation process. In fact, "cost accounting may be more important in many not-for-profit organizations than in the private sector. . . ."[39]

Proper determination of costs is certainly within the present capability of accounting, since costs are determined for a wide variety of organizations in the profit area with problems of determining costs much more sophisticated than for private foundations. Costs are determined for jobs, products, departments, cost centers, specific projects, and for anything else management needs information on.

Previously, in Chapter 6, it was recommended that the private foundation report its expenses on a functional basis, including administrative and overhead expenses allocated to the various programs being financed. The purpose of classification is to establish total costs of programs being financed. All evaluation involves comparisons, and the costs should be comparable. Proper reporting of costs will permit comparisons of the costs of a particular program being performed by different organizations or the same organization over different time periods.

The difficulties arise in measuring benefits. A private foundation engages in various projects or grants. To measure output, each grant or program would have to be evaluated independently and the sum of the individual evaluations would total an overall evaluation. How can the effectiveness of a grant or program be measured? A possible solution appears to be in cost-effectiveness analyses using social indicators.

Cost-Effectiveness Analyses Using
Social Indicators

I found in reading the literature on nonprofit organizations and in my interviews that to some degree the terminology cost-benefit analysis and cost-effectiveness analysis are used interchangeably.

Cost-benefit analysis is feasible in the profit sector since both costs and benefits can be quantified and measured. However, the measurement of benefit is difficult in the nonprofit area both conceptually and in implementation because of the lack of standards and measurement techniques. Benefits can and probably will have to be measured nonquantifiably. Then this type of analysis will more closely resemble cost-effectiveness analysis, which is defined as being "specifically directed to problems in which the output cannot be evaluated in market prices, but where the inputs can. . . ."[40] I prefer the terminology cost-effectiveness analysis to avoid an implication that benefits received can be quantified in the same sense as revenues.

Any measurement of effectiveness should have two attributes: it must be relevant, and it should have some degree of measurability. "Choosing appropriate measures of effectiveness is probably the most difficult, unique problem in cost-effectiveness analysis."[41] The elements of relevance is vital; to ignore it subjects accountants to valid criticism that they are measuring what is easy to measure regardless of its relevance to the solution of the problem on hand.

Arthur Toan indicated to me the three basic difficulties in the measurement process:

1. difficulty of the measurement process
2. no control population
3. lack of clearly defined or established goals

He points out that to evaluate effectiveness, goals that can be measured must be established. He indicated that presently there exist enough areas that can be measured.

For example, if a foundation is involved in a social program to improve "well-being," that goal cannot be measured directly; it is impossible to set up a control population to isolate other variables not under study so that the effect of the program can be clearly determined. In addition, clearly defining the objectives hoped to be achieved in improving "well-being" is difficult.

A possible solution is to use social indicators in cost-effectiveness analyses. Social indicators are the surrogate measures which "would give a reading both on the current state of some segment of the social universe and on past and future trends, whether progressive or regressive, according to some normative criteria."[42] These social indicators would function in the same way economic indicators do to indicate the health and well-being of our economy. The Committee on Measures of Effectiveness for Social Programs of the American Accounting Association recommended using social indicators when it said:

Many social goals are and will continue to be stated
in terms which defy direct measurement. For example,
one cannot directly measure "safeness" or "well-being."
It is necessary to locate surrogates which best represent that goal . . . such as accident free and bed free
days per unit time.[43]

Arthur Toan defined surrogate as something that reacts in the same
way as the real thing, but is easier to measure.[44]
    David Linowes, writing on the use of social indicators, said
that their use on a regularly monitored and periodically reported
basis could function in the same way profit indicators function in
the modern corporation.[45] He gives examples of some typical
indicators:

Calorie and protein consumption to evaluate nutritional
level; density of occupancy for housing; access to hospitals
for health care; level of reading, writing, and arithmetic
proficiency for education; freedom to walk the streets
at night; and safety in the home.[46]

Social indicators are always related to values and goals. They
act as measures of effectiveness and should be viewed as gauges
indicating the degree to which an objective has been accomplished.
Every social endeavor is complex, and no single one social indicator
can possibly evaluate the endeavor's success or failure. Any measurement system for a social program that relies on a single indicator
should be viewed as dubious. If the objective of a project is to
increase highway safety, some of the indicators of success might
be reduction in travel time, decrease in accident rate, number of
vehicles used, and speed of movement.[47] The quality of an educational program would require more than one indicator, since it
would be impossible for a solitary indicator to totally measure the
attribute. Hence, the number of degrees issued could not be the
sole indicator.[48] The quality of an educational program should be
determined by considering many aspects such as student grades,
quality of faculty, class size, facilities, and performance after
graduation.
    To develop a reliable means of measuring social programs,
social indicators should be combined into an overall index. To
properly develop an overall index requires, first, the weighting of
the relative importance of the various indicators and, second,
choosing the proper statistical techniques to reflect the relative
value of the indicators.[49] Touche, Ross, Baily and Smart took that

approach in pioneering a project in 1965 for Detroit's war on poverty. Their role was to work with the Mayor's Committee for Human Resource Development to structure an information and management system to deal with the war on poverty. The long-range objective was to outline a total management system to provide information on the following:

1. Measure the relative urgency of various client needs.
2. Measure the resources—manpower, money, equipment, supplies, etc.—available to meet these needs.
3. Develop techniques to assess the alternative plans proposed for the allocation of scarce resources.
4. Provide the methodology for responding to changes in concept or procedure with regard to any aspect of the program when the measurement program indicates the desirability of such change.
5. Set up an information feedback network that would serve management in its continuing effort to optimize its planning and action.[50]

Touche, Rosse, Baily, and Smart asked the question "How does one determine and definitely state the needs of socially disadvantaged persons in a particular area?"[51] Working with social scientists, administrators, and the socially disadvantaged persons themselves, 11 basic needs emerged and were weighted:

Characteristics	Weight
Health	20
Employment status	12
Work experience	13
Education and training	17
Housing	7
Family income	10
Public assistance income	4
Family stability	9
Social problems	6
Urban adjustment	2[52]

Robert Beyer concluded in his article describing Touche, Ross, Baily and Smart's work on Detroit's war on poverty that by using modern management techniques, the social accounting system met the needs of the community:

A built-in system of evaluation and feedback which continually assesses not only results, but the measurement system itself, thereby upgrading the organization, planning and implementation of resource allocation.[53]

POSSIBLE APPLICATIONS OF COST-
EFFECTIVENESS MEASURES TO
PRIVATE FOUNDATIONS

Private foundation endeavors cover the entire range of the physical and social sciences, arts, and humanities. It was discussed previously that social measurement must be an interdisciplinary undertaking. The question arises: Where will the accountant obtain the experts of the various disciplines to apply social measurement techniques to the foundation being evaluated? The answer is: The foundation itself. As a general rule, foundations restrict themselves to limited areas of activity and do not cover the entire spectrum. Foundations have experts on their own staff to evaluate the requests for grants.

Using an interdisciplinary approach, the foundation experts will set the criteria to be used to evaluate and measure effectiveness, and the accountant will then be in a position to report on the effectiveness of the grants. For example, assume that a foundation is considering a grant to improve the "well-being" of children from economically, culturally, or educationally deprived homes on New York's Lower East Side. The grant would be to open a center to provide tutoring, counseling, health care, and cultural activities on a one-to-one basis. The grantee believes that providing these services on a one-to-one basis is the best approach to improving the "well-being" of the culturally and economically deprived children.

The foundation approves the grant providing both money and its own expertise in the area. How can the accountant later report on the success or failure of this endeavor?

Determining the total cost of the grant would not present the accountant with any problems different than those encountered in determining costs in an industrial enterprise. Using appropriate cost-accounting techniques, described previously, the accountant would be able to determine the total cost of the grant, which is the starting point of cost-effectiveness analysis.

However, the output "well-being" cannot be determined or measured directly. To prepare a cost-effectiveness analysis of the grant, measures of output are needed. Surrogates or social indicators that reflect on "well-being" should be substituted. Examples could be:

1. Health of children
2. Reading and arithmetic skills
3. Delinquency rates
4. Cultural expansion within the child
5. Vocational skills
6. Urban adjustment

7. Social adjustment
8. School drop-out rate

The social scientists employed by the foundation would be the ones to determine how to measure the success or failure of the grant for each social indicator listed.

LIMITATIONS ON MEASURES
OF EFFECTIVENESS

Some social scientists say that measuring the effectiveness of social programs simply cannot be done. For example, the social damage of alcoholism might be quantitatively measured as lost days of work. However, to the humanist, the main tragedy of alcoholism is its impact on the family. In many cases, the alcoholic functions in the work situation, but the home suffers from the alcoholic, whether or not he misses a day's work.[54]

Alice Rivlin, writing for the Brookings Institution, said: "It is my hunch that analysts would be wasting time and effort if they gave high priority to making dollar estimates of the benefits of social action programs. . . ."[55] She uses the example of evaluation of a class to demonstrate the limitations on measuring effectiveness.

A test may not be a valid measure of what the students have learned, either because it is poorly constructed or because the test-takers do not care whether they do well on it. . . .

A teacher's score on a verbal test may not matter as much as her sympathy, her sense of humor, or her confidence in her students.[56]

I agree that it is futile to attempt to place values on social output. Her second point deals with the surrogates used to measure effectiveness. The Committee on Concepts of Accounting Applicable to the Public Sector of the American Accounting Association considered this problem and responded by saying that "in cases of programs for which no really relevant output measures can be identified and quantified, nothing is to be gained by counting the uncountable."[57] Arthur Toan also emphasized that not everything can be evaluated, but presently, there exist enough areas that can be measured.

Another valid criticism is in the criteria and measurement selection. Alice Rivlin points out that:

No one likes to fail. Rightly or wrongly, the administrator of a successful experimental project will receive

more acclaim and greater opportunities for advance-
ment than the administrator of an unsuccessful project.
Under the circumstances will there not be a temptation
to cheat a bit—to choose the most favorable measuring
instruments. . . .58

Malvern Gross also said that social measurements will encourage
the organization being measured to do well in the measurement
process without considering the merits of the program.

Accountants are aware that this problem exists. It is unreasonable to expect individuals to act against their own self-interest in
the interests of the overall enterprise. Charles Horngren discusses
this problem in motivation accounting and he stresses the need for
goal congruence. He says the first question to ask is:

Does the system provide a global emphasis so that all
major goals and their relationships are considered as
far as possible when managers act? Expressed another
way, does the system specify goals and subgoals to encourage behavior that blends well with top-management
goals?59

Horngren gives the example of taxi drivers in Moscow to illustrate
his point. Taxi drivers in Moscow were placed on a bonus system
on mileage. As a result, the suburbs of Moscow were full of empty
cabs driving down the streets to increase their bonuses.60 William
Niskanen discussed the problems of choosing proxy measures and
illustrated with the classic story of the Soviet nail factory. Success
was initially measured by total weight of output. As a result, the
factory turned out only huge railroad spikes, although there was a
surplus of these. The objective was changed to the total number of
nails produced. In short order, the factory switched its entire
production to brads, tacks, and staples.61

The criticisms are valid, yet this does not mean that the measurements of effectiveness should be ignored. Robert Beyer recognized
the limitations of accounting in Detroit's war on poverty. He asks:

But what about the measurement? Is it foolproof? Far
from it. At the outset it will be full of flaws. But the
important thing—and one that planners increasingly
are coming to recognize—is that even a relatively uncertain system of measurement is more desirable than no
measurement at all.62

Lee Seidler, writing on this theme, recognized the flaws in social
accounting. However, he said that such flaws will constitute valid

criticism only if they result in answers which are less valid than no answers at all.[63] The accountant is faced each day with the task of providing information, much of it imperfect. Every aspect of his measurement system is full of imperfections; yet he measures. The reason is that imperfect information is better than no information, provided the imperfections are understood by the user.

Another criticism focuses on who will choose the criteria and determine the measurement techniques. Earlier, I noted the feasibility of using the foundation itself as a prime source for setting objectives and determining the measurement process. An implied criticism of this approach is that the foundation being evaluated will determine the criteria and measurement techniques. However, that is precisely the technique that accountants used in the world of business. Historically, management selected the accounting principles, not the accountants. At one time, generally accepted accounting principles meant principles that had widespread management acceptance in reporting financial position and results of operations. Management had a range of accounting principles to choose from and only in recent years has the accounting profession attempted to limit the alternatives available. Management will choose the accounting principles that will reflect its stewardship in the best light. This has not acted as a deterrent to accountants, since they have been attesting to financial statements prepared on this basis for many years, while recognizing the limitations of the financial statements. There have been cases of outright fraud, cases of misrepresentation, and all kinds of data manipulation in the reporting process. However, overall, it has been determined by the users that this information is better than no information.

The accounting profession plays an active role in the setting of accounting standards; a role based on long experience in the measurement process. It is, therefore, not unreasonable to expect the nonprofit managements to play a similar role in establishing standards and measurement techniques. It is reasonable to expect that social accountability would parallel the history of financial reporting "in which imprecise measures were sorted out, and the surviving measures retained because of their utility which, in turn, was enhanced through usage."[64] Many companies, upon adopting budgets, reported that at first, the budgets were very imprecise but over a period of time, as experience with them grew, the budgets became more precise and more useful. Lee Seidler wrote that it is not necessary to solve all the problems of social accounting before practice can be undertaken.[65]

There is disagreement with the position of Seidler. Taylor, writing on the illusions of social accounting, says that "measurement of performance relating to undefined goals is an unrealistic and illogical expectation."[66] He criticizes Seidler for advocating a social audit system as a new path in accounting when it is devoid of any measurement system. Taylor concludes that no meaningful determination of the excess of benefits over costs is possible without a common unit of measure. "There is no way to compare the inflow of social utility against the sacrifice of social utility for particular actions taken."[67] He criticizes the suggested use of surrogate measures such as the number of minority employees hired during the year because it does not involve a measurement of benefits.[68] He also points out that the euphoric appeals to social accounting ascribe superior knowledge to practicing accountants not supported by objective evidence. Taylor concludes that social measurement as an accounting function is untenable because the valuations of specific social projects are "necessarily personal and subjective value judgments."[69]

Dilley, in discussing the expanded scope of audits, says:

Once the program objective has been determined, performance of that objective must be measured. How does one measure the effectiveness of health care provided to the aged? If 60 percent of the pertinent population received care, but 40 percent did not, is that "effective" or not? Should the quality of the health care be considered? Additional questions arise, ad infinitum.[70]

RECOMMENDATIONS

Measuring Social Output

I believe it would be desirable to measure social output not only of private foundations but of all charitable, scientific, or educational institutions whether in the public or the private sector. However, standards for measuring social output simply do not exist. Under the present state of the art, measuring social output of private foundations would be extremely difficult, if not impossible, both in concept and in implementation.

Private foundations do not carry out charitable, scientific, or educational activities directly. They make grants to carry out these objectives. Therefore, in order to measure the social output of the foundation it would be necessary to measure the social output of each grant. The types of grants made, in my opinion, defy measurement given the present state of the art. For example, the Panamin Foundation makes grants to preserve the Tasaday people in their primitive stone-age existence in the Philippines. Can the benefits of preserving these people be measured and compared against the costs of maintaining them? During the Second World War, some American foundations contributed monies in an attempt to save the Jews in Europe from annihilation. Can the benefits of saving the Jews in Europe from Hitler be quantified and measured? The Atran Foundation and the Chanin Foundation provided grants to help author Irving Howe to write World of Our Fathers, an historical work describing the journey of the East European Jews to America and the life they found and made. Can the knowledge derived from this book be quantified and measured? The Kress Foundation made a grant for the cleaning and preservation of the facade of San Petronio in Bologna, Italy. Can the benefits of saving this architecture be quantified and measured? The Kress Foundation devotes itself primarily to the field of art. It states in its annual report that it is interested in programs designed to increase the national competence in conservation and restoration of works of art.[71] Can any of its grants in this area be quantified and measured in terms of benefits? Many private foundations, especially smaller ones, make grants directly to charitable, scientific, religious, or educational organizations. The foundation grants may be made to organizations such as the Red Cross, The United Way, Boy Scouts, and similar organizations. How can these grants be quantified and measured?

In an interview with Robert Goldman of the Ford Foundation,[72] we discussed the problem of quantifying and measuring social output of private foundations. He informed me that the Ford Foundation does not attempt to evaluate in terms of cost-benefit analysis. They make no attempts to evaluate in terms of monetary benefits. He said that in his opinion it would be impossible to quantify and measure the benefits of foundation grants.

He also indicated another difficulty in attempting to measure output—the problem of isolating the foundation's contribution to the overall benefits. For example, if a community development organization receives support from various foundations and governmental agencies, it becomes very difficult to isolate the Ford Foundation's contribution to overall results. Arthur Toan also spoke about the difficulties in isolating the foundation's contribution to benefits. He said that multiple causes and effects and timing questions can make measurement difficult.[73]

In an experiment, the variable under study is observed and the other variables must be held constant, otherwise it becomes impossible to determine whether it is the variable being studied that is producing the cause and effect or the variables not under study. If a private foundation makes a grant to improve health care in a poverty area, unless all the other factors affecting health care are held constant (which is impossible to do), then it becomes difficult,

if not impossible, to measure the foundation's contribution to health
care.

By definition, private foundations are involved in the process of
initiating thought and action, experimenting with new and untried
ventures, and dissenting from prevailing attitudes.[74] The output of
private foundations does not lend itself to quantification and measurement. In my opinion, progress will be made in this area when other
disciplines made more of a contribution to the measurement process.
Although at the present time, in my opinion, measuring social output
is not feasible, it does not mean that no changes are necessary in the
reporting practices of private foundations. There is much the private
foundation can do to fully and completely disclose its activities to
those interested in its activities. The remaining sections of this
chapter will be devoted to my recommendation to improve the quality
of the foundation's reporting practices in terms of social output.

Disclosure of Grant Application Procedures

Many foundations revealed the criteria for applying for grants.
Some were much more specific than others in listing the requirements. Since one of the users of the annual report is the potential
grantee, it serves both the foundation and a grantee's interest to
disclose the application procedure to avoid an unnecessary waste
of time and resources on both sides because of inappropriate or
incomplete applications. Jack Gould of the Edna McConnell Clark
Foundation said that revealing the criteria will keep the foundation
from being "snowed under" by grant applications that are not of
interest to the foundation. It would cut down on the number of proposals. He pointed out that nine out of every ten proposals are
turned down.[75]

The starting point is for the foundation to indicate its areas of
interest. The Mary Reynolds Babcock Foundation states that the
foundation is interested in education, primarily private higher
education, in social welfare organizations, and in the arts.[76] Next,
the foundation should state in specific terms the procedure for applying for a grant. The Babcock Foundation indicates the procedure
for applying to it for a grant.

Application Procedure—the Foundation prefers to receive,
well ahead of deadline dates indicated below, a two- or
three-page proposal statement outlining the central idea
of the proposal, the time schedule, needs, costs, personnel and what hopefully will be accomplished. All
applicants must send copies of IRS certificates indicating

their tax-exempt status. . . . An application must be
presented over the signature of the head of the organization, division, or department making the request. In
all cases the chief administrative officer, or his immediate delegate, should indicate approval of the proposal.[77]

I am not suggesting that each foundation adopt the same criteria
for grant applications, but that it should fully disclose its criteria.
The John Bulow Foundation lists 16 requirements in its grant application procedure with items such as current roster of the principal
administrators, faculty, or staff, and giving for each: formal education, professional experiences or special qualifications, and length
of service.[78]

It would be useful and appropriate for each foundation to then
indicate the procedure for processing the grants by the foundation.
The Bush Foundation tells the reader that all commitments of grant
funds are made by the Board of Directors. The board meets at least
quarterly. The Grants Committee, a five-man subcommittee of the
board, discusses all grants prior to final board action and makes
recommendations of final action to the board. Furthermore, all
grant proposals to be considered by the Grants Committee are first
investigated by the foundation's staff. The results of the investigations are made available to the Grants Committee and the board.[79]
The Moody Foundation presents a flow chart to visually describe the
procedure used by it to evaluate grant requests. The chart traces
the step-by-step procedure a grant application follows as it flows
through the foundation.[80]

Disclosing the criteria would not interfere with foundation
management in the carrying out of its job since each foundation,
following my recommendations, is free to choose its own criteria
for the selecting, processing, and approving of grant applications.

Disclosure of Grant Awards

In Chapter 6 I recommended that private foundations report their
grant expense on a functional basis. Almost all of the foundations
studied revealed in a schedule who received grants and the amounts.
This schedule is not a substitute for functional reporting and both
should be supplied. The reasons for functional reporting are given
in Chapter 6. A listing of grantees and amounts is useful to potential
grantees because it enables them to determine whether the foundation
would be interested in a particular project.

Previously, I discussed the difficulties of measuring social output.
However, difficulties in measurement should not act as a total bar to

supplying information on social output. There is much information
that the private foundations can supply on their social output. Grants
are the social output of private foundations because this is the primary activity of private foundations by definition.

The first step is to disclose the objectives of the grant and this
would be obtained from the grant application. Each application
should, and they probably all do, give the objectives of the proposal.
What does the grantee hope to accomplish? The objectives may be
quite specific or broad. A grant proposal may be to develop a strain
of corn that is highly resistant to a certain type of insect or the
proposal may have as its objective the education of America in a
new art form. Thus, the foundation should disclose for each grant
the objectives sought. The second step is to disclose why a particular
grant was approved. This step is asking the private foundations to
disclose the reasoning behind the acceptance of a particular grant.
What criteria did the foundation use in approving the grant? I recognize that subjective factors play an important role in the selection
process. In some areas, such as the arts, it may be all subjective
the reasons for awarding a particular grant. Even in these circumstances, it would still be useful for the foundation to disclose the
criteria used for awarding the grant. For example, if a foundation
awards a grant to an art student to continue his education in a particular art form, it would be useful for the foundation to disclose the
factors that led it to award this student a grant. The factors may
have been:

1. Student's portfolio
2. Opinion of outside experts
3. Opinion of foundation officials
4. Recommendations of recognized authorities
5. Personal interview

I do not intend to infringe on a foundation's freedom to choose
and determine criteria for the awarding of grants. This is the
foundation's reason for existing and I do not see any reason why
they should abdicate this responsibility to any other group. I do not
in any way imply that standard or uniform criteria should exist or
play a role in the selection of a grant. The spectrum of foundation
activity makes uniform or standard criteria impossible, and even
if it were possible, I doubt its desirability.

Disclosure of information on the criteria used by a foundation
in making a grant will provide information on what the foundation
hopes will be accomplished by the grant. The same way the American
people are entitled to know the expected benefits of any governmental
program, so are the American people entitled to know the expected
benefits of a grant made by a private foundation.

Reporting the Results of Grants

Reporting the results of grants would cause the foundation to reflect more deeply on goals and objectives. I suspect that in many cases grants are paid without careful consideration of the objectives to be achieved and the ways of evaluating the results. Jack Gould said that he would like to see some refreshing candor in the financial statements of foundations. He pointed out that although the grantee followed all the requirements of the grant, it still may not have accomplished its mission. Furthermore, reporting failures may help other foundations avoid the same pitfalls.[81]

I do not pretend to have the competence to suggest to any foundation how it should go about evaluating a grant. Neither I, nor any other accountant, by training, possesses the knowledge to set up a procedure for evaluating grants in the arts, sciences, humanities, or other social sciences. This is a task to be left to experts in their respective fields. However, it is vital that they reveal, if possible, the successes and failures of their grants. A grant made to develop a new hybrid type of corn may either have been successful or not. It may be relatively easy to report on this type of activity. It becomes much more difficult to report success or failure in the arts and social sciences. If a foundation funds an art exhibit in a locality, success or failure does not exist. It might be sufficient to report on the number of people viewing the exhibit and to include critiques of art critics who have attended the exhibit.

If a foundation made a grant to curb high-school drop-outs, then the foundation might report on the success or failure of the grant in achieving its objective. The grantee may have used a mix of factors in the experiment such as the hiring of competent teachers, using innovative programs, purchasing audio-visual materials, constructing well-equipped facilities, and using programmed teaching materials. The evaluation would have to involve each one of these factors and its role in the overall success or failure. Again, I must emphasize difficulties in evaluating these types of programs. A decrease in the dropout rate could have resulted from the feeling on the part of the student that someone cares and the above listed factors might not have played any significant role in achieving its objective.

Robert Goldman indicated to me a typical evaluation on the part of the Ford Foundation's Division of National Affairs. He used the example of a grant to sponsor a public-interest law firm. The Ford Foundation would hire an outside consultant to evaluate the grantee. The evaluator would talk to people involved such as government officials, judges, and defense attorneys. The evaluator would be interested in their opinion of the competency of the public-interest law firm. In addition, the number and kinds of cases selected, the number of wins, percentage of suits in a particular field, are all taken into consideration in the evaluation. The Ford Foundation would then receive a report that is studied for two purposes: to learn from experience, and to know whether to make a renewal or modifications of the grant.[82]

For the same reasons that the Ford Foundation finds it useful to receive an evaluation to be used for future planning, so would it be useful to others outside the foundation and it is for this reason that the private foundations should disclose their evaluation on the grants made. If a foundation does not perform any evaluation, it should so state.

My interviews indicate to me that there would be objections raised to disclosing this information. The basic reason is that disclosure would interfere with foundation management in the carrying out of its job. It infringes upon management's freedom of action. Management must have some leeway without public scrutiny. It would open the foundation to undue pressure because of disagreements with the evaluation methodology and conclusions reached.

Historically, in the world of business, any time additional disclosure requirements were mandated, business objected and gave as one of its reasons—competition. It would harm the business to disclose to its competitors the additional disclosure requirements. This was the argument against disclosing sales and cost of sales information and it is one of the arguments today against disclosing profits by line of business for diversified companies. The argument against disclosure has merit because disclosure does provide additional information which may be useful to a competitor. However, this argument is not valid in the nonprofit sector. As semipublic institutions, private foundations are under an obligation to fully and completely disclose themselves. It may be true that full and complete disclosure of the results of grants may interfere with the management's freedom of action, but that is the price they must pay for their tax-exempt status. In many ways, private philanthropic organizations are similar to government agencies and a cloak of secrecy is as dangerous for private philanthropic organizations as in government. Enjoying privileges bestowed upon them by the American public, private foundations must conduct themselves in the full light of public scrutiny. The public is entitled to receive information and arguments against supplying the information must be considered against this standard.

I have created a hypothetical foundation making a hypothetical grant to illustrate the methodology that, if used where possible, would improve upon the present reporting scheme in use by private foundations. I do not imply that the private foundations should rigidly adhere to the type of format that I have chosen to illustrate how a foundation may go about reporting the results of a grant. Foundations should be encouraged to experiment with different formats in presenting this information.

Grant-Lower Manhattan Drug Program

The ABLE Foundation funded a new type of drug-treatment program for the residents of New York City residing in the area commonly referred to as the "Lower East Side." The funding was for a three-year period beginning in 1972 and ending in 1975. The program was a new type, incorporating methadone, intensive counseling and psychotherapy, vocational training, and techniques to improve reading skills.

The ABLE Foundation and the officials of the drug program agreed to use the following criteria to evaluate the effectiveness of the drug program:

1. Decline in use of narcotics
2. Improvement in social attitudes
3. Attendance in the program
4. Gainful employment
5. Improvement in reading skills
6. General psychological adjustment

The ABLE Foundation and the officials of the drug program agreed to use the following methodology to evaluate the effectiveness of each criteria:

1. Number of drug-free days to be determined by medical examinations, that is, urine analysis.
2. Number of arrests.
3. Attendance records at the center.
4. Length of time on job, absenteeism, number of jobs.
5. Metropolitan Reading Test—a standard test widely employed to measure the reading achievement. It is used in New York City schools.
6. Thematic Apperception Test—a standardized psychological test administered by a trained psychologist. It is designed to measure motivation, aggression, hostility, needs, social adjustment, maturity, interaction with others.

The effectiveness of the program was to be compared to two different groups, both containing individuals with similar socioeconomic backgrounds, and both residing in the same neighborhood. One group would be untreated drug addicts obtained from the waiting

list of this program. The second group would be individuals in a
private methadone maintenance program where the emphasis is on
methadone with some counseling.

Total cost of program	$750,000
Number of addicts treated	100
Breakdown of costs by components	
Rent for facilities	$ 20,000
Methadone	12,000
Psychologists	250,000
Vocational training	300,000
Social workers	100,000
Administrative expenses	68,000
Total	$750,000

The results of the grant are summarized in Illustration 7.1.
The grantee and the foundation agree that the results reveal a significant improvement in the treated group over the control group but
that the patients in an ordinary methadone maintenance program did
almost as well as the grantee group.

Cost–Benefit Analysis

Program	Costs Per Patient 3-Year Period
Lower East Side Program	$7,500
Untreated	—
Ordinary Methadone Program	$1,500

A cost-benefit analysis reveals that it cost five times as much per
patient under the grantee program as compared to the ordinary
methadone maintenance program without producing significantly
better results. Thus, this type of program would not be warranted
over the usual methadone maintenance program.

Untreated patients have a cost to society in terms of welfare costs,
lost productivity and taxes, and incarceration costs. Illustration 7.1
reveals that the number of arrests per patient declined by approximately 50 percent in both programs, assuming the costs of maintaining an inmate in prison are $20,000 a year per inmate. A decrease
in the number of arrests will lead to a decrease in time spent in
prison and assuming four arrests average one conviction, then
halving the number of arrests will half the convictions. The untreated
group shows an average of eight arrests per person during the three-
year period.

ILLUSTRATION 7.1

Hypothetical Drug Program: Analysis of
Criteria—100 Patients, Three-Year Period
Ending December 31, 1975

Per patient	Grantee Group	Untreated Group	Ordinary Methadone Program
1. Number of drug-free days	20	1	19
2. Number of arrests	4	8	4.2
3. Attendance at the program	80%	—	70%
4. Gainful employment			
a. Length of time on job	3 months	2 weeks	$3\frac{1}{2}$ months
b. Absenteeism rate	15%	50%	17%
c. Number of jobs	4	4.3	4.5
5. Metropolitan Reading Test—% improvement in reading skills	40%	1%	10%
6. Thematic Apperception Test—scale 1-10			
a. motivation	3	.5	2.8
b. aggression	8	8.8	7.9
c. hostility	8.3	9.2	8.1
d. needs	9.1	8.6	9.2
e. social adjustment	1.9	1.7	1.9
f. maturity	2.1	.3	1.8
g. interaction with others	3.8	2.1	3.6

Source: Compiled by the author.

Incarceration Costs—Untreated Patients

| 8 arrests | = | 2 convictions (6 months each sentence) |
| 2 convictions | = | $20,000 (cost of one year in prison |

Incarceration Costs—Ordinary Methadone Program

| 4 arrests | = | 1 conviction (6 months) |
| 1 conviction | = | $10,000 (cost of 1/2 year in prison) |

The ordinary methadone maintenance program saves society
$10,000 over a three-year basis. The cost of the methadone main-

tenance program averages $1,500 per patient for the same three-year basis. The net benefit in terms of dollars is $8,500.

Classification System for Grants

It would be extremely useful for statistical purposes if a uniform classification system for grants was adopted by private foundations. Fund raisers, governmental agencies, and others interested in the grants made by private foundations would be benefited. Presently, the Foundation Center is the primary source for grant information. It compiles a "Source Book" to relate the needs of fund seekers to the activities of foundations.

The Foundation Center collects the raw data from annual reports, tax returns, and information submitted directly to it from private foundations. The center then classifies the grant information by area of activity. Adopting a standard classification system would shift the classification burden to the private foundation to whom it properly belongs. The private foundation making the grant is the logical one to classify it because it possesses more information on the grant than anyone else. The Foundation Center's classification relies on information which may not be complete. A standard-grant classification system would permit the compiling of more accurate information on foundation grants.

A classification system similar to the Standard Industrial Classification Code should be adopted and used by each private foundation to classify all its grants. I believe that a three-digit code would be sufficient to achieve its objectives. The starting point is to categorize foundation grants by major area of activity:

1. Education
2. International activities
3. Humanities
4. Welfare
5. Sciences
6. Health
7. Religion

Each major area of activity should then be broken down into major subcategories. For example, under education, the following subcategories could be used: higher education, elementary schools, junior high schools, and high schools. To further subdivide the subcategories of each major area of interest would be the next classification:

1. Libraries
2. Scholarships
3. Publishing
4. Vocational training
5. Educational associations
6. Aid to teachers
7. Fellowships
8. Adult education
9. Buildings

Therefore, a grant to provide aid to teachers in elementary schools would be coded 126.

The major area of the humanities could be subdivided on the following bases: music, performing arts, language and literature, history, and museums. A scholarship granted to a student in the performing arts would be classified 362.

My purpose here is not to derive the actual classification system but to illustrate how one can be derived. A standard classification system for grants would be very useful and I conclude that one should be adopted by private foundations.

NOTES

1. Commission on Foundations and Private Philanthropy, Foundations, Private Giving, and Public Policy (Chicago, Ill.: University of Chicago Press, 1970), p. 135.

2. American Accounting Association, Report of the Committee on Accounting for Not-for-Profit Organizations, Supplement to Vol. 46 of the Accounting Review, (1971), p. 96.

3. United States General Accounting Office, Standards for Audit of Government Organizations, Programs, Activities and Functions (Washington, D.C.: U.S. Government Printing Office, 1972), p. 1.

4. Lee Seidler, "Accountant: Account for Thyself," The Journal of Accountancy, June 1973, p. 43.

5. David F. Linowes, Strategies for Survival (New York: AMACON, 1973), p. 15.

6. Ibid., p. 17.

7. Ibid., p. 23.

8. Elmer Staats, Comptroller General of the United States, Speech given to AICPA Council at its meeting in Colorado Springs, Journal of Accountancy, June 1973, p. 10.

9. Nester E. Terleckyj, "Measuring Progress Toward Social Goals: Some Possibilities at National and Local Levels," Management Science (August 1970), p. B-765.

10. U.S. Department of Health, Education and Welfare, Towards a Social Report (Washington, D.C.: U.S. Government Printing Office, 1969), p. 95.

11. "Report of the Committee on Measures of Effectiveness for Social Programs," The Accounting Review, Supplement to Vol. 47, 1972, p. 340.

12. GAO, op. cit., p. i.

13. Committee on Accounting Practices for Not-for-Profit Organizations, 1971, op. cit., p. 127.

14. Sybil C. Mobley, "Opportunities for Accountants in the Socio-Economic Area," CPA Journal, December 1973, p. 1052.

15. Robert Beyer, "Pilots of Social Progress," Management Accounting, July 1972, p. 11.

16. Robert L. Elliot, "Accounting in the Technological Age," The Journal of Accountancy, July 1972, p. 72.

17. M. E. Frances, "Accounting and the Evaluation of Social Programs: A Critical Comment," The Accounting Review, April 1973, p. 250.

18. C. West Churchman, "On the Facility, Felicity, and Morality of Measuring Social Change," The Accounting Review, January 1971, p. 33.

19. Beyer, "Pilots of Social Progress, op. cit., p. 11.

20. Committee on Not-for-Profit Organizations, 1971, op. cit., p. 125.

21. David F. Linowes, "Socio-Economic Accounting," The Journal of Accountancy, November 1968, p. 41.

22. Ibid., p. 40.

23. Ibid., p. 41.

24. Robert Beyer, "The Modern Management Approach to a Program of Social Improvement," The Journal of Accountancy, March 1969, p. 39.

25. "Report of the Committee on Non-Financial Measures of Effectiveness," The Accounting Review, Supplement to Vol. 46, 1971, p. 167.

26. Social Measurement (New York: American Institute of Certified Public Accountants, 1972), p. 45.

27. Ibid., p. 46.

28. Committee on Non-Financial Measures of Effectiveness, op. cit., p. 189.

29. "Budgeting à La McNamara," The Journal of Accountancy, February 1966, p. 14.

30. "Program Budgeting and Rand Corp.," Management Accounting (NAA), November 1968, p. 64.

31. William Zimmer, Robert Rogow, and Thomas Zimmer, "Budget Planning: How PPBS Can Be Useful to Associations," Association Management, November 1971, p. 40.

32. "Program Budgeting and Rand Corp.," op. cit.

33. Report of the Committee on Accounting Practices of Not-for-Profit Organizations, 1971, op. cit., p. 129.

34. Harry D. Kerrigan, Fund Accounting (New York: McGraw-Hill, 1969), p. 209.

35. "Program Budgeting and Rand Corp.," op. cit.

36. Kerrigan, op. cit., p. 216.

37. Roderick K. Maclead, "Program Budgeting Works in Non-Profit Institutions," Harvard Business Review, September-October 1971, p. 50.

38. Ibid., p. 52.

39. Committee on Accounting Practices for Not-for-Profit Organizations, 1971, op. cit., p. 127.

40. William A. Niskanen, "Measures of Effectiveness," Cost-Effectiveness Analysis, ed. Thomas A. Goldman (New York: Frederick A. Praeger, 1967), p. 18.

41. Barry G. Kind, "Cost-Effectiveness Analysis: Implications for Accountants," The Journal of Accountancy, March 1970, p. 45.

42. Eleanor Bernert Sheldon and Wilbert E. Moore, "Monitoring Social Change in American Society," Indicators of Social Change, eds. Eleanor B. Sheldon and Wilbert E. Moore (New York: Russell Sage Foundation, 1968), p. 4.

43. "Report of the Committee on Measures of Effectiveness for Social Programs," The Accounting Review, Supp. to Vol. 47 (1972), p. 364.

44. Interview with Arthur Toan, July 15, 1974.

45. Linowes, Strategies for Survival, op. cit., p. 40.

46. Ibid.

47. "Report of the Committee on Concepts of Accounting Applicable to the Public Sector, 1970-1971," The Accounting Review, Supp. to Vol. 47 (1972), p. 102.

48. Committee on Measures of Effectiveness for Social Programs, op. cit., p. 348.

49. Ibid.

50. Beyer, "The Modern Management Approach to a Program of Social Improvement," op. cit., p. 38.

51. Ibid., p. 40.

52. Ibid., p. 42.

53. Ibid., p. 38.

54. C. West Churchman, The Systems Approach (New York: Delacorte Press, 1968), p. 85.

55. Alice M. Rivlin, Systematic Thinking for Social Action (Washington, D.C.: Brookings Institution, 1971), p. 59.

56. Ibid., p. 75.

57. Committee on Concepts of Accounting Applicable to the Public Sector, op. cit., p. 105.

58. Rivlin, op. cit., p. 112.

59. Charles T. Horngren, Cost Accounting: A Managerial Emphasis, 3rd ed. (Englewood Cliffs, N.J.: Prentice-Hall, 1972), p. 155.

60. Ibid., p. 156.

61. Niskanen, op. cit., p. 20.

62. Beyer, "Modern Management Approach to a Program of Social Improvement," op. cit., p. 39.

63. Lee J. Seidler, "Dollar Values in the Social Income Statement," World, Peat, Marwick, Mitchell & Co., Spring 1973, p. 23.

64. Raymond A. Bauer and Dan H. Fenn, Jr., The Corporate Social Audit (New York: Russell Sage Foundation, 1972), p. 66.

65. Seidler, "Dollar Values in the Social Income Statement," op. cit., p. 23.

66. Thomas C. Taylor, "The Illusions of Social Accounting," The CPA Journal, January 1976, p. 25.

67. Ibid., p. 27.

68. Ibid.

69. Ibid., p. 28.

70. Steven C. Dilley, "Expanded Scope Audits–Untapped Opportunities?", The CPA Journal, December 1975, p. 32.

71. Kress Foundation, Annual Report, 1973, p. 5.

72. Interview with Robert Goldman, Program Officer-Head of Project Evaluation Division of National Affairs of the Ford Foundation, October 22, 1975.

73. Interview with Arthur Toan, op. cit.

74. U.S. Congress, House, Committee on Ways and Means, Treasury Department Report on Private Foundations, 89th Cong., 1st Sess., 1965, p. 5.

75. Interview with Jack Gould, Financial Vice President, Edna McConnell Clark Foundation, June 11, 1974.

76. The Foundation Center Source Book 1975/1976, Volume I (New York: The Foundation Center, 1975), p. 21.

77. Ibid.

78. Ibid., p. 69.

79. Ibid., p. 57.

80. Moody Foundation, Annual Report, 1972, p. 24.

81. Interview with Jack Gould, op. cit.

82. Interview with Robert Goldman, op. cit.

CHAPTER

8

PUBLIC POLICY
IMPLICATIONS

PUBLIC'S RIGHT TO INFORMATION
ON FOUNDATIONS

Foundations are private entities created under state law by either incorporation or trust agreement. The creator is usually one or a small group of individuals. The question arises as to why the public is more entitled to information on foundation activities than would be the case of a business corporation or trust. Some foundations subscribe to the theory that since they are private and nongovernment funded, the public does not possess any inherent right to oversee their activities.

The public interest derives from three attributes that private foundations possess: gifts to private foundations are deductible in computing the taxable income of the donor; gifts to private foundations are deductible in computing the net taxable estate for death-tax purposes of the donor; and the subsequent earnings from the donated property are almost totally immune from income taxes. This tax exemption dates back as far as the Revenue Act of 1894, which provided tax exemption for charitable, religious, or educational purposes.[1]

Prior to 1942, exempt status was usually granted by the government with only the slightest consideration. Proof of exemption took the form of a general affidavit and rejections by the Internal Revenue Service were infrequent. After the organization received its exemption, formal contact was lost by the government as no subsequent returns were required to be filed. The prevailing attitude of the government was that these organizations, once exempt from taxation, were outside the jurisdiction of the Internal Revenue Service. In 1942, the Treasury Department adopted several new measures to improve its knowledge of the activities of all exempt organizations. Refinements for establishing tax exemption were made with the adoption of special forms for exemption applications. In addition, the Treasury Department required tax-exempt organizations to file annual information returns with the Internal Revenue Service on Form 990.

Subsequently, the Internal Revenue Service made available at its offices a public portion of the Form 990-A for public scrutiny and these documents became the basis for providing information on private foundations.

Private foundations operate under a tax exemption granted to them by the American people through Congress. This exemption is not an inherent right of private foundations or any other entity. The objective of the tax laws is to spread the tax base as much as possible so that everyone pays a part of the cost of running the government since everyone enjoys the benefits of government. The government requires a certain amount of revenue to perform its functions and it uses the income tax laws as the principal means of raising revenue. Thus, exempting one sector means that the non-exempt sector must bear the additional burden.

The private foundation is not required to obtain tax exemption. Obtaining tax exemption is a voluntary act on the part of the foundation and in exchange for tax exemption, it is agreeing to commit its assets to the public domain. Thus, private foundations are in the nature of public trusts; their activities limited to scientific, charitable, religious, or educational purposes.

Unlike other charities, private foundations lack a direct constituency. For example, churches have congregations, schools have student bodies, symphony orchestras have audiences, and governmental agencies have voters. However, private foundations do not have a congregation, student body or alumni association, audience, or a voting body. Their constituency is the general public. That a public interest exists in private foundations is without dispute. A member of a church's congregation is certainly entitled to information on the church's finances and activities. In the same way, the American people are entitled to detailed information on the private foundation's finances and activities. The public interest demands this information.

Congress recognized the public's right to information when it said, in passing the Tax Reform Act of 1969, that the general public was entitled to be informed of the foundation's activities and financial position. Congress concluded that the experience of the last two decades indicated that more information is needed on a current basis and that the information should be readily accessible to the general public.[2]

PUBLIC INTEREST IN ACCOUNTING
STANDARDS

Congressman Wright Patman, the Commission on Foundations and Private Philanthropy, and the Accounting Advisory Committee to the Commission on Private Philanthropy and Public Needs all complained about the absence of accounting standards in the nonprofit sector. Congressman Patman, in investigating private foundations, had to compile his own statistics to gather information on the assets, liabilities, net worth, and accumulation of net income. Information was needed on interest income, dividend income, rents and royalties, capital gains and losses, other income, contributions received, investments, number of shares owned in corporations, percentage of ownership, book value of the shares owned, and market value of the shares owned. Information was also needed on expenses attributable to gross income, administrative and operating expenses, contributions, and gifts, grants, scholarships paid.[3]

Congressman Patman secured the information by sending out a questionnaire to selected private foundations, giving as the reason for this procedure: "We went directly to the foundations because that was the only way to secure information adequate for our purposes."[4]

The Commission on Foundations and Private Philanthropy expressed concern for the absence of uniform standards for financial reporting by private foundations. The commission recognized that uniformity of definitions, basis of measurement, and reporting practices is essential to compile valid statistical data, and in order to permit comparisons between foundations. In addition, "the total value of assets owned by foundations collectively is highly relevant to the formulation of public policy."[5]

The Accounting Advisory Committee, in its report to the Commission on Private Philanthropy and Public Needs, concluded that the present financial reporting practices of philanthropic organizations require substantial improvement.

Alternative accounting principles now exist from which most philanthropic organizations may choose. Accordingly, transactions handled in one way by an organization may be handled in a different way by another.[6]

The Commission on Private Philanthropy and Public Needs was established in 1973, as a privately initiated and funded citizens' panel.[7] It had two main objectives. First, to study the role of voluntary charitable giving in the United States. Second, to make recommendations to Congress, the voluntary sector, and to the

American public at large on how to improve private giving. Recognizing the growing demand for accountability of all nonprofit organizations, the commission urged that uniform accounting standards be adopted by similar nonprofit organizations.

One obstacle in the path of accountability is the tangle of accounting definitions and principles that are in effect among non-profit organizations, which makes examination of any particular organization's basic finances often difficult if not impossible, especially for non-experts, and compounds the problems of comparing one organization with another.[8]

The Foundation Center, in describing the adjustment of private foundations to the Tax Reform Act of 1969, said the following:

Foundations are still adjusting to the specific as well as the implied information requirements of the tax law. A number of larger foundations and even some small ones maintained high standards of reporting for many years prior to the new legislation and continue to do so. Many others are moving along a scale from traditional reluctance to make any disclosures toward greater openness, even beyond the minimum requirements of the law, but a fairly large number are still unresponsive.[9]

Daniel Robinson discussed the increasing attention being paid to financial reporting for nonprofit entities. He concluded:

The reasons for this interest in public reporting by the public sector are not difficult to find. The increasing investment of contributed and tax dollars, the competition for scarce resources and, in some cases, the abuses leading to lack of credibility have provided a collective impetus toward standardization and uniformity in communication of financial data by each of the respective special groups within the public sector.[10]

My empirical study of reporting practices of private foundations reveals that, presently, too many alternative accounting standards are being used in financial reporting. Some foundations use the accrual basis, while others use the cash basis. Some foundations record the acquisition of fixed assets and subsequent depreciation, while others treat similar acquisitions as an expense in the period

of acquisition. Contributions received by foundations are handled
in alternative ways. Capital gains are treated as principal by some
foundations, while others treat them as income. Foundations value
their investment portfolios on different bases, with cost, market,
and lower of cost or market all being used. Some foundations deduct
grants paid from income, while others deduct them from principal.

In the same legal and economic circumstances, some foundations
use fund accounting, while others do not. The number, type, and
terminology used for financial statement presentation is bewildering
with every conceivable alternative being used. Furthermore,
terminology, which has a specific meaning to the profit sector,
is used with a different meaning by foundations. My study reveals,
for example, that of the 75 foundations presenting an income statement separately, 30 different titles are used. Of the 45 foundations
presenting a combined income and changes in principal statement,
34 differently titled statements resulted.

The result of all the alternative accounting principles available
and being used is that comparisons of one foundation over different
time periods or different foundations over the same time period are
difficult, if not impossible. For example, if a foundation purchases
a building and treats it as an expense in the year of acquisition, it
becomes difficult to compare the cost of services provided by the
foundation over different time periods. Furthermore, it becomes
difficult to compare this foundation with other foundations who have
capitalized fixed-asset acquisitions, or with still other foundations
who are renting quarters.

IS GOVERNMENT ACTION NECESSARY TO
IMPLEMENT ACCOUNTING STANDARDS?

Is government action necessary to implement accounting standards
for private foundations? This question will be discussed in this section.
The related question of whether government action is desirable to
implement accounting standards for private foundations will be discussed in a subsequent chapter.

In the United States, the private sector has been the primary
agent for setting accounting standards. Beginning in the mid-1930s,
the Committee on Accounting Procedure of the AICPA issued Accounting Research Bulletins with the aim of improving financial reporting.
Later on, the Accounting Principles Board of the AICPA issued
Opinions of the Accounting Principles Board with the same objective
as the Committee on Accounting Research. Recently, the Financial
Accounting Standards Board has been formed with the objective of
improving financial reporting. This agency is independent of the
AICPA.

Recently, the AICPA issued audit guides for hospitals, colleges and universities, and voluntary health and welfare organizations. These guidelines do not possess the same level of authority as pronouncements of the Financial Accounting Standards Board, but are authoritative.

Thus, the private sector does possess considerable background, expertise, and authority to implement accounting standards. The corollary question as to whether it is in the public interest to allow the private sector to assume primary responsibility for creating and enforcing accounting standards for private foundations will be discussed in a subsequent chapter.

COST-BENEFIT ANALYSIS OF IMPLEMENTING
ACCOUNTING STANDARDS

Will the benefits to be derived from implementing standards of accounting outweigh the cost involved in the implementation? Obviously, the answer to this question cannot be quantified in terms of dollars and cents. There is always a cost involved in changing the status quo. Professional groups are involved, research is involved, and changed formats, additional analysis, and new reports all have a cost factor.

The beneficiaries will be the American people and the foundations themselves. A fuller and better understanding of foundation activities will cause the public to have more confidence in and sympathy towards the private foundations. Shedding the light on foundation financial activities will enable the American public to understand and evaluate the scope, extent, and achievements of foundation endeavors. It will permit better comparisons to be made of the success or failure of private foundations in carrying out charitable, religious, or educational activities. The best ally of the private foundations is an informed public. The private foundations must assure the public that they are working in the public interest, and are worthy of public trust.

To lose that trust would be disastrous to the private foundations. Poor and inadquate financial reporting may result in new and harsher laws than were imposed in the Revenue Act of 1969. There exist today a much greater awareness and concern with the public interest. Our institutions are under attack, and no institution is immune from public scrutiny. The tax burden in heavy, and any sectors enjoying tax advantages are and will be called upon to justify their special status.

The Commission on Foundations and Private Philanthropy asked the following question:

when the Congress was enacting the Tax Reform Act of 1969, philanthropy generally and the foundations

specially seemed to lack the active support of a broad
based public constituency. The vocal part of the public
seemed far more ready to decry the faults of some
foundations than the silent part was ready to come to
the support of what was worth preserving in others.
Why?[11]

For the success of the foundations in the future, it is vital that
they enjoy public support. Public support will not be forthcoming
in the absence of meaningful financial information. In addition,
one of the objectives of the Commission on Private Philanthropy
and Public Needs is to strengthen and make more effective the practice of private giving. Private foundations, as well as other charitable
institutions, need funds to operate. The demands made upon them
are far in excess of their financial capabilities. It is certainly in
their interest, as well as in the public interest, to increase the flow
of charitable funds made available to them so that they can carry out
their objectives.

The interviewees revealed to me the fact that private foundations
receive requests for grants far in excess of their financial resources.
Private foundations, in providing useful information, will permit the
reader to ascertain for himself this reality.

The benefits to be derived by the private foundations and the
general public from implementation of accounting standards far
outweigh its cost.

WILL STANDARDS OF ACCOUNTING
INTERFERE WITH THE MISSION OF
PRIVATE FOUNDATIONS?

Will standards of accounting act as a straitjacket inhibiting
foundations from carrying out their mission? Will additional disclosure requirements cause the foundations to become timid rather
than innovative? Any discussion of setting accounting standards for
private foundations must consider these two questions.

The purpose of accounting standards is to make for comparable,
understandable, and useful financial reporting. The objectives of
accounting standards are not to impose limitations on foundations,
but to assure that similar economic transactions by different foundations are reported in a similar way.

Accounting standards in no way dictate or even indicate appropriate foundation activity. Accounting standards will not interfere
with the following activities: areas of foundation interest, procedure
for grant selection, methods of evaluation of prospective grantees,

methods of evaluation of grants, size of staff, or any other management function.

However, foundations will have to bare more of their soul and this may act as an inhibiting factor on some foundations. No doubt, some foundations would prefer to work in secret and not be exposed to public view. The same problem is faced in the profit sector when accounting standards are introduced that will modify some companies' accounting practices. No doubt, there are some companies that would prefer to have less than the whole truth told, who would prefer to continue misinforming and misleading investors, and who would argue that the proposed accounting standards will stifle their business.

This does not imply in any way that opposition to any accounting standard is because of a lack of ethics or morality on the part of the opponent. My purpose here is not to disparage the integrity, honesty, or motivation of any opponent to any accounting standard. No doubt some foundations believe that implementing accounting standards with increased disclosure will cause them to shy away from innovative, or controversial, programs. However, the general public is entitled to have information on all the financial activities of private foundations, and if it is not forthcoming voluntarily, then they will demand government action. The private foundations cannot enjoy the benefits bestowed upon them by the general public without submitting an accounting to the public.

During the Congressional debate on the Revenue Act of 1969, some foundations testified that the proposed law would interfere with their activities and would act as an inhibiting factor. What the law accomplished was to set limits on certain activities. Far from inhibiting foundations, the guidelines and limits enable the foundations to function in a more positive environment.

Previously, I maintained that the adoption of accounting standards will increase public confidence in private foundations. Increased public support may give the private foundations the confidence to engage in more controversial and innovative programs. Thus, standards of accounting will not interfere with the mission of private foundations, but may provide an environment where it will be easier for foundations to function and hence for foundations to be even more innovative in seeking out new programs.

THE EFFECTS OF ACCOUNTING STANDARDS
ON LARGE FOUNDATIONS VERSUS
SMALL ONES

Is it feasible and desirable to have one set of accounting principles and disclosure requirements for all private foundations, regardless

of their size, or should the financial statements of small foundations
(assets less than one million dollars) be exempt from conforming
with the accounting principles and reporting requirements proposed
in this study? The size of foundations range from small (assets less
than one million dollars) to very large (assets in excess of 100 million
dollars). The implementation of accounting standards involves a
cost. Are the attributes of a very large foundation compared to a
small foundation similar enough to warrant both to be bound by the
same standards?

In the profit sector exists businesses of different sizes, different
types of ownership, and different types of products and services
produced. There are certainly as many differences between General
Motors and a local manufacturer, as there are between the Ford
Foundation and a small local foundation.

Large and small foundations are created in the same way, either
by incorporation under a state's not-for-profit laws or by a trust
agreement. Both have boards of directors and both engage in charitable, religious, and scientific activities. The scope of activities
and the nature of the grants are quite different. However, the large
foundation and the small foundation possess more similar attributes
than is the case of a large manufacturer versus a small one. Yet,
in the business sector, we have a unitary applicability of accounting
standards. But in recent years there has been a trend on the part
of the SEC to introduce differential disclosure on companies subject
to its jurisdiction. Differential disclosure applies different criteria
to corporations depending upon their size.

Despite this trend, I believe that it is both feasible and desirable
to have one set of accounting principles and disclosure requirements
apply to all private foundations, regardless of their size. Accounting
standards determine the kind of information that is furnished to the
reader of the annual report. The information requirements of a
reader does not change simply because of the size of the foundation.
Exempting small foundations from proposed accounting standards
would give these foundations more freedom to continue under the
present state of affairs, with the result that accounting standards
and reporting practices would not improve for small foundations.

An authoritative accounting body that would permit small foundations to use accounting standards that it disapproves of for large
foundations would have difficulty in justifying its position.

I discussed already the public interest in having private foundations conform to accounting standards. The public needs assurance
that the financial information received is the best that can be presented
Financial information supplied in conformity with standards established
by authoritative accounting groups is the best assurance they can
receive. It is not in the public interest to exempt small foundations

from accounting standards, nor is it in the best interest of the small foundations to be exempt from accounting standards. Part of the criticism of private foundations is due to a lack of useful information about them. For small foundations to continue withholding information would invite more criticism and perhaps more adverse legislation.

Small foundations have, in effect, chosen to go "public." The choice was made when they applied for and received tax exemption. They cannot reap the benefits without accepting the responsibilities. Even though the proposed accounting standards will involve an additional cost to them, the public interest requires that they adequately and fully disclose their financial activity.

The Study Group on the Objectives of Financial Statements concluded:

> An objective of financial statements is to serve primarily those users who have limited authority, ability, or resources to obtain information and who rely on financial statements as their principal source of information about an enterprise's economic activities.[12]

I do not see how users would derive any benefit from excluding small foundations from the proposed standards. My empirical study revealed that small foundations' present accounting practices are inadequate and exempting them from improving their accounting standards and disclosure practices would allow them to continue in a state of inadequacy.

WILL ACCOUNTING STANDARDS ENABLE THE FOUNDATION TO BETTER UTILIZE ITS RESOURCES?

One of the questions I asked foundation officials in my interviews was—Who uses the annual report? The officials said other foundations were one of the users of the annual report. It is not surprising that when faced with a problem, or a need for certain information, foundations turn to other foundations for the information. There are public-policy implications in how foundations manage their resources. Society has a legitimate interest in knowing how much was produced for society by the foundations and if they are managing their own investments in ways that could produce the best possible investment return for the greatest possible payout to charity. The public interest is benefited to the extent foundations efficiently manage their resources. The greater the investment return, the more that can be spent for charity.

Foundation managers need information on interest, dividends, and capital gains realized and unrealized. A foundation manager may be trying to decide whether to manage the portfolio himself or hire an outside investment service. In order to decide, he may turn to other foundations to see what their experience has been with these alternatives.

In trying to judge and compare his foundation's total rate of return with other foundations, the foundation manager needs information on the market value of assets; however, different foundations value their assets differently. Information may be sought on stock-turnover rate, types of investment, investment philosophy, and other pertinent investment information.

The Commission on Foundations and Private Philanthropy sought information on foundation performance in investing its assets with the aim of making recommendations to improve it, if deficient. The commission concluded that its estimates of the total return on foundation assets were necessarily imperfect, since different foundations value their assets differently.[13]

To make comparisons, the information must be supplied on a comparable basis; hence, the need for accounting standards. The better the information, the better the decisions and the foundations themselves will benefit and so will the general public. Better foundation investment performance makes more funds available to be paid out each year by the private foundation for charitable, religious, and scientific purposes.

Useful, comparable, standardized information on how they spend their resources will provide foundations with information that will enable them to do a better job of spending their funds. Information on areas of interest, types of grants, recipients, and in-house support is all of interest to foundations. It will tell them what other foundations are doing and perhaps how successfully. It will supply information on the present status and trends of the future.

Foundations need information to guide them in carrying out their objectives. It is only logical that they turn to other foundations for guidance. A foundation may want information on the role of board members in grant making, frequency of foundation board meetings, frequency with which board members suggest new program areas or types of recipients, and type and quality of monitoring of grants. Information may be desired on administrative expenses—how much does it cost to run the foundation? Do certain types of grants require in-house support and if so, of what type?

Standards of accounting and disclosure requirements that will ensure that this type of information is supplied in a useful, under-standable, and comparable fashion will enable the private foundation to better utilize its resources.

NOTES

1. J. S. Seidman, Seidman's Legislative History of Federal Income Tax Laws 1938-1861 (New York: Prentice-Hall, 1938), p. 1016.

2. U.S. Congress, Senate, Tax Reform Act of 1969, 91st Cong., 1st Sess., 1969, Report 91-552 (New York: Commerce Clearing House, 1969), No. 51, p. 52.

3. U.S. Congressional Record, 87th Cong., 2nd Sess., 1962, Vol. 128, No. 147, pp. 15943-16007, and U.S. Congress, House, Select Committee on Small Business, Tax-Exempt Foundations and Charitable Trusts: Their Impact on Our Economy, 87th Cong., 2nd Sess., 1962.

4. U.S. Congress, Select Committee on Small Business, Tax-Exempt Foundations and Charitable Trusts: Their Impact on Our Economy, 87th Cong., 2nd Sess., 1962, p. 2.

5. Commission on Foundations and Private Philanthropy, Foundations, Private Giving, and Public Policy (Chicago, Ill.: University of Chicago Press, 1970), p. 152.

6. Accounting Advisory Committee. Report to the Commission on Private Philanthropy and Public Needs (1974), p. 4.

7. Report of the Commission on Private Philanthropy and Public Needs, Giving in America (Washington, D.C.: Commission on Private Philanthropy and Public Needs, 1975), p. 1.

8. Ibid., p. 165.

9. Foundation Directory, 3rd ed. (New York: Russell Sage Foundation for the Foundation Library Center, 1967), p. x.

10. Daniel D. Robinson, "Private Philanthropy and Public Needs," The Journal of Accountancy, February 1976, p. 46.

11. Commission on Foundations and Private Philanthropy, op. cit., p. 6.

12. Report of the Study Group on the Objectives of Financial Statements, Objectives of Financial Statements (New York: AICPA, 1973), p. 17.

13. Commission on Foundations and Private Philanthropy, op. cit., p. 73.

CHAPTER

9

ROLE OF THE
ACCOUNTING PROFESSION

ACCOUNTING PROFESSION'S STAKE IN
ACCOUNTING STANDARDS FOR
PRIVATE FOUNDATIONS

The objectives of financial statements are to communicate information to the user about the enterprise under study. The Accounting Principles Board of the AICPA identified seven attributes that financial accounting should possess to properly meet its objectives.

First, the information supplied should be relevant. Information that does not meet this attribute is useless, regardless of any other attributes it may possess. Second, the information supplied should be understandable. Accounting information to be useful must be intelligible. The data presented must be expressed in a form and with terminology adapted to the users' capabilities of understanding. Third, the information supplied should be capable of independent verification. Therefore, independent measurers using similar measurement techniques should be able to duplicate the results. Fourth, the information supplied should be neutral. The information should be directed toward the common needs of all users rather than trying to be helpful to a few users at the expense of others. Fifth, the information should be supplied on a timely basis so that it is communicated early enough to be used for making economic decisions. Sixth, the information supplied should be comparable. Similar economic transactions should be reported in a similar way. This permits comparability within a single enterprise over different time periods and different enterprises over the same time period. Seventh, the information provided should be complete.[1]

The Study Group on the Objectives of Financial Statements affirmed that these seven objectives are the appropriate objectives of financial reporting.[2] The accounting profession has assumed the responsibility for implementing these objectives which are applicable to profit as well as nonprofit entities.

Private foundations have been criticized for poor, inadequate, and incomplete financial disclosure. Eleanor Taylor wrote a book on public accountability of foundations in which she complained that many private foundations took the position that they were free of any obligation to report their activities.[3] Congressman Wright Patman complained that the information supplied by the private foundations was inadequate and therefore he had to go about gathering his own data. He then criticized the public accounting profession for the shortcomings of foundation accounting:

> The accounting data furnished by far too many of the
> foundations is defective in many ways. This has posed
> problems in the preparation of our report. The lack
> of uniformity in accounting procedures, and the account-
> ing practices generally in the foundation industry, should
> be a matter of concern to the certified public accountant
> profession.[4]

The Commission on Foundations and Private Philanthropy expressed dismay over the tiny fraction of foundations issuing any annual report. The commission was aware of the dangers caused by a lack of information when it wrote that "the sense of privitism which many foundations have displayed serves neither the public interest nor their own."[5] The commission said that suspicion exists about foundations, nurtured by the paucity of available information.[6]

The accounting profession has the primary responsibility for improving the accounting standards and disclosure requirements for private foundations. It has the responsibility to implement the seven objectives of financial reporting as they pertain to private foundations. The accounting profession has the obligation to develop and implement accounting standards that will give a complete, clear, understandable, and comparable picture of the foundations' financial activities and achievements.

Failure of the accounting profession to assume its responsibilities for promulgating accounting standards and reporting requirements for private foundations will inevitably result in the public sector assuming responsibility for accounting standards and reporting requirements. Thus, by continuing a course of nonaction, the private sector will abdicate its jurisdiction over the creation of accounting standards, and the government will fill the void.

HISTORICAL ROLE OF THE ACCOUNTING
PROFESSION IN PROMULGATING
ACCOUNTING STANDARDS FOR
PRIVATE FOUNDATIONS

Why does the accounting profession have primary responsibility
for setting accounting standards for private foundations? The answer
lies in the authority possessed by the accounting profession to pro-
mulgate accounting standards in general.

Before the stock market crash of 1929, the basic philosophy of
the United States toward business was laissez faire. The stock
market crash of 1929 had profound social, political, and economic
implications for the entire country. The whole structure of the
capital markets was in a state of disarray. Public confidence in the
securities market was destroyed. Investigations disclosed that
investors were swindled, defrauded, lied to, and tricked in every
conceivable way. The New York Stock Exchange realized that survival was at stake and sought the help of the American Institute of
Accountants (now the American Institute of Certified Public Accountants) to improve the information being supplied to stockholders and
potential stockholders. A special committee on cooperation with
stock exchanges was appointed, and George O. May was appointed
chairman.

In 1933, the New York Stock Exchange adopted a policy of
requiring listed corporations to have their financial statements
attested to by certified public accountants. In 1934, the American
Institute of Accountants issued a pamphlet entitled "Audits of
Corporate Accounts," containing the correspondence between the
Institute and the New York Stock Exchange. The pamphlet contained
five broad accounting principles that were considered as so generally
accepted that they should be followed by all listed companies.

The Securities Acts of 1933 and 1934 gave the Securities and
Exchange Commission authority to prescribe uniform accounting
standards. The Securities Acts provided for certification of financial
statements by independent certified public accountants. The requirement that registrants must have their financial statements audited
by certified public accountants gave a tremendous boost to the accounting profession and the authority of the institute. The position of the
auditors was strengthened in their attempts to encourage their clients
to adopt sound accounting principles.

No doubt the authority of the SEC to prescribe uniform accounting
standards prodded the accounting profession to improve accounting
standards.

The AICPA formed a committee on accounting procedure and
established a research department in 1938. The purpose of this

committee was to narrow the areas of difference and inconsistency
in accounting practices and to further the development of generally
accepted accounting principles through the issuance of pronouncements
that would serve as standards for determining the suitability of
accounting practices reflected in financial statements.[7] The committee
issued 51 bulletins until its demise in 1959. The committee specifically stated that it

> has not directed its attention to accounting problems
> or procedures of religious, charitable, scientific,
> educational, and similar non-profit institutions, munici-
> palities, professional firms, and the like. Accordingly
> . . . its opinions and recommendations are directed
> primarily to business enterprises organized for profit.[8]

The basic purpose of the committee was to identify existing
accounting practices and to recommend one or more alternatives
as being superior to other procedures which also received a certain
measure of recognition. Although the Committee on Accounting
Procedure of the Institute directed all its energies to the profit sector,
by stating that it did not direct its attention to the nonprofit sector,
it implied that the nonprofit sector was within its scope of authority.

In 1959, the Accounting Principles Board of the AICPA was
formed to supercede the Committee on Accounting Procedure. The
board's charter states the institute's purpose to be as follows:

> The general purpose of the Institute in the field of finan-
> cial accounting should be to advance the written expression
> of what constitutes generally accepted accounting principles,
> for the guidance of its members and of others. This means
> something more than a survey of existing practice. It
> means continuing effort to determine appropriate practice
> and to narrow the areas of difference and inconsistency
> in practice.[9]

The purpose of the Accounting Principles Board was to develop
the basic assumptions or postulates on which accounting principles
rest and to advance the state of the art from "what is" to "what ought
to be" accounting principles. In addition, the AICPA set up a research
program under a director of Accounting Research. The purpose of
the research program was to provide information and guidance for
the issuance of Accounting Principles Board Opinions.

The Accounting Principles Board issued 31 opinions until its
demise in 1973. All 31 dealt with profit-directed enterprises.
Accounting Principles Board Opinion No. 22 concluded that the

accounting policies adopted and followed by not-for-profit entities should be presented as an integral part of their financial statements.[10]

In 1973, the Financial Accounting Standards Board, an agency independent of the AICPA, was given primary responsibility for promulgating accounting standards in the United States. To date, it has not issued any pronouncements on the nonprofit sector except that in Financial Accounting Standards No. 12, dealing with accounting for marketable securities, the board stated that the provisions of this standard do not apply to not-for-profit organizations.[11]

Within the past few years, the AICPA has issued three industry audit guides for nonprofit organizations, a hospital audit guide, a college and university audit guide, and a voluntary health and welfare organizations guide. The purpose of these guides is to assist the independent public accountant in examining and reporting on financial statements of these nonprofit organizations. In 1974, the National Health Council, National Assembly for Social Policy and Development, Inc., and the United Way of America issued a revised edition of "Standards of Accounting and Financial Reporting for Voluntary Health and Welfare Organizations."[12]

In 1972, the AICPA sent out a letter to private foundation financial executives informing them of the formulation of a Committee on Private Foundations. The objective of this group was to evaluate accounting and reporting practices of private foundations and to recommend changes that would attempt to establish uniform accounting standards for private foundations.[13] In addition, the letter requested their aid in accomplishing its objective. This committee's existence was terminated in June 1973.

The AICPA established a "task force" to study accounting and reporting problems of private foundations. In the beginning of 1976, this "task force" was changed to a Sub-Committee on Non-Profit Organizations. The general objective of this subcommittee is to set forth and define accounting principles for all nonprofit organizations other than those covered by an audit guide. In interviews with Richard C. Lytle, Technical Coordinator of the AICPA, and Thomas Kelley, Director of the Accounting Standards Division of the AICPA, it was revealed to me that nothing has been officially published but that in the near future the subcommittee hopes to publish a brief statement of the issues and the subcommittee's present views on the issues.[14]

Malvern Gross, Jr. wrote that he doubted whether the "task force" would issue any definitive rules because the AICPA was no longer the primary rule-making body of the accounting profession.[15] Gross stated that in his opinion, the Financial Accounting Standards Board was unlikely to consider accounting problems of nonprofit organizations for many years because of other more pressing problems.[16] Gross noted that the task force was in the process of preparing a position paper interpreting the three nonprofit industry guides as to their applicability to private foundations.[17]

An Accounting Advisory Committee, not affiliated with the AICPA, was formed to make recommendations to the Commission on Private Philanthropy and Public Needs. The Accounting Advisory Committee issued a report to the Commission on Private Philanthropy and Public Needs in October 1974 in which the committee dealt with the following: the adequacy of present accounting principles and reporting practices of each major type of philanthropic organization; the desirability and practicability of establishing a single set of accounting principles and reporting practices for all philanthropic organizations; a survey of present federal and state regulatory financial reporting requirements and the extent to which uniform reporting exists; and a study of the financial information appropriate for regulatory agencies.[18]

In 1957, the Committee on Accounting Concepts and Standards of the American Accounting Association, an organization comprised mainly of teachers of accounting in the colleges, issued a publication entitled "Accounting and Reporting Standards for Corporate Financial Statements," in which the committee said that the objectives of accounting are the same for profit, as well as nonprofit entities.

> The primary function of accounting is to accumulate
> and communicate information essential to an under-
> standing of the activities of an enterprise, whether
> large or small, corporate or non-corporate, profit
> or non-profit, public or private.[19]

In 1966, the Committee to Prepare a Statement of Basic Accounting Theory of the American Accounting Association issued "A Statement of Basic Accounting Theory." The Committee attempted to close the gap existing between profit and nonprofit accounting. The publication stated:

> The Committee's statement envisages application of
> the accounting process not only to business operated
> for profit, but also to the activities of individuals,
> fiduciaries, governmental units, charitable enterprises,
> and similar entities. Information systems are designed
> to serve managers and others in carrying out the
> organizational objectives of entities in which profita-
> bility is not the sole or even an important objective
> as well, of course, as in business entities. Economic
> considerations, broadly conceived, are of major impor-
> tance in planning action and controlling operations to

achieve the planned objectives for all entities. While
the Statement may, because of certain illustrations,
appear to be directed primarily toward profit-making
enterprises, virtually all of the observations and recommendations are applicable with equal force to organizations with other objectives. [20]

In 1971, the Committee of Accounting Practices of Not-for-
Profit Organizations issued its report with three objectives in mind:
first, to review accounting practices of non-profit entities; second,
to assess accounting practices in the light of the standards suggested
in the Statement of Basic Accounting Theory; and third, to suggest
changes for further improvement in the form and content of reports. [21]
The committee stated that it attempted to be forward-looking and
concentrate its attention on "what should be" rather than "what is." [22]
    Another Committee of the American Accounting Association,
the Committee on Non-Financial Measures of Effectiveness, was
charged with the difficult task of searching out developments in the
area of nonfinancial measures used in business or nonbusiness
profit-making, and suggest their applicability to accounting. [23] The
Committee on Concepts of Accounting Applicable to the Public Sector
issued its report in 1972. The objective of this committee was to
identify the accounting standards applicable to public sector programs
and organizations. [24]

DEFICIENCY OF ACCOUNTING PRACTICES
OF PRIVATE FOUNDATIONS IN COMPARISON
WITH THE PROFIT SECTOR

    My empirical study of the annual reports of the private foundations
reveals that presently too many alternative accounting standards are
used in financial statement preparation. While it is true that alternative accounting procedures exist in the profit sector, the alternatives
available have been reduced through the years. The same is not true
for private foundations. Some foundations record acquisitions of
fixed assets and subsequent depreciation, while others immediately
charge these expenditures to expense. Capital gains are treated as
principal by some foundations, while others treat them as income.
Different foundations handle contributions received differently.
Foundations choose to value their investment portfolios on different
bases, with cost, market, and the lower of cost or market all being
used. Some foundations deduct grants from income, while others
deduct them from principal. Even the timing of the deduction for
grants varies with some foundations deducting grants when paid; others

deduct grants when the foundation commits itself to the grantee; yet others deduct grants when funds are appropriated for a specific area of foundation activity. Some foundations use the cash basis of accounting, while others use the accrual basis.

Accounting standards for private foundations are deficient in comparison with accounting standards existing in the profit sector. Accounting treatment of items that have been resolved for many years in the profit sector still exist and are unresolved in the private foundation sector. In the same economic and legal circumstances, some foundations use fund accounting, while others do not. In the profit sector, in similar circumstances, the financial statements would have to be prepared on a consolidated basis and it would violate generally accepted accounting principles for them to be attested to on any other basis.

The extent and variety of terminology used in the financial statements and the various combinations of financial statements presented by private foundations simply do not exist in the profit sector where terminology used and format of presentation is much more standardized.

REASONS FOR DEFICIENCY OF ACCOUNTING PRACTICES OF PRIVATE FOUNDATIONS IN COMPARISON WITH THE PROFIT SECTOR

The lack of accounting standards and reporting requirements for private foundations has not received much attention from the accounting profession for various reasons. Malvern Gross, Jr. gave as one of the reasons when he said that in his opinion, the Financial Accounting Standards Board "is unlikely to consider accounting problems of nonprofit organizations for many years, in view of other, more pressing problems."[25]

The accounting profession is faced with tremendous pressure from the profit sector. It has the responsibility to improve accounting standards and reporting practices for profit-oriented entities. If it falters in its task, the SEC stands ready to pick up the "slack." In addition, with the new wave of public awareness and consumerism, there has been a rash of law suits directed against public accounting firms in connection with their involvement in alleged deficient accounting and reporting practices. It appears to be a case, starting with the stock market crash of 1929, of the accounting profession putting out one fire only to have to dash off to put out another fire, and then discovering that the original fire wasn't fully extinguished.

The same situation does not exist in the nonprofit sector. The results of a lack of standards in the nonprofit sector are not as visible as in the profit sector, where investors or creditors make financial decisions based on the data attested to by accountants. The lack of standards in the profit sector could and has caused, among other things, lawsuits directed at the public accountants for false or misleading information. This process is not at work for private foundations, and other nonprofit entities, where the users generally have a much more indirect or even remote relationship with the nonprofit organization, and the lack of comparable, meaningful, and useful information will not result in lawsuits. While some nonprofit organizations have a direct constituency to whom they are responsible, private foundations do not have any direct constituency since they are private, self-funded, and with their own board of directors not directly accountable to anybody.

ADDITIONAL RESEARCH INDICATED

Further research is needed on the presentation of financial statements. My recommendations, based on my empirical study and analysis of private foundation annual reports, is one solution to the problem. Other formats may have merit. Private foundations, grantees, government officials, public accountants, and others interested in private foundations, all should be surveyed and exposed to the recommendations made in this study. Their ideas, comments, suggestions, and recommendations should be solicited to get as much "feedback" as possible. Quite often, a concept good in theory may, as a practical matter, be difficult to implement for reasons unknown to the researcher. For example, one of my recommendations is to use as much nontechnical language as possible in the financial statements. It could conceivably turn out that most users would prefer not less technical language, but more technical language.

Some of the foundations may indicate that some of the additional disclosure requirements that I recommend would work a hardship on them and may interfere with their mission. For example, disclosure of selection criteria in grant making may cause the rejected grantees to claim they met the criteria and should, therefore, receive the grant. Other foundations may object because it infringes upon management's freedom of action; other foundations may object because it would merely encourage potential grantees to write grant proposals to meet the criteria set forth. However, other foundations may say that the disclosure will reduce the number of applications that the foundation is not interested in and the resultant costs of processing the applications.

Additional research is needed in measuring the "output" of private foundations. The type of research involved is interdisciplinary and more work is needed by other disciplines outside of accounting, before any measuring of private foundation social performance can take place. Case studies are needed in tracing the proposed grant through the foundation to its ultimate conclusion. Further research is needed on how programs are evaluated for selection, how in-progress grants are monitored, and how completed grants are evaluated.

WHO SHOULD DO THE RESEARCH?

The basic theoretical research should be done under the auspices of the American Accounting Association. Most of the members of this association teach in the colleges and are engaged in research. In fact, many of its members possess a Ph.D. degree which emphasizes research capability. The difficult and vexing fundamental research needed for social measurements can be best handled by the American Accounting Association, since its members have the best credentials for carrying on basic research in accounting. This type of research involves considering the social, economic, and legal conditions surrounding the foundation. The research will involve different disciplines and the researchers will have to possess a broad background and considerable expertise in measurement techniques, many of them clearly outside the scope of the usual accounting measurement techniques. In my opinion, this type of research is best done in an academic environment, outside of the daily pressures of the actual accounting practice.

However, the process of implementing new accounting standards and reporting practices should be left to the practitioner and not the theoretician. Accounting is utilitarian in nature. It exists because it is useful. Accounting principles, if they are to be accepted, must be practical. New accounting standards may be theoretically sound but they must be evaluated and implemented in the light of experience and common sense. Therefore, implementing new standards of accounting and reporting requirements should fall on those who possess the practical experience to know whether the standard proposal is practical and capable of implementation.

The AICPA and the Financial Accounting Standards Board have a history of implementing new accounting standards to be used for financial reporting. The AICPA represents the certified public accountants in practice and the Financial Accounting Standards Board presently possesses the authority to issue accounting pronouncements that constitute "generally accepted accounting principles." These two groups possess the experience and expertise to implement accounting standards that are practical and capable of being implemented.

IMPLEMENTING STANDARDS OF ACCOUNTING

The best way for accounting standards for private foundations to be implemented would be for the Financial Accounting Standards Board to issue a "Statement of Financial Accounting Standards" on accounting standards and reporting requirements for private foundations.

The code of professional ethics of the AICPA provides the following:

> A member shall not express an opinion that financial statements are presented in conformity with generally accepted accounting principles if such statements contain any departure from an accounting principle promulgated by the body designated by Council to establish such principles which has a material effect on the statements taken as a whole, unless the member can demonstrate that due to unusual circumstances the financial statements would otherwise have been misleading.
> In such cases his report must describe the departure, the approximate effects thereof, if practicable, and the reasons why compliance with the principle would result in a misleading statement.[26]

In 1973, the Council of the AICPA designated the Financial Accounting Standards Board as the body to establish accounting principles pursuant to Rule 203. The Financial Accounting Standards Board possesses adequate authority to issue pronouncements binding on the accounting profession.

The first step should be for the Financial Accounting Standards Board to issue a discussion memorandum on accounting standards for private foundations, to be followed by an exposure draft. The exposure draft is in the nature of applied research. It would expose the recommendations of the Financial Accounting Standards Board to public view. All interested parties would be able to present their views in writing or orally in public hearings. Private foundations, government officials, grantees, and public accountants would all have an opportunity to express their views on the exposure draft.

The Financial Accounting Standards Board presently utilizes the exposure draft concept on establishing accounting standards and the Accounting Principles Board of the American Institute of Certified Public Accountants also utilized exposure drafts before issuing finalized Accounting Principles Board Opinions. Issuing an exposure draft would not present the Financial Accounting Standards Board with any unique problem that it has not handled previously.

After consideration of the response to the exposure draft, the
Financial Accounting Standards Board would then issue a statement
on accounting standards and reporting requirements for private
foundations. This statement would be binding on all certified public
accountants in the United States who are members of the AICPA.
The practical effect of issuance of accounting standards for private
foundations would be that in order for a private foundation to have
its financial statements attested to by an independent public accountant, the private foundation would have to abide by the accounting
standards set by the Financial Accounting Standards Board.

A private foundation not having its financial statements attested
to by an independent public accountant would not be bound by the
pronouncements of the Financial Accounting Standards Board nor of
the AICPA. My empirical study reveals that not all private foundations have their financial statements audited. Legally, there is no
requirement that private foundations must submit to independent audit
of its financial statements.

The only type of authority that the Financial Accounting Standards
Board can assert over the nonaudited private foundations would be a
moral or intellectual authority. The Financial Accounting Standards
Board would be saying to these foundations that the accounting standards recommended are the result of the work of various experts on
foundation accounting and reporting requirements, and represent in
their opinion the best procedures and practices to improve private
foundation accounting and reporting practices.

In my opinion, moral persuasion will not be enough. Accounting
acceptability rests on its usefulness. Accountants and others disagree on the goals and objectives of accounting. Different people
honestly disagree as to what is useful and what is not. The recommended accounting standards will be ignored by those foundations
who consider them disadvantageous or simply not useful.

I conclude that while an authoritative pronouncement by the
Financial Accounting Standards Board will constitute a giant step
toward improving the financial reporting practices of private foundations, that step alone will not be sufficient to insure that all foundations
abide by its pronouncements. It appears that some form of government intervention is necessary to fully ensure private foundation
compliance. The form and extent of government action necessary
to institute accounting standards for private foundations will be discussed in the next chapter.

NOTES

1. American Institute of Certified Public Accountants, Accounting
Principles Board, "Basic Concepts and Accountant Principles Under-

lying Financial Statements of Business Enterprises," Statement
No. 4 (New York, 1970), pp. 36-38.

    2. Report of the Study Group on the Objectives of Financial
Statements, Objectives of Financial Statements (New York: AICPA,
1973), p. 67.

    3. Eleanor K. Taylor, Public Accountability of Foundations
and Charitable Trusts (New York: Russell Sage Foundation, 1953),
p. 114.

    4. U.S. Congress, House, Select Committee on Small Business,
Tax-Exempt Foundations and Charitable Trusts: Their Impact on
Our Economy, 87th Cong., 2nd Sess., 1962, p. 5.

    5. Commission on Foundations and Private Philanthropy,
Foundations, Private Giving, and Public Policy (Chicago, Ill.:
University of Chicago Press, 1970), p. 154.

    6. Ibid.

    7. American Institute of Certified Public Accountants, Committee
on Accounting Procedure, "Restatement and Revision of Accounting
Research Bulletins," Accounting Research Bulletin No. 43 (New York,
1953), p. 5.

    8. Ibid., p. 8.

    9. Weldon Powell, "The Development of Accounting Principles,"
The Journal of Accountancy, September 1964, p. 38.

    10. American Institute of Certified Public Accountants, Account-
ing Principles Board, "Disclosure of Accounting Policies," Opinion
No. 22 (New York, 1972), p. 435.

    11. Financial Accounting Standards Board, "Accounting for
Certain Marketable Securities," Statement of Financial Accounting
Standards No. 12 (Stanford, Conn., 1975), p. 3.

    12. Standards of Accounting and Financial Reporting for Voluntary
Health and Welfare Organizations (Exposure Draft) (New York:
National Health Council, 1974).

    13. Walter J. Reich, Chairman, Committee on Private Founda-
tions of the American Institute of Certified Public Accountants,
Letter to Private Foundation Financial Executives, December 15,
1972.

    14. Interview with Richard C. Lytle, Technical Coordinator of
the AICPA, April 21, 1976, and interview with Thomas Kelley,
Director of the Accounting Standards Division of the AICPA, April 21,
1976.

    15. Malvern Gross, Jr., Financial and Accounting Guide for
Nonprofit Organizations, 2nd ed. (New York: Ronald Press, 1974),
p. 275.

    16. Ibid.

    17. Ibid.

18. Accounting Advisory Committee. Report to the Commission on Private Philanthropy and Public Needs (1974), p. 4.

19. Committee on Accounting Concepts and Standards, American Accounting Association, Accounting and Reporting Standards for Corporate Financial Statements (Iowa City, Iowa: American Accounting Association, 1957), p. 1.

20. American Accounting Association, A Statement of Basic Accounting Theory (Evanston, Ill.: American Accounting Association, 1966), p. 2.

21. "Report of the Committee on Accounting Practices of Not-for-Profit Organizations," The Accounting Review, Supp. to Vol. 46 (1971), p. 83.

22. Ibid., p. 82.

23. "Report of the Committee on Non-Financial Measures of Effectiveness," The Accounting Review, Supp. to Vol. 46 (1971), p. 166.

24. "Report of the Committee on Concepts of Accounting Applicable to the Public Sector, 1970-1971," The Accounting Review, Supp. to Vol. 47 (1972), p. 78.

25. Gross, Financial and Accounting Guide . . . , 2nd ed., op. cit., p. 275.

26. American Institute of Certified Public Accountants, Code of Professional Ethics, Rule 203, March 1, 1973.

10

THE INTERNAL REVENUE SERVICE AND CONGRESS

CONGRESSIONAL OR IRS INVOLVEMENT IN THE
DEVELOPMENT OF ACCOUNTING STANDARDS
AND REPORTING PRACTICES OF
PRIVATE FOUNDATIONS

Following the stock market crash of 1929, Congress passed the Securities Acts of 1933 and 1934 and created the Securities and Exchange Commission (SEC) to monitor the securities market. Congress considered using its own accountants to audit the corporations to be subject to the law. However, since public accountants already had the necessary experience and personnel to do the work efficiently and economically, Congress decided to allow the private sector to do the audits.[1]

The Securities Acts of 1933 and 1934 gave the SEC authority to prescribe uniform accounting standards. The Securities Acts provided for certification of financial statements by independent public accountants. The SEC decided to allow the private sector to set the accounting standards and they would enforce them. The AICPA assumed primary responsibility for the development of accounting standards.

I believe it is in the public interest to allow the private sector to set the accounting standards for private foundations. Faced with a far more serious situation, the SEC chose not to exercise its authority to prescribe uniform accounting standards for companies subject to its jurisdiction. The public interest was involved then, too. What has resulted is a system of accounting standards being set in the private sector, and the involvement of the government in its enforcement. This system has worked reasonably well in the United States.

I see no reason for introducing a new procedure in the area of accounting standards for private foundations. Government involvement in the development of accounting standards for private foundations would be necessary if no feasible alternatives existed. However, the private sector does have the experience and the expertise, based on long experience, in setting accounting standards. This was the specific function of the Accounting Principles Board of the AICPA before its demise and is the specific function of the Financial Accounting Standards Board, a private, nongovernmental agency.

Governmental control of accounting under the Interstate Commerce Commission, bank regulatory agencies, and in the utilities field has not resulted in financial statements that are superior to those of unregulated companies. In fact, they are inferior.

> They (railroads) are discovering that ICC accounting
> is more like Achilles' heel than Athene's aegis in that
> it has developed a past pattern of reported net income
> amounts which can no longer be sustained.[2]

Railroads are required by ICC regulations to use a system of accounting called "betterment accounting." Under this system, the initial cost of laying track, including rails, ties, other track materials and grading, is capitalized. However, no depreciation is taken and the asset is carried on the balance sheet at original cost so long as the track is in use at that location. All subsequent expenditures to replace track structure are charged to expense when made, even though replacement cost is frequently greater than the original cost.[3] This system is in direct conflict with accounting for industrial enterprises where depreciation accounting is the norm and has been so for many decades.

The effect of direct government intervention in the setting of accounting standards for private foundations may be to stratify accounting standards in their present form.[4] The private sector possesses the flexibility to constantly be updating and adopting new ideas, new concepts, and new theory as it develops. The government does not possess this flexibility. The trend in recent years is to get away from the concept of big government doing everything. The movement is to shift the controls away from Washington. There is a realization that government cannot and should not be doing everything. Things that can be done in the private sector should be done in the private sector and I see no reason why the private sector should not assume primary responsibility and authority for improving accounting practices of private foundations.

The government, to a certain extent, is already involved in the area of private foundation financial reporting. Under prior law, a portion of the private foundation's tax return (990-A) was considered a public document and hence available to anyone who wished to examine it at the Internal Revenue Service. Congress, in the Tax Reform Act of 1969, added a requirement that an information return (990-AR) be available for public inspection at the foundation's office. In lieu of the 990-AR, a private foundation that prepares an annual report containing all the information specified on the 990-AR will satisfy the law. Congress recognized that the general public is entitled to information on foundation financial activities. Congress said that the experience of the last two decades indicated that the public is entitled to more current information on a current basis and that this information should be made more readily available.[5]

The Form 990-AR is not a substitute for an annual report. It does not set accounting standards for its preparation. It does not give a detailed analysis of the financial activities of the private foundation and it does not require the disclosure that I have recommended to reveal the private foundation completely and fully to public view.

The government has taken a step, and in my opinion, a wrong step to improve the information received about the financial activities of the private foundations. In the next section, I will discuss the role that government should play in improving the accounting standards and reporting practices of private foundations.

CONGRESSIONAL OR IRS INVOLVEMENT IN THE ENFORCEMENT OF ACCOUNTING STANDARDS AND REPORTING PRACTICES OF PRIVATE FOUNDATIONS

Previously, I have discussed the role the accounting profession should assume in the development of accounting standards and reporting practices of private foundations. I will discuss in this section the role that the government should assume for the same objective.

The accounting profession possesses the experience, know-how, and expertise to develop accounting standards and reporting practices for private foundations but it lacks the authority to fully implement its recommendations. The accounting profession, through the Financial Accounting Standards Board, can impose its authoritative pronouncements on every private foundation that desires to have its financial statements audited by the independent public accountant. However, private foundations are not required by law to have their financial statements audited by independent public accountants, such as is the case with the SEC and the corporations coming under its provisions. If a private foundation disagrees with the accounting standards and reporting practices recommended by the accounting profession, it can avoid being subject to them by not having its financial statements audited by independent public accountants.

Since it is in the public interest to have standards of accounting and reporting practices adhered to by all private foundations, then government action is necessary. A law is needed to require that every private foundation, in order to maintain its tax-exempt status, must have its financial statements audited annually by independent public accountants. A law of this type would not be unique. The Securities Acts of 1933 and 1934 require it of corporations subject to the law. Many governmental programs and activities are presently requiring independent audits. The new pension reform act requires that every welfare benefit plan and every qualified and unqualified retirement plan of employers engaged in interstate commerce with certain exceptions must have the opinion of independent public accountants that the financial statements are fairly presented.

The government, in passing this type of law, would not become involved with the development of accounting standards and reporting practices of private foundations. The government would become involved with the enforcement of the standards. Requiring every private foundation to be audited by independent public accountants would cause an additional cost to be incurred by private foundations not presently being audited by independent public accountants. However, private foundations voluntarily file for tax-exempt status, and they must assume the responsibilities that tax exemption gives them. One of these responsibilities is to tell fully, and completely, their story in financial terms.

An audit by independent public accountants is not a duplication of an audit by the IRS. The objective of an IRS audit is to verify whether the foundation is complying with all applicable tax law and regulation. The purpose of an audit by independent public accountants is to add credibility to the financial statements presented. Each type of audit is necessary, and rather than duplicate each other, they complement each other. The IRS has made significant advances in providing public access to foundation information, but as the tax enforcement authority it must give primary emphasis to insuring compliance with the tax laws, and hence the provision of public information remains a minor concern.

REPEAL OF THE EXCISE TAX ON INVESTMENT INCOME

The Tax Reform Act of 1969 imposes a 4 percent excise tax on the net investment income of private foundations.[6]

The House Committee on Ways and Means said:

Your committee believes that since the benefits of
government are available to all, the costs should be
borne, at least to some extent, by all those able to
pay. Your committee believes that this is as true for
private foundations as it is for taxpayers generally.
Also, it is clear that vigorous and extensive administration is needed in order to provide appropriate assurances
that private foundations will promptly and properly use
their funds for charitable purposes. This tax, then,
may be viewed as being in part a user fee.[7]

This tax, in effect, removes part of the tax exemption of private
foundations. The Commission on Foundations, Private Giving, and
Public Policy argued against the tax, giving as its reasons: while
the initial rate is low, it creates a bad precedent and could easily
be raised; it is counterproductive to encourage charitable giving and
then impose a tax which reduces the amount available for foundation
grants; and the tax flows into general government funds and is not
earmarked for improved regulation of foundations.[8] The Commission
on Private Philanthropy and Public Needs recommended that the
excise tax be repealed and replaced by a fee on all private foundations
based on the actual costs of auditing them.[9] The Commission noted
that for the years 1971-73, the tax raised $157 million, while the
costs of auditing private foundations for these three years amounted
to $55 million.[10]

I believe that the excise tax on private foundations should be
repealed, and furthermore, private foundations should not be charged
with the cost of auditing them. This tax applies only to private
foundations and to no other charitable organization. There is an
implication that foundations are second-class charities. The tax is
a penalty for some of the questionable activities carried on by some
private foundations. I agree with the provisions of the Tax Reform
Act of 1969 curbing self-dealing, involvement in business, and
unreasonable accumulation of income. It was necessary to end
these abuses. The business of private foundations is to engage in
charity and not become part of some tax-planning scheme to avoid
the payment of income taxes.

However, the activities carried on by the private foundations
and their donors and substantial contributors were, to a great extent,
sanctioned by the courts. The law either was unclear or failed to
prohibit undesirable activities. Why should the private foundations
be penalized for the failure of Congress, in the past, to pass appropriate laws? Private foundations were doing what the law permitted

them to do and now to penalize them is manifestly unfair. When the IRS discovers an area of tax abuse in some segment of our economy, it doesn't assess the segment with additional taxes because of the additional audit work involved in monitoring that segment. The abuses of private foundations are not of recent origin. Congress was aware of tax abuses engaged in by private foundations when it passed the Revenue Act of 1950 but failed to take appropriate action. Congress bears a major share of the blame for the abuses and to assess a penalty tax on private foundations for Congressional inaction is unwarranted.

FOUNDATION INVOLVEMENT IN BUSINESS

The use of private foundations to maintain control over businesses was a tax abuse. The basic abuse was one of unfair competition. Dividends paid by a business to its stockholders are taxable to them, while dividends paid by a business to a private foundation are tax-free to the foundation. If a commercial corporation wanted to acquire a new subsidiary, it would have to use after-tax dollars. For example, if the acquisition price is one million dollars, then the corporation must earn two million dollars, since one million is paid in taxes. This is not the case if a private foundation is involved because the contribution to the private foundation is tax deductible. The corporation, by utilizing a private foundation, can contribute funds to the private foundation and receive a tax deduction and the private foundation can then acquire the subsidiary.

The Treasury Department Report on Private Foundations revealed that a large number of foundation-owned enterprises proceeded from year to year earning substantial profits, but making little or no distributions to the parent foundation.[11] The ability to defer indefinitely the realization of profits from commercial enterprises, an ability frequently not shared by ordinary shareholders in a business, makes it possible for the foundation-owned business to modernize and expand more rapidly than in the case of a non-foundation-owned business. Private foundations were able to circumvent the laws on unreasonable accumulations by allowing the funds to accumulate in the business entity under its control.

In Chapter 2, I described many abuses involving "lease-backs" and "bootstrap sales" to charities in which foundation ownership of the business was part of the device to avoid payment of tax by the seller of a business. The private foundation may run a business in such a way to unfairly compete with other businesses whose owners must pay taxes on the profits earned from the business.

It is a matter of public policy to create an environment where businesses compete on a fair and equal basis. Public policy is violated when private foundations control a business. Congress, in the Tax Reform Act of 1969, limits private foundations to owning 20 percent or less of the voting stock in a business, [12] the objective being to curb unfair competition. [13] The question is: Does a limitation of 20 percent ownership of stock in a business achieve its objectives?

Public policy dictates that private foundations should not be involved in running commercial enterprises. The business of private foundations is charity and not business. Passive investments in business are permissible as a source of foundation income. It has always been proper, and rightfully so, for foundations to earn interest, dividends, rents, and royalties. These are passive sources of income. However, in my opinion, allowing foundations to own 20 percent of the stock in a business violates the concept of noninvolvement in business.

There is no fine line separating the percentage of stock ownership required to become involved in management of a corporation as distinguished from a passive investment. Experts in corporation finance say that in some situations, 15 percent or 10 percent or even less stock ownership may be sufficient to exercise control or to substantially influence management. [14] John Kenneth Galbraith wrote in the New Industrial State about the shift of power from owners to managers within the modern large corporation. The point Galbraith makes is that it doesn't require much stock ownership to effectively control the corporation.

> A small proportion of the stock is represented at stockholders' meetings for a ceremony in which banality is varied chiefly by irrelevance. The rest is voted by proxy for the directors who have been selected by the management. The latter, though their ownership is normally negligible, are solidly in control of the corporation. [15]

Under the equity method of ownership for investments in common stock, an investor recognizes its share of the profits of an investee in the period earned by the investee rather than in the period in which the investee declares a dividend. The Accounting Principles Board, in a pronouncement extended the usage of the equity method to investments in common stock of all unconsolidated subsidiaries. [16] The Board concluded that the equity method should be followed even though the investor holds 50 percent or less of the voting stock, if such investment gives the investor ability to exercise significant influence over operating and financial policies on investee.

Ability to exercise that influence may be indicated in
several ways, such as representation on the board of
directors, participation in policy making processes,
material intercompany transactions, interchange of
managerial personnel, or technological dependency. . . .
The Board recognizes that determining the ability of an
investor to exercise such influence is not always clear
and applying judgment is necessary to assess the status
of each investment. In order to achieve a reasonable
degree of uniformity in application, the Board concludes
that an investment (direct or indirect) of 20% or
more of the voting stock of an investee should lead to a
presumption that in the absence of evidence to the con-
trary an investor has the ability to exercise significant
influence over an investee.[17]

Thus, the Accounting Principles Board concluded that a 20
percent stock ownership was significant enough to influence operating
and financial policies so that the investment no longer could be termed
a passive one. Mutual funds whose objective is investment without
influencing management generally set a limit of approximately 5 percent or less as the maximum stock ownership they will acquire in
any one corporation.[18]

Congress, in the Tax Reform Act of 1969, curbed foundation
involvement in business by limiting their ownership of stock in a
business to 20 percent or less. The objective being to limit foundations to making passive investments rather than influencing or
controlling businesses. To achieve this objective, the 20 percent
limitation should be reduced to less than 5 percent. I realize that
any level set is arbitrary but since mutual funds limit themselves
to approximately 5 percent stock ownership, then using the same
percentage will ensure that foundation investments are passive.

DONOR-CONTROLLED FOUNDATIONS

Under present law, it is possible for an individual to establish
a private foundation, dominate its affairs throughout his life, and
pass its management to members of his family upon his death. The
tax statutes impose no restrictions as to who may serve on the board
of directors or as to the number of board members required in a
foundation. Quite often, especially in smaller foundations, the
donor or creator of the foundation and/or members of his family
constitute the majority or the entire board of directors.

The problem is whether a donor-controlled foundation will be more likely to reflect a particular narrow perspective and be inaccessible to a wide range of opinions and ideas. Supervision of the activities of a foundation may remain within the influence and power of a narrow and homogeneous group indefinitely. Furthermore, there is no assurance that persons more representative of the public will ever gain access into the foundation's governing body.[19]

Both the Commission on Foundations and Private Philanthropy and the Commission on Private Philanthropy and Public Needs reported that no evidence exists that donor-controlled foundations are not doing as an effective job as uncontrolled foundations.[20] Both believe that it would be desirable to encourage private foundations to broaden their boards of directors to get a diversity of views and to allay some of the public suspicion of privatism on the part of private foundations. Neither commission believes that this is an appropriate matter for legislation but that private foundations should be encouraged to diversify their boards. The Commission on Private Philanthropy and Public Needs recommended that a new category of independent foundations be established by law. These independent foundations would enjoy the same tax benefits as public charities in return for a diminished role on the foundation's board by the foundation's creator and/or substantial contributor or members of his or her family.[21]

I believe that legislation would be inappropriate to broaden the boards of private foundations to achieve diversity. What criteria will the government use to determine how much representation should be on the board for racial minorities, religious minorities, and ethnic minorities? What proportion of the board should labor, management, businessmen, lawyers, bankers, and public officials represent? I do not see the importance of diversity in a particular foundation since private foundations, like most other American institutions, represent the broad spectrum of America. Thus, we have private foundations on the political "left" and others on the political "right." Some are liberally oriented, while others are conservatively oriented. Any religious, racial, or ethnic group is free to create their own charitable organizations, including private foundations, to further the religious, scientific, charitable, or educational goals of that group.

I believe that legislation is necessary to broaden boards, not for diversity of representation and views, but for a very different reason. As a general rule in taxation, no deduction is permitted for a contribution until the donor separates himself from the ownership of the assets donated. Thus, if a donor pledged money to charity, no deduction would be allowed until the charity actually received the money. However, if the donor contributes the money to a private foundation, even one in which he exercises full control, he still is entitled to receive a deduction for the money contributed. We then have a situation where the donor has separated himself from legal ownership of the assets donated but still maintains economic control over the assets. Donald C. Young, in an article on donor-foundation dealings, said:

> Many of the difficulties in the charitable area appear to derive from the willingness of the tax law to permit control by a donor or person under his influence. It may be that this permitted control is the necessary price of maintaining the flow of private charity, but one can only conjecture so long as the proposition is not put to a test by the enactment of more stringent legislation. In the meantime, preservation of the public interest will depend, in the last analysis, upon the dictates of conscience of philanthropists.[22]

A solution to this problem must balance public policy considerations involved in charitable deductions against decreasing the flow of funds to charity. Tight limitations on donor control of a private foundation may result in fewer foundations being created and less money available for charitable activity.

The Treasury Department recommended to Congress that after the first 25 years of the existence of a private foundation, the donor and related parties should not be permitted to compose more than 25 percent of the managing board of the foundation.[23] Congress did not enact this recommendation into law in the Tax Reform Act of 1969.

A possible solution to this problem, and one that I believe is more feasible than setting a time limit on the donor divesting himself of control over the foundation, would be not to allow a charitable deduction for a donation to a private foundation in a situation where the donor or his family control the private foundation. The deduction for contributions is a matter of legislative grace and public policy implications mandate that the donor should be separated from his gift before he receives a tax deduction. The deduction would be allowed at the point where the donor and/or his family relinquish majority control over the private foundation.

Whether limiting the charitable deduction in this manner will discourage the setting up of new private foundations is a complex question and one to which I do not have the answer. However, the objectives of the tax law are not to encourage charitable contributions at any cost. The whole area of charitable deductions for income and estate tax purposes is full of restrictions and limitations. Even at the risk of reducing the creation of new foundations or contributions

to presently existing foundations, public policy considerations dictate
that those receiving a charitable deduction should legally and economically separate themselves from the assets being donated to charity.
It is unrealistic and unnecessary to require that the creator totally
divorce himself from the foundation he is creating in order to receive
a charitable deduction for contributions to the foundation. The law
should require that the creator relinquish majority control to independ
ent board members.

IMPOSING A SIZE REQUIREMENT ON
PRIVATE FOUNDATIONS

Private foundations play an important part in the work of private
philanthropy in the United States. Private foundations can provide
for areas into which government cannot or should not advance. They
are well qualified to inaugurate new and untried programs and they
are free to act flexibly and quickly to new ideas and concepts. They
can experiment with new methods and technology in science, art,
social science, and the humanities. Private foundations exist to add
something to private philanthropy. From my experience with private
foundations, it is my conclusion that small foundations do not add
much of a contribution, besides money, to private philanthropy.

Small foundations mostly make grants to other charitable organizations, unlike the large foundations that make grants for specific
purposes such as a grant for research in a certain type of heart
disease. Hence, many small foundations act as conduits. They
receive funds from the creator and pay them out to other charitable
organizations and not really adding anything of value in their role of
intermediary.

Table 10.1 reveals that 82 percent, or 18,349 of small foundation
have assets of less than $200,000. The average size of a grant for
this subset is under $1,000. Fifty-seven percent of small foundations
have assets of less than $50,000. The relationship of total grants
($143,947) to assets ($176,138) indicates that many of these foundations act as conduits, paying out and replenishing capital regularly,
leaving small balances in endowment.

Small foundations generally have no staff, no employees, or
anyone knowledgeable in charitable, scientific, and educational work.
Large foundations such as the Ford Foundation or the Rockefeller
Foundation have a staff of people who are active in evaluating and
recommending grants. They perform a valuable service in their
fields of endeavor whether it be science or the humanities. These
foundations, by their expertise, make a valuable contribution to
private philanthropy.

TABLE 10.1

Small Foundations

Asset Range	Foundations		Total Assets		Total Grants		Grants	
	Number	Percent	Dollars	Percent	Dollars	Percent	Number	Percent
$200,000 to $1 million	4,072	18	1,818,186	70	183,256	44	108,067	29
$50,000 to $200,000	5,668	25	605,086	23	92,516	22	106,843	29
Under $50,000	12,681	57	176,138	7	143,947	34	152,630	42
Totals	22,421	100	2,599,410	100	419,719	100	367,540	100

Source: Foundation Directory, 3rd. ed. (New York: Russell Sage Foundation for the Foundation Library Center, 1967), p. 13.

Small foundations do not have the resources to engage in the same type of activities as larger foundations. Thus the smaller foundations contribute their funds to other charitable organizations such as Red Cross, United Funds, and so on. I believe that it is in the public interest to require private foundations to be of a certain size before they can receive tax exemption. This would not be an unusual requirement. Colleges, before they can open, must meet certain requirements on such items as physical plant, faculty, library facilities, and recreational facilities. Similarly, a hospital must meet and pass many requirements before it can open its doors.

It is a relatively easy task to obtain a tax exemption for private foundations. The major test is whether the foundation charter provides that its assets will be used exclusively for charitable, religious, scientific, and educational purposes, and that no part of its net income will inure to the benefit of any private individual. Size is no criteria for obtaining exemption and it is as easy for a small foundation to obtain tax exemption as it would be for a large foundation.

A donor receives a contribution deduction when he donates assets to the private foundation and not when the private foundation pays it out. Therefore, if the private foundation merely acts as a conduit, private philanthropy is harmed by the extra layer between it and the donor. If it were more difficult for smaller private foundations to obtain tax exemption, then potential creators would probably contribute their donations directly to the ultimate beneficiary—charity.

I do not have any easy answers for setting criteria for the establishment of private foundations. A possible solution would be for private foundations to create an accreditation committee, similar to accreditation agencies for colleges. The task of this accreditation committee would be to set forth the minimum attributes that a private foundation should possess in order to function effectively. More research is needed in the area of small foundations. More information is needed on their finances and their activities so that intelligent decisions can be made about their future.

PERPETUAL LIFE OF PRIVATE FOUNDATIONS

Various proposals have been made that a time limit be imposed on the life of private foundations.[24] These proposals stem from the tax abuses engaged in by some private foundations. Chapter 2 of this study describes the various tax abuses engaged in by private foundations and Congressional attempts to curb these abuses. Placing a time limit on the life of private foundations is viewed by some critics as a solution to the variety, extent, and scope of the tax abuses engaged in by some private foundations.

I do not see any rationale to curbing the life of private foundations in order to curb their tax abuses. It is a case of the cure killing the patient. This radical proposal would only be valid if private foundations, as an institution, posed some danger to America. Only if one views private foundations as evil or undesirable does the proposal, then, make sense. The tax abuses engaged in by private foundations such as self-dealing, delay in benefit to charity, involvement in business, and control of corporate and other property have been dealt with in the Tax Reform Act of 1969.

I have seen no evidence to warrant the conclusion that private foundations should be destroyed. Congress must bear a part of the responsibility for the "excesses" of private foundations. It would be unfair to penalize so heavily the private foundations for activities condoned and permitted by law. Private foundations have, in the past, and will continue in the future, to play a vital role in the private philanthropy sector of our society. Nothing that they have done in the past warrants treating them as second-class charities.

FOUNDATION GRANT MAKING IN SENSITIVE AREAS

Tax law provides broad guidelines for permissible foundation activity. Foundations derive their tax-exempt status under the statute, which provides tax exemption for:

Corporations and any community chest, fund, or foundation, organized and operated exclusively for religious, charitable, scientific, testing for public safety, literary

or educational purposes, or for the prevention of cruelty
to children or animals, no part of the net earnings of which
inures to the benefit of any private shareholder or individual, no substantial part of the activities of which is
carrying on propaganda, or attempting, to influence
legislation, and which does not participate in, or intervene in (including the publishing or distribution of statements), any political campaign on behalf of any candidate
for public office.[25]

The Commission on Private Philanthropy and Public Needs noted:

Considerable uncertainty surrounds just what constitutes
a "substantial part" of an organization's activities or
"attempting to influence legislation". After forty years
of the tax-law provision, this uncertainty remains
unclarified by either the courts or the Internal Revenue
Service.[26]

Was the Ford Foundation's role in voter registration drives in
the Brownsville-Ocean Hill section of New York a permissible activity
or was it, as some critics charged, an attempt to increase voters in
certain districts to insure the election of certain candidates?
Private foundations have a wide latitude in deciding the recipient of
the grant and for what purpose the money will be used. As long as the
grants fall within the purview of being religious, scientific, educational
or charitable, the activity is permissible. For example, the Bollinger
Foundation subsidized research into such matters as the phenomenology
of the Iranian religious consciousness and the origin and significance
of the decorative types of medieval tombstones in Bosnia and Herzego-
vina.[27] I am not suggesting that government should determine which
areas should be given priority by the foundations or which areas are
worthy and which areas are unworthy of investigation. As long as
private foundations confine themselves to permissible religious,
scientific, and charitable activities, it would be inappropriate for
the government to intervene. Government intervention would ultimately
lead to government control and would result in a tremendous weakening,
if not destruction, of the role that private foundations play in private
philanthropy in the United States. However, the government does
have the right to intervene if foundation funds are being spent for
activities that are beyond the range of being religious, scientific,
charitable, or educational in scope.
Neat, categorical, and easily administered guidelines do not
exist to guide foundations in making grants in twilight zones. For
example, if a foundation wanted to make a grant to a researcher

interested in testing Shockley's hypothesis that blacks are biologically intelectually inferior to whites, what, if anything should the government do? Many people would consider this activity outside the scope of legitimate scientific inquiry. Furthermore, since Negroes are taxpayers, they may object to a research project, indirectly subsidized with their tax dollars, that is repugnant to them as well as other Americans. Is the IRS the agency to evaluate and determine whether an activity of this type is within the purview of being scientific or educational?

The IRS is charged with administering the tax law. The Internal Revenue agents possess expertise in tax law and accounting but they do not possess any special knowledge that would permit them to evaluate and judge foundation endeavors in sensitive areas. Furthermore, it would be unfair to a private foundation that, in good faith has made such a grant and then later discovers upon an audit by the IRS that it has violated the law and now suffers the adverse consequences.

The solution is to set up some type of procedure whereby a private foundation can request a ruling beforehand on the proposed grant in a sensitive area and then receive a ruling as to the permissibility of the proposed grant. A request for a private ruling is a technique used by taxpayers who wish to know the tax consequences of a certain course of action before it is undertaken. Quite often, in a proposed reorganization or merger, a ruling, in which all the facts are stated, is requested from the IRS so that the tax consequences will be known beforehand rather than after the reorganization or merger is consummated. Private foundations should be permitted to avail themselves of a similar administrative technique. However, the IRS personnel do not possess the necessary expertise to judge the propriety of such proposed grants.

A committee should be formed to advise the IRS on grants in sensitive areas. The committee would be made up of experts from the various disciplines. A good place to obtain members would be from the academic world. Thus, a proposed grant involving a sensitive area would be submitted to the committee who would be free to request additional pertinent information from the foundation or the prospective grantee on the proposed grant. A committee of this type would be in a much better position to evaluate and judge a proposed grant since its members would be knowledgeable in the area under inquiry.

Submitting a proposed grant to this committee would be on a voluntary basis. The private foundation would have a choice either to submit the proposed grant prior to acceptance or not to do so. If the foundation chooses to request the advance ruling, it will know the government's position on a particular grant before it funds it, rather than after it funds the grant.

FOUNDATION PAYOUT PROVISIONS

Private foundations were engaged in two related abuses. First, private foundations were unreasonably accumulating their net income, and second, foundations were investing in or receiving as a contribution unproductive assets. Current law deals with these two abuses by requiring a foundation to distribute its entire net income (excluding long-term capital gains) on a current basis or a percentage of the fair market value of its investment assets—whichever is higher. The Tax Reform Act of 1969 set the minimum investment return at 6 percent for 1970 and requires the Secretary of the Treasury to adjust the 6 percent for future years as money rates and investment yields vary, in order to maintain a payout requirement with the same effect for other years as the 6 percent had for 1969.28

I agree in principle with the payout requirements of the Tax Reform Act of 1969, but I believe that the enacted provision has deficiencies. Taxes should be neutral in their effect on economic activity unless by design it is desired to favor one segment of the economy over another. Congress has created a tax law that is not neutral in its effect on private foundation investments. Current law requires the private foundation to distribute its entire net income; however, capital gains are excluded from the distribution requirement. A private foundation earning capital gain income can better shield it from the payout requirements than would be the case if the foundation were to earn ordinary income. For example, a foundation with investment assets of $1 million would be required to distribute at least $60,000 currently. If the investment earned $90,000 in ordinary income (dividends, interest, rents, royalties), then the foundation would be required to distribute the $90,000 currently. However, if the foundation earned $40,000 in ordinary income and $50,000 in capital gains, then the foundation would be required to distribute $60,000 (minimum payout requirement). In the latter situation, the foundation would be able to retain $30,000 more than in the former case.

It appears that current law is introducing a new factor into foundation investment decisions which may be at variance with the overall objectives of the payout provisions. Current law is making investments with capital gain appreciation more desirable than those with a current income yield. Changing the law to include long-term capital gains as income for payout purposes would not be desirable because it would cause private foundations to be locked into their investments. Private foundations would become reluctant to sell investments which may have appreciated in value because selling them would require a distribution of the appreciation in value.

The law should be amended to repeal the requirement that private foundations distribute their net income on a current basis. A flat payout rate based on the fair market value of investment assets should be the sole payout requirement. The Secretary of the Treasury should be given authority to set the payout rate annually based on the following criteria: total rate of return of private foundations, mutual funds, pension funds, profit-sharing funds, and other similar endowment funds, and rate of inflation. Thus, the law should be changed to deal with the economic reality of total rate of return on investment. Investment performance should be measured by total rate of return on investment—the measure used to evaluate mutual funds, pension funds, profit-sharing funds, and other similar funds. Total rate of return includes current ordinary income plus realized and unrealized capital gains. It is a much better yardstick to use in measuring private foundation investment performance. It does not discriminate between different types of investments and would be neutral in its effect on the selection of foundation investment portfolios.

The other factor that must be considered in selecting the flat payout rate is the rate of inflation. Failure to consider the rate of inflation in setting a payout requirement can mean a slow death sentence for a private foundation if the payout rate is set at a level that impairs the foundation's ability to maintain its principal intact in terms of real dollars. An ideal payout rate would be one that permits a foundation with average investment performance to maintain its principal, in terms of real dollars, intact. Foundations whose investment performance is better than average would grow in size and foundations whose investment performance is below average would see a decline in assets in real dollars.

NOTES

1. John L. Cary, "The Origins of Modern Financial Reporting," The Journal of Accountancy, September 1969, pp. 43-44.

2. Philip I. Coleman, "Is Railroad Accounting Off the Track?" The Journal of Accountancy, October 1970), p. 65.

3. Ibid., p. 67.

4. It should be noted that while this may be true in certain sectors of the economy, the SEC and the Cost Accounting Standards Board have been quite active in setting new accounting standards and reporting requirements and both these agencies have demonstrated competence and flexibility in their efforts to improve accounting standards and reporting practices.

5. U.S. Congress, Senate, Tax Reform Act of 1969, 91st Cong., 1st Sess., 1969, Report 91-552 (New York: Commerce Clearing House, 1969), No. 51, p. 52.

6. Sec. 4940, Tax Reform Act of 1969.

7. U.S. Congress, House, Tax Reform Act of 1969, 91st Cong., 1st Sess., 1969, Report 91-413, Part 1 (New York: Commerce Clearing House, 1969), no. 35, p. 19.

8. Commission on Foundations and Private Philanthropy, Foundations, Private Giving and Public Policy (Chicago: University of Chicago Press, 1970), p. 167.

9. Report of the Commission on Private Philanthropy and Public Needs, Giving in America (Washington, D.C.: Commission on Private Philanthropy and Public Needs, 1975), p. 166.

10. Ibid., p. 167.

11. U.S. Congress, House, Committee on Ways and Means, Treasury Department Report on Private Foundations, 89th Cong., 1st Sess., 1965, p. 33.

12. Section 4943, Tax Reform Act of 1969.

13. H.R., 1969, op. cit., p. 27.

14. Interview with Dr. Stephen Feldman, Chairman of the Finance Department, Hofstra University, January 26, 1976.

15. John Kenneth Galbraith, The New Industrial State (New York: Signet Books, 1968), p. 61.

16. American Institute of Certified Public Accountants, Accounting Principles Board, "The Equity Method of Accounting for Investments in Common Stock," Opinion No. 18 (New York, 1971).

17. Ibid., p. 355.

18. Feldman, op. cit.

19. Treasury Department Report on Private Foundations, op. cit., p. 56.

20. Commission on Foundations and Private Philanthropy, op. cit., p. 138, and Commission on Private Philanthropy and Public Needs, op. cit., p. 172.

21. Commission on Private Philanthropy and Public Needs, op. cit., pp. 172-73.

22. Donald C. Young, "Donor Foundation Dealings," New York University Twenty-Second Annual Institute on Federal Taxation (New York: Matthew Bender & Co., 1964), p. 1006.

23. Treasury Department Report on Private Foundations, op. cit., p. 57.

24. Ibid., p. 13.

25. Sec. 501(c) (3), I.R.C. 1954, as amended.

26. Commission on Private Philanthropy and Public Needs, op. cit., p. 180.

27. U.S. Congress, House, Select Committee on Small Business, Tax-Exempt Foundations and Charitable Trusts: Their Impact on Our Economy, fourth installment, 89th Cong., 2nd Sess. (1966), p. 9.

28. Sec. 4942, Tax Reform Act of 1969.

APPENDIX A

INTERVIEWS WITH CERTIFIED PUBLIC
ACCOUNTANTS

Name	Affiliation	Date of Interview
Delford Edens	Partner in Haskin & Sells	July 31, 1975
Malvern Gross, Jr.	Partner in Price Water-house & Co.	June 18, 1974
John Harrigan	Manager in Peat, Marwick & Mitchell	May 22, 1974
Timothy Racek	Partner in Arthur Andersen & Co.	May 22, 1974
Howard Ray	Partner in Peat, Marwick & Mitchell	June 26, 1974
Quentin Squires	Partner in Main Lafrentz & Co.	June 17, 1974
Joel Whitman	Partner in Price Water-house & Co.	May 20, 1974

Question 1. Who are the users of the financial statements?

Answer. The seven certified public accountants identified the following users: (1) board of directors and trustees; (2) regulatory agencies; (3) other foundations; (4) contributors; (5) potential grantees; (6) those interested in the activities of a particular foundation; (7) general public.

Question 2. What should be the primary objective of the financial statements?

Answer. The interviewees gave the following objectives: (1) should inform the reader of the resources available to carry out foundation activities and what they did with those resources; (2) should show the reader what happened; (3) should reflect on the stewardship of the funds; (4) should present financial position.

Question 3. Should the foundation be evaluated on its performance in investing its assets?

Answer. All the interviewees indicated that foundation performance should be evaluated; however, they expressed reservations as to who would perform the evaluation.

None indicated that it should be the accountant. Six of the seven interviewees favored the market method for valuing securities, one favored cost.

Question 4. Should the private foundation be evaluated on its effectiveness in carrying out its social programs?

Answer. Five interviewees responded with a "yes" but all five commented on the difficulty of establishing evaluation criteria and the difficulty of measurement itself. One interviewee responded with a "no" to this question because of the difficulties in setting criteria and measuring performance. One interviewee also replied with a "no" and he gave similar reasons but in addition he was afraid that attempts at measurement would encourage foundations to do well in the measurement process without considering the merits of the program.

Question 5. Should the financial statements be prepared on a fund basis or as a set of unified statements?

Answer. Five of the interviewees indicated that fund accounting is appropriate only if legally required or where legally the principal is to remain intact. One interviewee said that fund accounting must be used. One interviewee said that the financial statements should be prepared on a consolidated basis.

Question 6. Should the foundation disclose the criteria used to determine which projects to finance?

Answer. Six interviewees responded with a "no." The reason being that specific disclosure would interfere and infringe on the boards in doing their job properly. The six all agreed that the foundation in general terms should disclose their areas of interest and activity. One interviewee answered with a "yes" to the question but he did not think it was essential.

APPENDIX B

INTERVIEWS WITH FOUNDATION OFFICIALS

Name	Affiliation	Date of Interview
Kierman Bracken	Comptroller, Ford Foundation	June 19, 1974
Stewart Campbell	Treasurer, Duke Endowment	June 10, 1974
David Freeman	President, Council on Foundations	May 13, 1974
Jack Gould	Financial Vice President, Edna McConnell Clark Foundation	June 11, 1974
Kenneth Herr	Treasurer, Mellon Foundation	May 28, 1974
Mary Hotter and R. Cassans	Treasurer and Assistant Treasurer, Kress Foundation	May 31, 1974
Leo Kirschner	Controller, Rockefeller Foundation	May 16, 1974
William Mebane	Secretary-Treasurer, Alfred P. Sloan Foundation	May 31, 1974

Question 1. Who are the users of the financial statements?

Answer. The nine foundation officials identified the following users: (1) boards of directors or trustees; (2) regulating agencies; (3) Congress; (4) other foundations; (5) potential grantees; (6) colleges; (7) those interested in the activities of a particular foundation; (8) general public.

Question 2. What should be the primary objectives of the financial statements?

Answer. The interviewees gave the following objectives: (1) accountability; (2) clear and understandable presentation of how the monies have been invested and spent; (3) inform the reader of the financial activities.

Question 3. Should the foundation be evaluated on its performance in investing its assets?

Answer.   Five of the interviewees said "no" to this question. The
               major reasons being that it serves no worthwhile pur-
               pose and the Tax Reform Act of 1969 is, in effect, an
               evaluation. The three interviewees that said "yes"
               expressed reservations as to who will do the evaluating.
               The interviewees were evenly divided on valuing securi-
               ties at cost versus market.

Question 4.   Should the private foundation be evaluated on its effec-
               tiveness in carrying out social programs?

Answer.   Five interviewees responded with a "no" to this question
               giving the following reasons: (1) too difficult; (2) too
               impractical; (3) would be misinterpreted by the public;
               (4) just cannot be done. The three who responded with
               a "yes" also expressed reservations about the difficulty
               and practicality of evaluating. One of the interviewees
               favoring evaluation said that reporting failures may
               help other foundations avoid the same pitfalls.

Question 5.   Should the financial statements be prepared on a fund
               basis or as a set of unified statements?

Answer.   Six interviewees indicated that the financial statements
               should be prepared on a consolidated basis giving the
               following reasons: (1) fund basis serves no purpose;
               (2) fund basis is not meaningful; (3) fund basis is very
               difficult to comprehend and confuses readers; (4) con-
               solidated basis is more useful. One interviewee favored
               a fund basis approach only if legal restrictions exist.
               One interviewee preferred a fund basis.

Question 6.   Should the foundation disclose the criteria used to
               determine which projects to finance?

Answer.   Six interviewees responded with a "no" to this question
               giving the following reasons: (1) would interfere with
               management's job; (2) it is difficult to reveal criteria
               that do not exist; (3) it would prevent the foundation
               from changing criteria. One interviewee said "yes"
               to this question because it is a matter of full disclosure,
               and if criteria are expressed well, it will keep the
               foundation from being snowed under with requests that
               the foundation is not interested in. One interviewee
               said that foundations are already disclosing the criteria.

APPENDIX C

INTERVIEWS ON SOCIAL MEASUREMENT

Interviewee: Joseph Dodwell
Position: Affiliated with Coopers & Lybrand, Certified Public
        Accountants, recognized authority on operational auditing.
Date of interview: June 20, 1974.

Q 4.   Should the foundation be evaluated on its effectiveness in
        carrying out its social programs?

A.   In the private sector, much research has been done on pro-
        ductivity, but not in the public sector. Private foundations
        do not have measurement standards. There is no demand
        on the part of the directors of the foundation that there be
        a measurement of the foundation.

        Mr. Dodwell said that he feels the researcher's project
defines a tremendous need but the forthcoming answers will
be few, if any. The public has an interest in foundations
due to the tax grant. There is no inherent need on the part
of the trustees to be productive and to be measured. Public
should demand more measures of effectiveness.

        In certain areas of activity, foundations are comparable
to government programs and should be subject to the same
measurements. For example, in the area of education, the
efficiency and effectiveness of the institution can be determined
by classroom size, teacher effectiveness. In the absence of
anything, something is better than no standard at all.

        The foundation can supply the following:

1. Type of evidence they receive before making the grant.
2. Standards and criteria used to make the grants. Study
   may show that no criteria exist.
3. Are there different or more stringent criteria for
   larger grants than smaller ones?
4. How is the effectiveness of the grant measured?

Researcher's project may prod Congress into forcing foundations to set standards and means of measurements. This is
an important area which has not received any attention and
which should be studied.

Interviewee: Arthur Toan
Position: Partner in Price Waterhouse & Co., Certified Public
   Accountants, chairman of AICPA committee on social
   measurement.
Date of Interview: July 15, 1974.

Q4. Should the foundation be evaluated on its effectiveness in
   carrying out its social programs?
A. The actual recipient will be the one to look at in order to
   determine success. The foundation does influence the way
   the resources flow. Output can be measured in several ways
   such as intermediate steps. What was the result of the process being carried out by the organization? It can be determined how efficient the organization is where the output is a
   fairly direct one. Multiple causes and effects and timing
   questions can make measurement difficult.

   There are enough areas that can be measured, but not
everything can be evaluated. Some progress is being made
in the area of social measurement. The three difficulties
of social measurement are:

  1. Difficulty of measuring instruments
  2. No control population
  3. Goals not clearly defined or established

Goals must be established that can be measured. If the
overall goal is to improve health in the Bronx, then specific
measurements would be items such as number of chest
x-rays. The question of the impact of the clinic on the
health of a community cannot be determined because the
effect of the clinic on the community cannot be isolated.
   There is a need for more critical and candid reporting
and talk about the failures. Many foundations probably have
qualitative data in their files but qualitative data is much
more difficult to transmit to the public, but it can be done.
   A surrogate is something that reacts in the same way
as the real thing, except that it is easier to measure. Imperfect measurements are better than just operating on
hunches. Operating on hunches exposes the decision maker
to maximum danger.

BIBLIOGRAPHY

ANNUAL REPORTS

Alfred P. Sloan Foundation. Annual Report. 1973.

Edwin Gould Foundation for Children. Annual Report. 1972.

Ford Foundation. Annual Report. 1972.

Jessie Smith Noyes Foundation. Annual Report. 1972.

Kresge Foundation. Annual Report. 1972.

Lilia Babbitt Hyde Foundation. Annual Report. 1970.

Louis and Maud Hill Family Foundation. Annual Report. 1972.

McGregor Fund. Annual Report. 1973.

Moody Foundation. Annual Report. 1972.

Robert Wood Johnson Foundation. Annual Report. 1972.

Rockefeller Foundation. Annual Report. 1973.

Samuel H. Kress Foundation. Annual Report. 1973.

Turrell Fund. Annual Report. 1971.

ARTICLES AND PERIODICALS

Alvin, Gerard. "Accounting for Investments and Stock Rights:
    The Market Value Method." CPA Journal, February 1973,
    pp. 126-31.

Backer, Morton. "A Model for Current Value Reporting." CPA
    Journal, February 1974, pp. 27-33.

Baldwin, Rosecrans. "Depreciation for Non-Profit Organizations—
An Opposing View." New York Certified Public Accountant,
August 1963, pp. 549-57.

Bastable, C. W. "Collegiate Accounting Needs Re-evaluation."
Journal of Accountancy, December 1973, 51-57.

Beams, Floya A. and Paul E. Fertig. "Pollution Control Through
Social Cost Conversion." Journal of Accountancy, November
1971, pp. 37-42.

Beaver, William H. "Reporting Rules for Marketable Equity
Securities." Journal of Accountancy, October 1971, pp. 57-61.

Beyer, Robert. "The Modern Management Approach to a Program
of Social Improvement." Journal of Accountancy, March 1969,
pp. 37-46.

____. "Pilots of Social Progress." Management Accounting, July
1972, pp. 11-15.

Brummet, R. Lee. "Accounting for Human Resources." Journal
of Accountancy, December 1970, pp. 62-66.

"Budgeting à La McNamara." Journal of Accountancy, February
1966, pp. 14-17.

Cary, John L. "The Origins of Modern Financial Reporting."
Journal of Accountancy, September 1969, pp. 35-48.

Cerisano, Michael P. "SMS: Social Measurement Systems for the
Future—A Practitioner's Preview." CPA Journal, May 1974,
pp. 25-30.

Chambers, R. J. "The Missing Link in Supervision of the Securities
Market." Abacus, September 1969, pp. 16-36.

Churchman, C. West. "On the Facility, Felicity, and Morality of
Measuring Social Change." Accounting Review, January 1971,
pp. 30-35.

Clausen, A. W. "Toward an Arithmetic of Quality." Conference
Board Record, May 1971, pp. 9-13.

Coleman, Philip J. "Is Railroad Accounting Off the Track?" Journal of Accountancy, October 1970, pp. 64-68.

Dickens, Robert. "Formulation of Accounting Principles for Non-Profit Institutions." New York Certified Public Accountant, June 1958, pp. 399-415.

Dilley, C. and Jerry L. Weygandt. "Measuring Social Responsibility: An Empirical Test." Journal of Accountancy, September 1973, pp. 62-70.

Dilley, Steven C. "Expanded Scope Audits—Untapped Opportunities? CPA Journal, December 1975, pp. 30-35.

"Editor's Notebook." Journal of Accountancy, November 1972, p. 39.

Elliot, Robert K. "Accounting in the Technological Age." Journal of Accountancy, July 1972, pp. 70-73.

____. "Measuring the Quality of Life." World, Peat, Marwick, Mitchell & Co., Spring 1973, pp. 15-29.

Frances, M. E. "Accounting and the Evaluation of Social Programs: A Critical Comment." Accounting Review, April 1973, pp. 245-57.

Friedman, Milton. "Does Business Have a Social Responsibility?" Magazine of Bank Administration, April 1971, pp. 13-16.

Gross, Malvern J., Jr. "An Accountant Looks at the Total Return Approach for Endowment Funds." CPA Journal, November 1972, pp. 977-91.

____. "Evolving Accounting Rules for Private Foundations." Foundation News, March-April 1975, pp. 34-39.

Hall, Parker J., III. "The Professional Investor's View of Social Responsibility." Financial Analysts Journal, September-October 1971, pp. 32-34.

Hylton, Delmer. "Needed: More Informative and Understandable Financial Statements for Governmental Units." Accounting Review, January 1957, pp. 51-54.

Kennedy, Roger. "Shareholder Responsibility in Institutional Investment." Trusts & Estates, April 1975, pp. 214-17.

King, Barry G. "Cost-Effectiveness Analysis: Implications for Accountants." Journal of Accountancy, March 1970, pp. 43-49.

King, Randle R. and David C. Baron. "An Integrated Account Structure for Governmental Accounting and Financial Reporting." Accounting Review, January 1974, pp. 76-87.

Levy, Robert A. "What Price Performance?". Barron's, July 5, 1971, pp. 11-12, 14.

Linowes, David F. "Socio-Economic Accounting." Journal of Accountancy, November 1968, pp. 37-42.

____. "An Approach to Socio-Economic Accounting." Conference Board Record, November 1972, pp. 58-61.

____. "The Accounting Profession and Social Progress." Journal of Accountancy, July 1973, pp. 32-40.

"The Macaroni Monopoly: The Developing Concept of Unrelated Business Income of Exempt Organizations." Harvard Law Review, April 1968, pp. 1280-94.

McKnight, W. A. "Letters to the Editor." New York Certified Public Accountant, July 1962, p. 435.

Malkiel, Burton G. and Richard E. Quandt. "Moral Issues in Investment Policy." Harvard Business Review, March-April 1971, pp. 37-47.

Markowitz, H. "Portfolio Selection." Journal of Finance, March 1952, pp. 77-91.

Mobley, Sybil C. "The Challenges of Socio-Economic Accounting." Accounting Review, October 1970, pp. 762-68.

____. "Opportunities for Accountants in the Socio-Economic Area." CPA Journal, December 1973, pp. 1050-52.

Moore, Michael. "Professional Development: The Future Is Now." Journal of Accountancy, May 1973, pp. 38-47.

Morgan, James N. and James D. Smith. "Measures of Economic Well-Offness and Their Correlates." American Economic Review, May 1969, pp. 450-62.

Morris, William A. and Bernard Coda. "Valuation of Equity Securities." Journal of Accountancy, January 1973, pp. 48-54.

Overhiser, John C. "Accounting Postulates and Principles for Non-Profit Organizations." New York Certified Public Accountant, May 1962, pp. 307-12.

Parker, James. "Accounting and Ecology: A Prospective." Journal of Accountancy, October 1971, pp. 41-46.

Piersall, R. W. "Depreciation and the Non-Profit Organization." New York Certified Public Accountant, January 1971, pp. 57-65.

Powell, Weldon. "The Development of Accounting Principles." Journal of Accountancy, September 1964, pp. 37-43.

"Program Budgeting and Rand Corp.," Management Accounting, (NAA), November 1968, pp. 63-65.

Regazzi, John H. "Why Aren't Financial Statements Understood?" Journal of Accountancy, April 1974, pp. 48-55.

Robinson, Daniel D. "Private Philanthropy and Public Needs." Journal of Accountancy, February 1976, pp. 41-54.

Ross, Howard. "Is It Better to Be Precisely Wrong Than Vaguely Right?" Financial Executive, June 1971, pp. 8-12.

Schulman, James S. and Jeffrey Gale. "Laying the Groundwork for Social Accounting." Financial Executive, March 1972, pp. 38-42.

Seidler, Lee J. "Dollar Values in the Social Income Statement." World, Peat, Marwick, Mitchell & Co., Spring 1973, pp. 14-23.

_____. "Accountant: Account for Thyself." Journal of Accountancy, June 1973, pp. 38-43.

Sharpe, William F. "A Simplified Model for Portfolio Analysis." Management Science, January 1963, pp. 277-92.

Staats, Elmer. "Address to AICPA Council at Its Meeting in Colorado Springs, May 9, 1973." Journal of Accountancy, June 1973, p. 10.

Steiner, George A. "Should Business Adopt the Social Audit?" Conference Board Record, May 1972, pp. 7-10.

Stone, Marvin. "The Age of Aquarius—Even for Accounting." Journal of Accountancy, August 1971, pp. 67-69.

Sugarman, Norman. "Current Issues in the Use of Tax-Exempt Organizations." Taxes, December 1956, pp. 795-808.

Swalley, Richard W. "The Benefits of Direct Costing." Management Accounting, September 1974, pp. 13-16.

Taylor, Thomas C. "The Illusions of Social Accounting." CPA Journal, January 1976, pp. 24-28.

Terleckyj, Nestor E. "Measuring Progress Toward Social Goals: Some Possibilities at National and Local Levels." Management Science, August 1970, pp. 765-78.

Treyner, Jack L. "How to Rate Management of Investment Funds." Harvard Business Review, January-February 1965, pp. 63-75.

Welles, Chris. "The Beta Revolution: Learning to Live with Risk." Institutional Investor, September 1971, pp. 21-27, 52-55, 58-62, 64.

Withey, Howard A. "Financial Reporting for Non-Profit Organizations." Journal of Accountancy, December 1967, pp. 40-53.

Woelfel, Charles J. "Exploring Opportunities in Social Accounting." CPA Journal, November 1973, pp. 1006-07.

Zimmer, William, Roger Rogow, and Thomas Zimmer. "Budget Planning: How PPBS Can Be Useful to Associations." Association Management, November 1971, pp. 40-43.

BOOKS

Bauer, Raymond A., ed. Social Indicators. Cambridge: MIT Press, 1966.

Bauer, Raymond A. and Don H. Fenn, Jr. The Corporate Social Audit. New York: Russell Sage Foundation, 1972.

Capron, William M. "Cost-Effectiveness Analysis for Government Domestic Programs." In Cost-Effectiveness Analysis, ed. Thomas A. Goldman. New York: Frederick A. Praeger, 1967.

Cary, W. L. and C. B. Bright. Law and the Lore of Endowment Funds. New York: Ford Foundation, 1969.

____. Developing Law of Endowment Funds: "The Law and the Lore" Revisited. New York: Ford Foundation, 1974.

Chambers, Raymond J. Accounting Evaluation and Economic Behavior. Englewood Cliffs, N.J.: Prentice-Hall, 1966.

Churchman, C. West. The Systems Approach. New York: Delacorte Press, 1968.

College and University Business Administration. Washington, D.C.: American Council on Education, 1968.

Commission on Foundations and Private Philanthropy. Foundations, Private Giving and Public Policy. Chicago: University of Chicago Press, 1970.

Commission on Private Philanthropy and Public Needs. Giving in America. Washington, D.C.: Commission on Private Philanthropy and Public Needs, 1975.

Edwards, E. P. and P. W. Bell. The Theory and Measurement of Business Income. Berkeley and Los Angeles: University of California Press, 1961.

Englander, L. Accounting Principles and Procedures of Philanthropic Institutions. New York: New York Community Trust, 1957.

Estes, Ralph W., ed. Accounting and Society. Los Angeles: Melville, 1973.

Galbraith, John K. The New Industrial State. New York: Signet Books, 1968.

Goldstein, Eli. The Quantification of Concern: Some Aspects of Social Accounting. Pittsburgh: Carnegie-Mellon University, 1971.

Gross, Malvern J., Jr. Financial and Accounting Guide for Non-Profit Organizations. New York: Ronald Press, 1972.

_____. Financial and Accounting Guide for Non-Profit Organizations, 2nd ed. New York: Ronald Press, 1974.

Henke, E. O. Accounting for Non-Profit Organizations. Belmont, Calif.: Wadsworth, 1966.

Hollis, Victor E. Philanthropic Foundations and Higher Education. New York: Columbia University Press, 1938.

Horngren, Charles T. Cost Accounting: A Managerial Emphasis, 3rd ed. Englewood Cliffs, N.J.: Prentice-Hall, 1972.

Johnson, Malcolm. "Bootstrap and Contingent Sales: The Implications of Clay Brown: Problems of the Seller, the Leasee Corporation and the Liquidated Corporation." In New York University 25th Annual Institute on Federal Taxation. New York: Matthew Bender, 1967.

Karrenbrock, W. and H. Simons. Advanced Accounting, 3rd ed. Cincinnati: South-Western, 1961.

Kerrigan, Harry D. Fund Accounting. New York: McGraw-Hill, 1969.

Lazarsfeld, Paul F. "Accounting and Social Bookkeeping." In Accounting in Perspective: Contributions to Accounting Thought by Other Disciplines, ed. R. R. Sterling and W. F. Bentz. Cincinnati: South-Western, 1971.

Linowes, David F. Strategies for Survival. New York: AMACOM, A Division of American Management Association, 1973.

Magat, Richard. "Foundation Reporting." In New York University Conference on Charitable Foundations. New York: Matthew Bender, 1969.

Niskanen, William A. "Measures of Effectiveness." In Cost-Effectiveness Analysis, ed. Thomas A. Goldman. New York: Frederick A. Praeger, 1967.

Rivlin, Alice M. Systematic Thinking for Social Action. Washington, D.C.: Brookings Institution, 1971.

Seidler, Lee J. and Lynn L. Seidler. Social Accounting: Theory, Issues and Cases. Los Angeles: Melville, 1975.

Seidman, J. S. Seidman's Legislative History of Federal Income Tax Laws 1938-1861. Englewood Cliffs, N.J.: Prentice-Hall, 1938.

Sheldon, Eleanor B. and Wilbert E. Moore, eds. Indicators of Social Change. New York: Russell Sage Foundation, 1968.

Simon, John C. "Foundations as Stockholders: Corporate Responsibility." In Conference on Charitable Foundations, Tenth Biennial New York University 1971 Proceedings. New York: Matthew Bender, 1971.

Snee, T. and L. Cusack. Principles and Practices of Estate Planning. Englewood Cliffs, N.J.: Prentice-Hall, 1964.

Taylor, Eleanor K. Public Accountability of Foundations and Charitable Trusts. New York: Russell Sage Foundation, 1953.

Weaver, Warren. U.S. Philanthropic Foundations. New York: Harper & Row, 1967.

Wormser, R. Foundations: Their Power and Influence. New York: Devin-Adair, 1958.

Young, Donald C. "Donor Foundation Dealings." In New York University 22nd Annual Institute on Federal Taxation. New York: Matthew Bender, 1964.

COURT CASES

Anderson Dairy, Inc. v. Commissioner of Internal Revenue, 39 TC 1027 (1963).

C. F. Mueller Co. v. Commissioner of Internal Revenue, 51-1 USTC Para. 9360 (1951).

Commissioner of Internal Revenue v. Clay Brown, 65-1 USTC Para. 9375 (1965).

Commissioner of Internal Revenue v. Teich Foundation, 69-1 USTC Para. 4239 (1969).

Erie Endowment v. Commissioner of Internal Revenue, 63-1 USTC Para. 9373 (1963).

Griswald v. Commissioner of Internal Revenue, 39 TC 620 (1962).

Labrenz Foundation v. Commissioner of Internal Revenue, T.C. Memo. 1974-296.

Ohio Furnace Co., Inc. v. Commissioner of Internal Revenue, 25 TC 179 (1959).

Oscar C. Stahl v. Commissioner of Internal Revenue, 22 TCM 996 (1963).

Roche's Beach Inc. v. Commissioner of Internal Revenue, 38-1 USTC Para. 9302 (1938).

Rueckwald Foundation v. Commissioner of Internal Revenue, T.C. Memo. 1974-298.

S. Friedland Foundation v. Commissioner of Internal Revenue, 56-2 USTC Para. 9896 (1956).

Sand Spring Homes v. Commissioner of Internal Revenue, 6 BTA 198 (1927).

Scripture Press Foundation v. Commissioner of Internal Revenue, 61-1 USTC Para. 9195 (1961), Sup. Ct. Cert. denied 368 U.S. 985 (1962).

Sico Foundation v. Commissioner of Internal Revenue, 61-2 USTC 9732 (1961).

Teich Foundation v. Commissioner of Internal Revenue, 48 TC 963 (1967).

Tell Foundation v. Wood, 58-1 USTC Para. 9111 (1957).

Trinidad v. Sagrada Orden De Predicadores, 263 U.S. 568 (1924).

University Hill Foundation v. Commissioner of Internal Revenue, 71-1 USTC Para. 9440, reversing 51 TC 548 (1969).

GOVERNMENTAL PUBLICATIONS AND
PUBLIC DOCUMENTS

Frequently Asked Questions About Accrual Accounting in the Federal Government. Washington, D.C.: U.S. General Accounting Office, 1970.

Standards for Audit of Governmental Organizations, Programs, Activities and Functions. Washington, D.C.: U.S. General Accounting Office, 1972.

Toward A Social Report. Washington, D.C.: U.S. Dept. of Health, Education and Welfare, 1969.

U.S. Congress, House. Committee on Ways and Means, Revenue Bill of 1938, 75th Cong., 3d sess., H.R. 1860 (1938).

____. Committee on Ways and Means, Hearings on Revenue Revision, 77th Cong., 2d sess. (1942).

____. Committee on Ways and Means, Treasury Department Report on Private Foundations, 89th Cong., 1st sess. (1965).

____. Committee on Ways and Means, Written Statements by Interested Individuals and Organizations on Treasury Department Report on Private Foundations, 89th Cong., 1st sess., vol. 1 (1965).

____. Committee on Ways and Means, Written Statements Submitted by Witnesses on the Subject of Tax Reform, (Feb. 18.-Feb. 20, 1969).

____. Committee on Interstate and Foreign Commerce, Institutional Investor Study Report of the Securities and Exchange Commission, 92nd Cong., 1st sess., vol. 2 (1971).

____. Hearings before the Special Committee to Investigate Tax-Exempt Foundations and Comparable Organizations, 83rd Cong., 2d sess. (1954).

____. Revenue Act of 1950, 81st Cong., 2d sess., H.R. 2319, (1949).

____. Revenue Act of 1950, 81st Cong., 2d sess., H.R. 3124 (1959).

____. Select Committee on Small Business, Tax-Exempt Foundations and Charitable Trusts: Their Impact on Our Economy, first installment, 87th Cong., 2d sess. (1962).

____. Select Committee on Small Business, Tax-Exempt Foundations and Charitable Trusts: Their Impact on Our Economy, second installment, 88th Cong., 1st sess. (1963).

____. Select Committee on Small Business, Tax-Exempt Foundations and Charitable Trusts: Their Impact on Our Economy, third installment, 88th Cong., 2d sess. (1964).

____. Select Committee on Small Business, Tax-Exempt Foundations and Charitable Trusts: Their Impact on Our Economy, fourth installment, 89th Cong., 2d sess. (1966).

____. Select Committee on Small Business, Tax-Exempt Foundations and Charitable Trusts: Their Impact on Our Economy, fifth installment, 90th Cong., 1st sess. (1967).

____. Select Committee on Small Business, Tax-Exempt Foundations and Charitable Trusts: Their Impact on Our Economy, sixth installment, 90th Cong., 2d sess. (1968).

____. Tax Reform Act of 1969, 91st Cong., 1st sess., Report 91-413 (pt. 1) (1969).

U.S. Congress, Senate. Hearings on Payne-Aldrich Tariff Act. 44th Cong., Rec. 151 (1909).

____. Final Report of the Commission on Industrial Relations, 64th Cong., 1st sess., Senate Document No. 415 (1916).

____. Revenue Act of 1950, 81st Cong., 2d sess., Rept. 2375 (1950).

____. Tax Reform Act of 1969, 91st Cong., 1st sess., Report 91-552 (1969).

U.S. Congress, Subcommittee of the Committee on Interstate and Foreign Commerce, Hearings on Investigation of Closing of Nashua New Hampshire Mills and Operations of Textron, Inc., 80th Cong., 2d sess. (1948).

U.S. Congressional Record, 87th Cong., 2d sess., vol. 108, no. 147 (1962).

PROFESSIONAL ORGANIZATIONS

Accounting Principles Board. "Reporting the Results of Operations." Opinion No. 9. New York: American Institute of Certified Public Accountants, December 1966.

____. "Basic Concepts and Accounting Principles Underlying Financial Statements of Business Enterprises." Statement No. 4. New York: American Institute of Certified Public Accountants, 1970.

____. "The Equity Method of Accounting for Investments in Common Stock." Opinion No. 18. New York: American Institute of Certified Public Accountants, March 1971.

____. "Reporting Changes in Financial Position." Opinion No. 19. New York: American Institute of Certified Public Accountants, March 1971.

____. "Disclosure of Accounting Policies." Opinion No. 22. New York: American Institute of Certified Public Accountants, April 1972.

____. "APB Accounting Principles." Current Text As of June 30, 1973. New York: American Institute of Certified Public Accountants, 1973.

Accounting Standards for Business Enterprises Throughout the World. Arthur Andersen & Co., 1974.

American Institute of Certified Public Accountants. Code of Professional Ethics. New York: American Institute of Certified Public Accountants, 1973.

Auditing Standards Established by the GAO, Their Meaning and Significance for CPA's, A Report. New York: American Institute of Certified Public Accountants, 1973.

Committee on Accounting Concepts and Standards. Accounting and Reporting Standards for Corporate Financial Statements. Iowa City, Iowa: American Accounting Association, 1957.

Committee on Accounting Procedure and Accounting Terminology. Accounting Research and Terminology Bulletins, Final Edition. New York: American Institute of Certified Public Accountants, 1961.

Committee on College and University Accounting and Auditing. Audits of Colleges and Universities. New York: American Institute of Certified Public Accountants, 1973.

Committee on Health Care Institutions. Hospital Audit Guide.
    New York: American Institute of Certified Public Accountants,
    1972.

Committee of Voluntary Health and Welfare Organizations. Audits
    of Voluntary Health and Welfare Organizations. New York:
    American Institute of Certified Public Accountants, 1974.

Committee to Prepare a Statement of Basic Accounting Theory.
    A Statement of Basic Accounting Theory. Evanston, Ill.:
    American Accounting Association, 1966.

Financial Accounting Standards Board. "Accounting for Certain
    Marketable Securities." Statement of Financial Accounting
    Standards No. 12. Stamford, Conn., 1975.

National Committee on Governmental Accounting. Governmental
    Accounting, Auditing and Financial Reporting. Chicago:
    Municipal Finance Officers Association, 1968.

Reich, Walter I., Chairman, Committee on Private Foundations
    of the American Institute of Certified Public Accountants.
    Letter to Private Foundation Financial Executives, December 15,
    1972.

"Report of the Committee on Accounting Practices of Not-for-Profit
    Organizations." Accounting Review, supp. to vol. 46, 1971,
    pp. 81-163.

"Report of the Committee on Concepts of Accounting Applicable to
    the Public Sector, 1970-1971." Accounting Review, supp. to
    vol. 47, 1972, pp. 77-110.

"Report of the Committee on Measures of Effectiveness for Social
    Programs." Accounting Review, supp. to vol. 47, 1972,
    pp. 337-96.

"Report of the Committee on Non-Financial Measures of Effective-
    ness." Accounting Review, supp. to vol. 46, 1971, pp. 165-
    211.

"Report of the Committee on Not-for-Profit Organizations, 1972-73."
    Accounting Review, supp. to vol. 49, 1974, pp. 225-49.

"Report of the Study Group on the Objectives of Financial Statements."
Objectives of Financial Statements. New York: American Institute
of Certified Public Accountants, 1973.

Social Measurement. New York: American Institute of Certified
Public Accountants, 1972.

Standards of Accounting and Financial Reporting for Voluntary Health
and Welfare Organizations—Exposure Draft. New York: National
Health Council, 1974.

Sprouse, Robert T. and Maurice Moonitz. "A Tentative Set of Broad
Accounting Principles for Business Enterprises." Accounting
Research Study No. 3. New York: American Institute of Certi-
fied Public Accountants, April 1962.

MISCELLANEOUS SOURCES

Accounting Advisory Committee. Report to the Commission on
Private Philanthropy and Public Needs, 1974.

Dermer, Joseph. How to Raise Funds from Foundations. New York:
Public Service Materials Center, 1971.

Foundation Center Source Book 1975-1976, vol. I. New York:
The Foundation Center, 1975.

Foundation Directory, 3d ed. New York: Russell Sage Foundation
for the Foundation Library Center, 1967.

Foundation Directory, 5th ed. New York: Foundation Center, 1975.

Foundation Grants Index 1972. New York: Foundation Center, 1972.

Guide to Foundation Annual Reports on Film, 1970. New York:
Foundation Center, 1972.

McVeigh, Thomas. Social Indicators: A Bibliography. Monticello,
Ill.: Council of Planning Librarians, 1971.

Mertens. Law of Federal Income Taxation. Mundelein, Ill.:
Callaghan & Co.

ABOUT THE AUTHOR

JACK TRAUB is Associate Professor of Accounting at Hofstra University, Hempstead, Long Island, New York. Prior to teaching, he was an Internal Revenue Agent in the Manhattan District where he was assigned to investigate private foundations for noncompliance with the tax laws.

Dr. Traub is a member of the American Institute of Certified Public Accountants, the New York State Society of Certified Public Accountants, and the American Accounting Association. He has published articles on taxation in The CPA Journal.

Dr. Traub was educated in the New York City school system and holds a Bachelor of Business Administration, Master of Business Administration, and a Doctor of Philosophy degree from the City University of New York. He is licensed as a Certified Public Accountant in New York State.

*COST-BENEFIT ANALYSIS: New and Expanded
Edition

E. J. Mishan

INTERNATIONAL ACCOUNTING AND FINANCIAL
REPORTING

Norlin G. Rueschhoff

PENSION AND INSTITUTIONAL PORTFOLIO
MANAGEMENT

Martin J. Schwimmer
Edward Malca

THE PROPERTY TAX AND ALTERNATIVE LOCAL
TAXES: An Economic Analysis

Larry D. Schroeder
David L. Sjoquist

*Also available in paperback as a PSS Student Edition